DATE DUE

IMAGI-NATIONS AND BORDERLESS TELEVISION

IMAGI-NATIONS AND BORDERLESS TELEVISION

Media, Culture and Politics Across Asia

AMOS OWEN THOMAS

SAGE Publications
New Delhi / Thousand Oaks / London

First published in 2005 by

Sage Publications India Pvt Ltd
B-42, Panchsheel Enclave
New Delhi 110 017
www.indiasage.com

Sage Publications Inc
2455 Teller Road
Thousand Oaks, California 91320

Sage Publications Ltd
1 Oliver's Yard, 55 City Road
London ECIY ISP

Published by Tejeshwar Singh for Sage Publications India Pvt Ltd, phototypeset in 10/12 Calisto MT by Star Compugraphics Private Limited, Delhi and printed at Chaman Enterprises, New Delhi.

Library of Congress Cataloging-in-Publication Data

Thomas, Amos Owen, 1954–
      Imagi-nations and borderless television: media, culture and politics across Asia/Amos Owen Thomas.
            p. cm.
      Includes bibliographical references and index.
      1. Television—Asia. I. Title: Imaginations and borderless television. II. Title.
HE8700.9.A78T48   384.55'095—dc22   2005   2005014163

ISBN: 0–7619–3395–6 (Hb)   81–7829–541–5 (India–Hb)
          0–7619–3396–4 (Pb)   81–7829–542–3 (India–Pb)

Sage Production Team: Anindita Pandey, Radha Dev Raj and Santosh Rawat

CONTENTS

LIST OF TABLES

LIST OF FIGURES

In the early 1990s as pan-Asian satellite television and the cable-fed "information superhighway" blazed a trail across the continent, the research for this book became topical. Over that decade Asian skies became increasingly congested with satellites beaming an array of commercial television channels transnationally. This growth in satellite platforms and transnational television channels in Asia, said to be the most rapid worldwide, needed to be analysed in the context of the globalisation of and by the media-communications industry. To date there have been periodic updates on various players in the market, but little analysis of their origins, development and interaction. The satellite, cable and terrestrial television industry across the largest continent moves at almost too rapid a pace for any individual to monitor. Hence this book does not purport to provide comprehensive and up-to-the-minute information, only to draw on such data to illustrate major trends and support critical analysis of the first decade. Still, any information on significant new developments or feedback on any inaccuracies of detail in this book are welcomed from readers.

In researching the growth of transnational television and advertising in Asia, I travelled to over 10 countries on the continent, most of them more than once. Over this past decade, my views on the issue of globalisation and approaches to researching the media industry have metamorphosed somewhat. Varied of schools of thought on globalisation across multiple academic disciplines—from sociology, political science, literary studies, communications to management, marketing and advertising—have been very influential in the shaping of my own thinking. As such this book is both a chronicle and creative outcome of a personal journey of discovery over the mid-1990s into the early 2000s within the television and advertising industries in Asia, not to mention the increasing convergent media, communications, telephony and information industries. I trust that its insights will be helpful to others who, like me, are fascinated by the media and eager to understand how the recent phenomenon of transnational television via satellite/cable is shaping and being shaped by our globalised world, at least from an Asian vantage point.

Amos Owen Thomas
Maastricht, The Netherlands
November 2004

ACKNOWLEDGEMENTS

In over a decade there were over 250 research respondents who granted me interviews, provided me with data or helped in various practical ways, without which this book might not have been possible. Many would actually prefer to remain anonymous. Still I would like to record my appreciation to them for the time and energy they put into cooperating with me, and hope that if they should read this book, they might discern their tangible contribution to knowledge.

Then, there are the many friends and relatives, literally around the world, who have been encouraging and supportive of my doctoral studies in more ways than they might have realised. They stayed in touch by phone, letters, email and in person, and cheered me on in weary times. They know who they are, and if they should read this book I would like them to know that they are very special to me and that I am very conscious of being in their debt.

Sadly, there are far too many to name without inadvertently leaving someone out. However, three of them are worthy of being singled out for special mention. Without the personal help over recent years of Geoffrey Abisheganaden, M.V. Samuel and Quek Swee Hwa, I would not have been able to complete the research long begun and so this book is dedicated to them. They have been "angels unawares", part of the divine choreography in my life for which I am grateful.

* * *

In covering the first decade of transnational television in Asia, research was conducted between the mid-1990s to the early 2000s, and work-in-progress was presented at various academic and policy conferences. Later versions of those papers were published as journal articles or submitted as chapters for edited books, in both disciplines of communications and business. The current book *Imagi-Nations and Borderless Television* represents a significant update, supplementation, reorganisation and integration of such earlier partial publications as those familiar with the latter would notice. Those publications are listed below in acknowledgement of the editors and reviewers who nurtured the research over the years, and for historical reference should it be thought needful by readers of the present book.

References

Thomas, Amos Owen (1995). "Asean Television and Pan-Asian Broadcast Satellites: Terrestrials Encounter the Extraterrestrial", *Media Information Australia*, 75, (February), pp. 123–29.

———— (1996). "Global-Diasporic and Subnational-Ethnic: Audiences for Satellite Television in South Asia", *Journal of International Communication*, 3 (2), pp. 61–75.

———— (1997). "Satellite Television and Greater China: Regional Media, National Policies", *Business & the Contemporary World: International Journal of Business, Economics and Social Policy*, 9 (4).

———— (1999). "Australia Television in Southeast Asia: Free-to-air yet Scarcely Rebroadcast", *Australian Journal of Communication*, 26 (2), pp. 97–111.

———— (1999). "Regulating Access to Transnational Satellite Television: Government Policies in North East Asia", *Gazette: International Journal for Communication Studies*, 61 (3–4), pp. 243–54.

———— (1999). "Broadcast Satellites in Asia: Global Actors on a Continental Stage", *Transnational Broadcasting Studies*, 1 (2); (Spring 1999). *www. tbsjournal.com.*

———— (1999). "Up-linked and Down-played: Understanding Transnational Satellite Television in Asia", *Media Asia*, 26 (3), pp. 132–38.

———— (2000). "Global Media, Globalised Culture: Contingency or Coincidence?", *Asia Pacific Media Educator*, 9, (July–December), pp. 4–23.

———— (2000). "West Asian Audiences for South Asian Satellite Television: Cosmopolitan Locals and Nostalgic Expatriates", *The Cypress Review*, 12 (2), Fall, pp. 135–50.

ADVENT AND AGENDA

T owards the turn of the twentieth century the media and communications industry in Asia underwent quite a radical transformation. The advent of transnational television at the start of the
twentieth century's last decade took Asian governments, broadcasters,
advertisers and consumers alike by surprise. Dating from CNN broadcasts of the first Gulf crisis of 1990–91, this borderless medium captured
the imagination of audiences in many countries who had been long
accustomed to unimaginative public broadcasting and commercial
broadcasting under government control. The transnational medium
soon fostered dramatic growth in the sales of satellite dishes and the
establishment of cable networks, illegal and quasi-legal, in many Asian
countries. Concurrently, there was the growth of the internet and wireless telephony which rode in on the burgeoning commercial communications infrastructure in Asia, making the continent a key regional
market. Hence, new borderless media in Asia, including transnational
television via satellite and cable, have been added to the on-going
debate among its intelligentsia about the controversial consequences
of globalisation.

GLOBALISATION AND CONVERGENCE

In recent decades globalisation has been a key concept across a number
of fields of human endeavour, but continued debate over its meaning
still seems to engender more hype than insight. Certainly, from the 1960s
through the 1980s the concept gained momentum with the increasing
risk of nuclear annihilation, awareness of environmental crises of plan-
etary proportions and the onset of a global economic recession. Then

in the 1990s, the growth of new communications technologies such as broadcast satellites, broadband cable, mobile telephony and the internet spurred further the debate about the possible liberating versus insidious effects of globalisation. These developments coincided fortuitously with the end of the Cold War and ascendancy of capitalism in the world economy to a position of unchallenged primacy. Asian nations were acutely conscious of the need to stay on the information superhighway, if they were not to be left behind in the capitalist world economy. Thus any book on transnational media in Asia must set its development within the wider context of political, economic, social and cultural globalisation at the end of the twentieth century.

Technological Transformation

Global media and communications have been revolutionised in recent decades through new electronic technologies such as geostationary satellites, optical fibre, digital transmission, cable television, mobile telephony, computer networks, online libraries and databanks, facsimiles and electronic mail and much more. Increasingly, business investments and government regulations concerning such media hardware and software are being made with the wider global context, and not just domestic imperatives, in mind. Advocates of these new technologies claim the ensuing unbridled access to information will lead to greater democratisation of societies and opportunities for economic growth to match those in the developed world. Sceptics point out that such technologies tend instead to reinforce the status quo of dependency of developing nations on developed nations, or even perpetuate the inequity within developing nations between their own capitalist elite and working classes. While the internet and mobile telephony might be at the cutting edge of communications technologies in the developed world, transnational television provides a far-reaching and pertinent case for evaluating the arguments of this debate in the context of Asia. It is this book's contention that it will be satellite and cable television as mass media that will continue to dominate the communications revolution for some years more. Certainly in Asia, they will drive digital connectivity and convergence, which will in turn accelerate the diffusion of those newer and more individualised communications technologies.

The phenomenal growth in satellite technologies in the second half of the twentieth century allowed global media corporations to circumvent national communications structures, and offer their media services to consumers in collaboration with advertisers. Globalisation of the media, particularly television, has been spurred by broadcast deregulation worldwide in recognition of the fact that such media technologies render national media sovereignty a quite unrealistic goal. Unimpeded media communication has been justified in the name of deregulation, a hallmark of the global capitalist economic system of the post-Cold War era. It is deemed an integral part of freer world trade in services as multinational corporations (MNCs) seek access to all media as a vital means of promoting consumption of the goods they produce. While advertising has underpinned this growth of commercial media in developing countries, the extent to which it does so has seldom been acknowledged adequately. On the one hand, business research has preferred to focus on maximising the effectiveness of marketing and advertising, while discounting the wider social implications of their practice. On the other hand, social science research has tended to ignore the underpinning role of marketing and advertising in the increasingly commercialised media, while being somewhat critical of certain business practices. It prefers instead to focus on the social impact of programming, issues of media ownership, audience consumption or government policies as befits its concerns about cultural imperialism and other media effects.

Development Sans Imperialism

Governments of developing countries have long feared cultural imperialism, perceived often as the erosion of their national and ethnic cultures, by television programming and other media products from the developed world. Newly independent countries in the 1960s and 1970s resented it as a form of neo-colonialisation by their former political masters and an impediment to the forging of a national identity. Across Asia the effects of transnational television from global sources were anticipated to be quite damaging. At best, audiences in the urban centres were perceived by leaders and commentators to be changing their media habits and, at worse, adopting unsustainable "Westernised" consumerist lifestyles *in toto*. Of course, there have been dissenting views which argue that cultures around the world could never become thoroughly homogenised. Some would point to a quite opposite trend towards differentiation through the de-massification of production and marketing, and suggest that cultures were becoming hybridised. In the media industry, this could foster in turn the reassertion of sub-cultural and minority ethnic identities within nation-states.

Development theorists in the mid-twentieth century, especially those from the modernisation school, consistently advocated the use of the media, particularly public television, as a major tool in promoting socio-economic development. The model adopted in the developing world, as in much of Asia, was of a dominant public broadcaster providing programming which promoted socio-economic development along with political and cultural integration. In reality, due to the high cost of local production, the public broadcaster usually featured largely imported entertainment programming and was highly dependent on advertising revenue from both domestic and global marketers. Ironically, it was this limited availability of television media for advertising amidst the rapid economic growth and the demand from affluent parts of Asia for better entertainment, that provided considerable impetus for the growth of transnational television via satellite and cable. While a few countries had liberalised their domestic television industries earlier as a consequence of political reform or deregulated to conform to global economic pressures, most were forced to react to the rapid change which swept the media industry over the 1990s.

QUEST FOR ANSWERS

In recent years, governments of diverse ideological persuasions have been instrumental in promoting the global integration of their national economies in return for economic benefits for their countries and thus their own political longevity. In the process of joining regional inter-governmental organisations (IGOs) or cooperating with large MNCs, these very governments, such as those of the Asian countries researched for this book, forfeit some measure of political control over their societies. Furthermore, political commentators and policy makers alike in developing countries have expressed reservations that commercial television broadcasting via transnational satellite could possibly foster

the misallocation of economic resources to consumer goods, and fer-
ment social disenchantment by promoting unattainable materialistic
expectations among their populace. Thus, quite rightly, any discussion
of globalisation via television in Asia needs to analyse its roots in and
consequences for political change within particular countries, their
participation in the world economic system and the role of MNCs.

So what impact can and does the new medium have directly on the
television and media-related industries of Asia, and indirectly on sociocultural change in its diverse nation-states? By and large, the evidence
cited in support of government policies concerning transnational television has been anecdotal and speculative in nature. The only other
data is proprietary market research commissioned by the broadcasters
and advertisers themselves, such as audience ratings, which largely
remain well-guarded commercial secrets and which in any case are
quite deficient in assessing broader societal impact. Adopting an empirical as well as critical approach, and utilising both qualitative and
quantitative data gathered from primary and secondary sources, this
book aims to understand the growth and development of transnational
television in Asia. Few studies of complex phenomena, even if qualitative and phenomenological, begin without a tentative conceptual
framework or some orientating ideas and the present book is no exception. Thus, key issues concerning the relationships between various
factors have been gleaned from the vast literature on globalisation to
help frame this exploration of the historical development of transnational television in Asia.

Economic and Political Globalisation

Why have governments in Asia perceived transnational television as
a threat? How have they sought to control its access and how successful
have these efforts been? What are the links, if any, between global capital, media corporations and political elite in transnational television
in Asia? More specifically, what are the ownership structures and
business alliances between satellite owners, transnational broadcasters,
domestic broadcasters, cable networks, advertisers, programme production houses and other cultural industries? These questions analyse
the policy and corporate context of the new medium in each country
and the answers will be identified through interview responses as well
as policy documents, legislation and other secondary sources.

Cultural and Social Globalisation

How has transnational television attracted sizeable audiences of particular cultural or socio-economic backgrounds in certain countries,
and why? Why has it not appealed much to other segments in these
and other countries? Has cultural change in each of the countries researched been influenced significantly by transnational television, and
if so, how? Or if not, what other factors might explain the changes
widely perceived in some segments of these societies? The extent of
globalisation of television audiences and cultural change in the
selected Asian countries will be assessed by analysis of industry data
such as household penetration, television ratings, audience profiles,
press clippings, academic research and government reports.

The advent of transnational television in Asia coincided with the
end of the Cold War, the transformation of General Agreement on
(GATT) into the World Trade Organisation (WTO), the rise of democracy movements, new technologies of communications and so on.
So it is difficult to assess the cultural and economic impact of transnational television on the general populace in isolation, although there
has been much journalistic reportage. There has also been some survey
research but this has been in pockets such as the urban youth or rural
villagers in particular countries. Nonetheless, transnational television
has a clearly discernible impact on the television industry in the various
countries and vice versa in the scramble for audiences and advertising.
With the decline of public broadcasting, the government was left as a
referee among the players, one that was sometimes ignored, seeking
to balance national cultural agenda with global economic imperatives.
It is this drama played out for over a decade from the early 1990s to
early 2000s in Asia that this book focuses on.

TRANSITION IN TELEVISION

With almost 500 million television households as of the start of the
twenty-first century, Asia has the highest television penetration worldwide; this is expected to rise further to 700 million within a decade.
Yet there is still need for systematic research on the politico-economic
and sociocultural context, as well as the media and marketing

consequences of transnational television broadcasting via satellite. This would invariably aid decision making by public policy makers, commercial broadcasters, advertisers and consumer movements alike. Television is an immense arena and there is much information available via industry journals and corporate websites, plus some proprietary information that is jealously guarded by industry insiders. This book seeks instead to further knowledge on how satellite and cable technology can and have transformed the media industries of developing countries in general. Any research in support of this aim would have to focus on the salient aspects of transnational broadcasting and its impact on specific markets using a specific set of methodologies. While the research will survey the responses to transnational television across most of Asia, it will progressively focus on key markets drawn from three regions, namely South Asia, Southeast Asia and Northeast Asia. Using a multi-method approach comprising key informant interviews on structures and strategies, and secondary data on audiences and policy (see Appendix C) it will attempt to provide comprehensive case studies for comparative analysis, systemisation of factors and theorising on globalisation.

Developments in transnational television in Asia over the decade 1992–2001 are surveyed in Chapter Two of the book, with a view to identifying and classifying the major players, both channel providers and satellite platforms, and their corporate ownership links, if any. This is followed by a literature review that surveys the phenomenon of globalisation, its antecedents, causes and dynamics. Both in the academic use of the term across different disciplines and the popular usage of the term in various professional fields, it has acquired a plurality of meanings. The concept of globalisation is critical to this study, yet its political-economic potential and sociocultural consequences remains unclear. Further issues surrounding the impact of transnational television gleaned from the extensive literature on social change, media theory, global communications, international marketing and advertising management are also interspersed within the latter of chapters of this book.

Following the discussion on politico-economic and sociocultural globalisation in the previous chapter, Chapter Four introduces an innovative six-fold typology by which to analyse government policies towards transnational satellite television, as well as the shifts that have occurred over the past decade. This typology is then applied to most of the countries in each of the three regions of South, Southeast and

Northeast Asia as a means of mapping out the policy responses of governments. In the subsequent Chapters Five to Seven, two or three countries are selected from each of the regions for their representation of the major markets within the Indian subcontinent, Malay Archipelago and Greater China for transnational broadcasters operating in Asia. These chapters examine developments with particular reference to their history, geography, cultural policies and broadcasting history, including the concurrent evolution of domestic commercial television in each country.

While the earlier chapters comprise primarily a historical record, Chapter Nine makes explicit comparison of the experience of transnational television in various countries through an inductively-derived analytical framework. Finally the anticipated socioethical consequences of media globalisation for rapid political, economic, social and cultural change in the developing countries of the region and beyond are highlighted from the author's personal standpoint in Chapter Nine. In seeking to provide a breadth of coverage across Asian regions, some depth of detail about countries and industry players has been sacrificed in this book. Furthermore, the field of transnational media progresses at a rapid pace in late twentieth-century Asia, and it is simply not possible to report, let alone analyse all up-to-the-minute developments in the region. Still, in adopting a systematic approach in analysis of media industries, this book should fill a void in research on developments during the early 1990s to the early 2000s, the decade following the advent of transnational television there. The end of the first decade of transnational television in Asia is now sufficiently past for the kind of critical reflection, long-term perspective and broad-based comparison across the region that this book seeks to provide.

Developments in media industries subsequent to the introduction of transnational television remains of interest to governments, citizens, social researchers, broadcasters and marketers alike, despite their often divergent agendas. Yet while much has been reported about it in industry media, systematic research on the critical issues has been scarce, the methodologies used rather limited and their findings somewhat inconclusive. Some of the preliminary findings of this research have been published by the author in academic and policy journals, or presented in conferences. This comprehensive book endeavours to chronicle salient aspects and analyse the impact of transnational television on the television and advertising industries in selected Asian countries. Therefore the research encapsulated in this book is proffered idealistically to governments, MNCs, civil society groups, advertising agencies, IGOs, broadcasters, academics, research institutions and all parties having an interest in broadcast media and newer communications technologies. Each readership may find its own selective path through the chapters, depending on the issues and regions it is primarily concerned with.

While the focus of this book is on Asia, it is believed that its experience with transnational television would be instructive for developing countries and transitional economies around the world. In particular those countries that have had strong public sector involvement in the media industry might draw lessons from the pressures of political and economic liberalisation and the struggle for influence over culture with multinational media organisations. It is hoped that, being independent of any vested interest, this research will provide these diverse groups with greater knowledge and critical insight which may facilitate either their involvement with or management of, and possibly strategic partnership, in the future development of transnational television in Asia and elsewhere in the developing world.

Transnational television took Asia by storm in the early 1990s, thrilling select audiences across the region, threatening domestic media and perplexing national governments. The true pioneer of this phenomenon was StarTV, which began its broadcasts in late 1991 and catered initially to a pan-Asian audience within its satellite footprint. While CNN preceded StarTV by many months, the former was then simply a relay of its global and largely US-centric programming. In the immediate years that followed, a number of other transnational broadcasters boosted this new industry in Asia, using either some channels created within the region or others that had already been operating globally. On the other hand, there were national broadcasters in the region that had long utilised satellites for domestic transmission, both prior to and after the advent of transnational satellites. Although they were largely available by virtue of signal spillover within their regions, some of these commercial and public broadcasters subsequently, and more so consequently, sought transnational audiences deliberately. Together, these global/regional broadcasters and their national/domestic counterparts transformed the television industry within Asia by capitalising on satellite, cable and later digital technologies.

TRANSNATIONAL BROADCASTERS

In this book, transnational television is defined as channels designed to cross national boundaries, whether or not intentionally, to gain wider audiences or to circumvent regulation. This is usually achieved through the use of satellite technology, often in conjunction with local cable networks though sometimes simply via spillover signals. The major transnational broadcasters operating in Asia over the 1990s may be classified by their origins, target markets and content (Table 2.1), though the demarcations are seldom clear-cut. For instance, some regional and global broadcasters have quite national target markets and vice versa, while some information channels incorporate some general and entertainment programming and vice versa. However, analysis of the various transnational channels primarily by their content and secondarily by their origins and target markets, seems the most appropriate method for getting a handle on the burgeoning industry.

Table 2.1
Major Transnational Television Broadcasters in Asia, Late 1990s/Early 2000s

Origin	Information	Entertainment	General
Global—commercial	CNN BBC World CNBC Asia-Pacific Discovery National Geographic Bloomberg	ESPN MTV HBO TNT/Cartoon MGM Disney	
Regional—commercial	ABN CTN Channel News Asia	SonyET CETV JET AXN	StarTV ZeeTV TVBI
National—public	Deutsche Welle Canal France Int'l		CCTV-4 & 9 DDI TCSI ABC Asia-Pacific NHK

Information Channels

Although CNN may be credited with establishing a bridgehead for transnational television in Asia, interest in its US-oriented international news waned soon after the First Gulf War. It was followed shortly after by various other news services such as BBC World and CNBC, and it soon became evident that the one that demonstrated regional relevance best would win the audience loyalty stakes. Hence, all the global news channels operating in Asia including CNN soon sought to internationalise their sources, moving away from their country-of-origin ethnocentrism and regionalising the news for their Asian markets. Otherwise audiences would have reverted to their increasingly technically sophisticated, if politically conservative, domestic-terrestrial broadcasters as their primary news source. Furthermore, regional broadcasters such as Asian Business News (ABN), Channel News Asia and Chinese Television News (CTN) soon entered the market to compete with the global channels in providing international news with Asian priorities and sensitivities.

CNN

Claiming then to be the only truly global network with transmissions available in 212 countries and territories worldwide via 12 satellites, CNN reached 150 million households, not counting offices and hotel rooms, by the late 1990s [CNN 1999]. By the time CNN entered the Asian market in 1991, much of its international news was being produced in London and Hong Kong [ibid. 1994], but it was still perceived as having an American flavour. CNN recorded steady growth in Asia over the 1990s through a strategy of regionalisation and strategic alliances with other transnational broadcasters. In 1992 CNN opened a New Delhi bureau and soon began broadcasting "Business Asia" daily in its Asia-Pacific feeds. From 1993 CNN was available to hotels and an estimated 50,000 households in Taiwan via cable subscription and was excerpted for use on Doordarshan, India's national network. By early 1995 CNN was available on cable systems in Hong Kong, the Philippines, Japan, Taiwan, Thailand, Singapore and Malaysia. Through such policies and practices it has endeavoured to overcome ethnocentrism [Flournoy 2001]. Recognising the critical drawcard of regionalised programming, CNN opened its own Asian production facilities in Hong Kong, began broadcasting "World News Asia" produced both there and in Atlanta and launched "Inside Asia", a current affairs programme. The first-ever survey of transnational television audiences in 1997 revealed that a substantial 21 per cent of high income Asians watched CNN in the last 30 days. A follow-up survey in 1999 confirmed that it reached more affluent adults than the other transnational news broadcasters such as BBC World and CNBC Asia-Pacific. As of the early 2000s, it was offering six different Asian regional programmes over 32 to 35 hours of airtime each week, though the mix varied by country and day of the week (Chang 2001).

BBC World

Launched in Asia in 1991 as part of the StarTV stable, it was the early leader in contextualised news broadcasting for Asia. It was dropped summarily in 1994 from the northern beam of AsiaSat1 by StarTV for offending the Chinese government, thus nominally halving its distribution. In early 1996 the channel parted company with StarTV and re-launched itself on PanAmSat satellites in the region: digitally-compressed off the satellite Pas-2 to reach Southeast and Northeast Asia, and via analogue off Pas-4 for South and West Asia. BBC World also had extensive distribution deals with cable networks in Hong Kong, Singapore, Thailand, Japan, the Philippines and Malaysia, not to mention other deals in South and West Asia [Cable & Satellite Asia 1996b: 20]. Its regionalisation began at the very start when most programmes were from the BBC's domestic UK broadcasts and supplemented with Asian programmes such as "Asia Today" and "Business Asia". By the end of 1999, BBC World had 14 to 15 hours of regional programmes on its broadcast feed to non-South Asian countries (Chang 2001). Having established its first commercial broadcasting model in Asia, BBC World entered the European television market in 1995, Latin America in late 1996 and the US in 1998, thus being able to claim by the end of the decade that it was in 150 million households in 200 countries and territories [BBC World 1999]. Unlike its renowned namesake, BBC World Service Radio which is multilingual, the television service broadcasts solely in English. Neither is the BBC World television channel funded by the British foreign affairs department like the radio service; it is a commercial subsidiary of the otherwise publicly-funded BBC, dependent on advertising and sponsorships. However, its commitment to editorial integrity has offended several governments in Asia, resulting in its virtual exclusion from many domestic cable and pay-TV networks (Atkins 2002: 136–47).

ABN

Although owned largely by western media interests, ABN was a distinctly regional channel dealing exclusively with commercial news. Its original partners, with a 29.5 per cent share each, were Dow Jones, TV New Zealand and Telecommunication Incorporation of the US. Regional participation involved smaller shares by Singapore Media

Ventures and Business News Network of Hong Kong. ABN programming was sourced from Dow Jones' 22 bureaux worldwide and the
staff of its publications, which included the *Far East Economic Review*
and the *Asian Wall Street Journal* [Asian Business News 1994]. By 1995
ABN reached 13 million homes in Southeast Asia directly, not counting a sizeable audience on some terrestrial television networks and
all cable networks in Taiwan and the Philippines which downlinked
selected programming for retransmission. A niche channel in comparison to other transnational services, it commenced as an 18-hour
per day service in English aimed at businesspersons based or travelling
in Asia, with subtitling in Chinese and Malay/Indonesian. Its flagship
programme was "Business Radar" which included a half-hour segment
called "The Asian Wall Street Journal On Air". ABN subsequently
migrated to PanAmSat's Pas-2 before moving on to the more powerful
Pas-4 in a bid to expand its market [APT-C 1995]. By 1995 it gained
half a million more subscribers in the US, through being relayed by
the International Channel Network there for an hour-and-a-half each
day in both English and Mandarin [Television Asia 1995a]. In early
1998 it merged with the US-owned CNBC due to sustained losses by
both channels as doubts grew on whether the regional market could
sustain two round-the-clock business channels. Though its brand name
ceased to be used, key personnel of ABN headed the new organisation
and CNBC's base of operations in Hong Kong were closed in favour
of ABN's in Singapore [ibid. 1998]. The geographical shift might have
reflected corporate concerns about China's political controls en-
croaching on media in the former British territory, though the choice
of Singapore was probably due to its status as a financial centre.

CNBC Asia-Pacific

A subsidiary of NBC of the US, this channel began broadcasting as
ANBC in November 1994 on Wharf Cable in Hong Kong, and later
diversified into a 24-hour business news channel CNBC Asia, and a
general entertainment channel NBC Asia [APT-C&S 1995: 97]. In
the mid-1990s CNBC and NBC had four channels each: the original
one in English, one for India, and two Mandarin channels for Taiwan
and for China respectively, demonstrating acute sensitivity to cultural
differences. These channels are carried on Pas-2, Palapa C2 and AsiaSat2
[Cable & Satellite Asia 1996b: 19]. By 1997 CNBC had 4.1 million

subscribers in the Asia-Pacific region for its 24-hour feeds. Though seemingly a smaller player than its business news rival, the free-to-air ABN, it was available on cable/pay-TV services and had segments on domestic broadcasters [Television Asia 1997]. By the end of 1999, it broadcast 10 Asia-related programmes and two national programmes for most Asian countries each week, totalling 56 hours or a third of its broadcast hours. Renamed CNBC Asia-Pacific upon the merger with ABN, it ventured further into localisation by forming partnerships with local channels and production houses in India, Japan and Taiwan for instance. This resulted in some of those markets having between 73 to 126 hours of regional and local programming per week (Chang 2001). By the early 2000s it had six feeds: CNBC Hong Kong, CNBC India, CNBC Singapore, CNBC Australia, Nikkei-CNBC Japan as well as the original pan-regional CNBC Asia Pacific.

CTN

Owned largely by Hong Kong interests, CTN positioned itself as the Chinese equivalent of CNN by providing all-Mandarin news and business reports as well as sports, lifestyle and documentary programming. Broadcasting out of its base in Hong Kong and utilising PanAmSat2, CTN targeted primarily the Taiwan market where it reached 80 per cent of the over 4 million households as early as the mid-1990s. Despite heavy investments in a digital satellite facility and a 25 per cent stake being sold to a Taiwanese programme distributor, by the mid-1990s doubts were expressed over whether CTN could maintain the high cost of news gathering worldwide [International Cable 1995]. Although having the potential to gain a sizeable following as a unique transnational Mandarin news service providing an alternative to public broadcast sources, CTN ran the risk of antagonising conservative governments in the People's Republic of China, Taiwan, Hong Kong and even Singapore. Since CTN failed to demonstrate market relevance by the late 1990s, it was sold to United Communications Group in Taiwan, which moved its Zong Tian channel to Taiwan and retrenched some staff at its Hong Kong headquarters [Television Asia 1999f]. In 2002 the now three-channel CTN was acquired by the China Times group, forming Taiwan's first media conglomerate incorporating television, the internet and print reaching the Chinese worldwide [Videoland.com 2003].

Discovery Asia

Begun in the US as far back 1985 but a relative latecomer to the Asian region, the educational and documentary network Discovery Channel was launched in January 1994 on both Palapa B2P and Apstar 1. Yet by the end of 1995, it was already available in 3.1 million households across Asia, 2 million of them in Taiwan where Discovery Asia incorporated Mandarin subtitles to increase its market share, on the Indovision package in Indonesia, on Wharf Cable in Hong Kong, as well as cable systems in the Philippines, Thailand, Japan and Korea [APTC&S 1995: 27]. To cater to cultural sensitivities in the Asian region, Discovery Asia utilised a Singapore base from the start to source and re-edit programming. Denying that concerns over media freedom in Hong Kong were a factor in the post-1997 era, Discovery Asia relocated its regional marketing and administrative offices as well to Singapore in 1996 [AMCB 1996a]. In the late 1990s it launched Animal Planet, later encrypting both it and Discovery Channel for Indian pay-TV and adding a Travel & Adventure channel. Its claim of 155 million subscribers throughout Asia by the early 2000s, through three channels, eight languages and 17 specific feeds seems reasonable given the near-universal appeal of its programming relative to business news and cultural entertainment [Discovery On-line 2004].

Others

National Geographic's inauguration in Asia in the late 1990s followed aggressive global expansion that saw its worldwide subscription touch 25 million. Though its rival Discovery Channel had a five-year headstart, National Geographic was launched on major satellite and cable networks in each market such as StarTV in India, Indovision in Indonesia, Astro in Malaysia, Eastern Television in Taiwan and Skycable in Philippines [Television Asia 1998c]. Inaugurated in 1999, Channel News Asia sought to provide businesspersons of the continent an English language news service with an Asian perspective. However, some argue that its regional news is characterised by political conservatism since it is controlled by investment corporations that are owned by the government of Singapore. Within a year of going pan-Asian via Apstar IIA and Palapa C2 satellites, Channel News Asia reached 12 million viewers in Indonesia, Philippines, Brunei, Papua New Guinea, India, Sri Lanka, Nepal, Hong Kong, Korea, Cambodia and the United Arab Emirates [Brown 2001f].

Entertainment Channels

The market for transnational satellite television that StarTV demonstrated as existing in Asia triggered the entry of a number of well
known global satellite broadcasters that specialised in providing entertainment programming. Beginning by rebroadcasting the staple fare
on their domestic US and European channels, they have gradually
learnt to adapt their programming to the interests of the Asian consumer and, no doubt, to accommodate the sensibilities of governments
in various domestic markets (Table 2.2). These broadcasters have done
so primarily to maintain a foothold among competitors, both transnational and domestic, in the potentially lucrative Asian audience
market.

Table 2.2
Regionalisation by Transnational Broadcasters in Asia
(Late 1990s/Early 2000s)

Broadcaster	Subtitling	Dubbing	Sourcing	Multichannel
StarTV	Yes	No	Yes	Yes
Discovery	Yes	Yes	Yes	Yes
HBO Asia	Yes	Yes	No	No
ESPN	No	Yes	Yes	Yes
CNN	No	No	Yes	No
TNT/Cartoon Network	Yes	Yes	No	No
CNBC Asia	No	No	Yes	Yes
MTV Asia	No	No	Yes	Yes

HBO Asia

Home Box Office (HBO) was inaugurated in Asia as a channel on
Singapore Cable Vision in June 1992, when its encrypted signal was
also uplinked from Singapore to Palapa B2P for transmission 24 hours
a day to Southeast Asia, and likewise to Apstar1 for Northeast Asia.
Its shareholders are US-based movie businesses such as Time-Warner
Entertainment, Paramount Pictures, Sony Pictures Entertainment
comprising Columbia and Tristar, and MCA/Universal, for whose
past, current and future movies HBO has exclusive pay-TV rights. Although HBO programming of more than 70 movies and other programmes per month (ranging from action, comedy, horror, thrillers,
westerns and classics to popular music concerts and family specials)
was neither local nor regional, it provided subtitles for these English

language programmes in Chinese, Thai and Indonesian to cater to the respective Asian markets. As of the mid-1990s, HBO had 600,000 subscribers and was available on Hong Kong's Wharf Cable, Indonesia's Indovision, as well as cable networks in Taiwan, Thailand, Singapore, New Zealand, Malaysia and the Philippines [APTC&S 1995: 31]. India was another prime target market given its sizeable English-speaking middle class, though HBO's satellite platforms did not cover the region till the late 1990s. In the competitive Taiwan market, it was able to claim penetrations of between 80 to 90 per cent; by 1998, its annual update stated subscriptions for HBO at 3.2 million with a further 2 million for its second channel, Cinemax [Cable & Satellite Asia 1998]. The widely reported 2003 Asia Pay Television Operators' Survey of the 57 million pay-TV viewers in over 15 Asian markets placed HBO amongst the most popular channels alongside Star Plus, Discovery and ESPN Star Sports, though no figures seem publicly available.

ESPN

In 1992 the US-based channel, Entertainment and Sports Program Network (ESPN) was launched in Asia in direct competition to Prime Sports in the StarTV stable. Its headquarters for the region was set up in Hong Kong. Its signal was then relayed from the US using the Intelsat 180 satellite, downlinked to Hong Kong where it was converted from NTSC to PAL and then uplinked to Palapa B2P, Apstar1, Pas-2 and Pas-4 [ESPN 1994]. Its early programming included NBA basketball, English premier league soccer, Indian test match cricket, PGA golf, Davies Cup tennis, Asian All-Stars table-tennis, volleyball and badminton. Learning from its experience in Latin America, ESPN soon customised its programming of sports in Asia, and translated it into a number of major languages including Mandarin, Cantonese, Hindi and Indonesian. By the mid-1990s it was available free-to-air in around 15 Asia-Pacific countries, on Indovision pay-TV in Indonesia, on Hong Kong's Wharf Cable, and on cable/pay-TV services in Thailand, Australia and New Zealand. Perhaps one secret of its growth has been its arrangements to supply programming duly dubbed to several major cable networks in China and India, as well as to domestic terrestrial stations throughout Asia. Out of 41 cable stations surveyed in China in the late 1990s, ESPN was on 21 and had a penetration of 95 per cent of stations with specialised sports channels, averaging 15 hours coverage per day [Broadcast Asia 1998]. Furthermore it achieved a strategic alliance with Prime Sports of the StarTV stable. By 2000 this had become a 50:50 joint venture known as ESPN Star Sports but often offering separate channels in national markets and claiming penetration of 135 million households across the region [Brown 2001a].

MTV

This service first commenced as part of the StarTV stable in 1992 but fell out two years later. It returned in mid-1995, this time transmitted on Apstar1, Palapa B2P and Pas-4. Beginning with a 24-hour channel, MTV Mandarin was available in 20 countries. It later launched a second English/Hindi channel, MTV Asia, targeted at India and the Philippines but also available in some 30 countries. MTV Asia also signed agreements to be distributed by domestic broadcasters as well, namely India's Doordarshan (DD) on its DD2 Metro channel and Indonesia's Anteve. MTV Mandarin, on the other hand, concentrated on retransmission by cable networks in Taiwan for 24 hours a day to 50 per cent of all cable households [APTC&S 1995: 33]. Perhaps seeking to emulate the success of its nemesis, Channel V, MTV programming in Asia included regional as well as international music videos. By the late 1990s, MTV had reached the 100 million households mark through its then three feeds: MTV Mandarin, MTV India and MTV Southeast Asia, and was cited by a pan-Asian survey as the most watched satellite channel among affluent young adults [Television Asia 1999c]. In the early 2000s it added a fourth broadcast feed to both South Korea and the Philippines, while maintaining significant blocks of programmes to Malaysia, Indonesia and Thailand on its Southeast Asia feed.

TNT/TCM & Cartoon Network

The Asian launch of this composite channel owned by Turner Broadcasting took place in October 1994, broadcast from Palapa B2P, Pas-2 and Apstar1. The Cartoon Network portion broadcast for 14 hours per day, drawing on a library of Hanna-Barbera, Warner Brothers and MGM cartoon programmes, up to 50 per cent of which were dubbed into Mandarin and Thai by the mid-1990s. Each night the TNT portion transmitted classic movies from MGM and Warner Brothers that were subtitled into Mandarin and Thai. Even though its programming drew on "western" library sources, TNT and Cartoon Network built a post-production and transmission centre in Hong Kong, an investment of US$10 million in the Asian market [APTC&S 1995: 43]. By early 2000s, it was rebranded as TCM and was claiming 23 million viewers served through its four feeds: the Indian subcontinent, East Asia, Taiwan and Australia/New Zealand [Television Asia 2001].

SonyET

Launched in 1995, later than StarTV and ZeeTV, it is now one of the leading commercial broadcasters targeting India where it claims 20.5 million households and the Indian diaspora in the UK, US, Middle East, South and East Africa and Fiji. The 24-hour channel is 60 per cent owned by Sony Pictures and 40 per cent locally owned by Ace Telefilms, and produces 4,000 hours of programming per year [Television Asia 2001]. Owned also by Sony Pictures Entertainment, AXN was launched as a stable-mate to SonyET in late 1997 and by 2001 was available in 44 million households in Asia, half of that in 18 countries on a 24-hour basis and another half in China through part-day broadcasts. AXN provides "action-adventure" programming for audiences in their twenties through three separate feeds: East Asia, South Asia and Taiwan (ibid.). This channel is discussed further in Chapter 5 on the Indian subcontinent where it is a significant player.

CETV

China Entertainment Television was founded in December 1994 to provide Mandarin language family entertainment catering to the Chinese mainland and thus to rival StarTV and TVBI. It was owned by Robert Chua, though partners from China and Indonesia were said to own 60 per cent of the channel [Green 1994]. It believed that its programming formula of "no sex, no violence, no news" would avoid controversy with the government of China and other conservative Asian nations. A third of its round-the-clock programming were produced locally, a third imported internationally (including from Discovery Channel) and a third rebroadcast from the Hong Kong public broadcaster RTHK. In March 1995 it was launched on Apstar as a 24-hour channel and by year-end CETV claimed it was carried into 28 million households via 100 cable networks in China, its main target. CETV was also available on 50 Taiwanese cable networks, on Singapore Cablevision and on Sky Cable in the Philippines as well [APTC&S 1995: 21]. A lack of rigorous market research to back its claim meant advertiser scepticism as the industry added to its slogan "no viewers, no ads" [Interview Chn 01.06]. Yet, less than a year later CETV received a US$29 million investment boost when the Hong Kong-based Lippo Group, the Malaysian-Chinese MUI group and the US-based International Media Corporation took equal shares in the firm [Hughes 1996a]. Hopes that with the handover of Hong Kong to China in 1997 CETV would be deemed a domestic Chinese channel in its own right had proved baseless. In the early 2000s CETV gained a financial lifeline from AOL Time Warner and was then said to have penetrated an estimated 33 million households across Asia via the AsiaSat 3S satellite [Brown 2000b].

General Channels

Commercial interests within the Asian region were quick to see that this new medium of satellite television offered a way to circumvent draconian laws forbidding commercial broadcasts nationally, or to broadcast in subnational minority languages. Apart from stimulating domestic broadcasters through competition, regional commercial channels were also able to reach similar ethnic groups across national borders, expatriates in other Asia regions, as well as diasporic communities across the world. Reaching these ethnic markets, uncatered for till then, meant tapping new regional markets for television programming as well as advertising, and providing new business opportunities for film and video producers that are based nationally.

Zee TV

Since its launch towards the end of 1992 on the southern beam of a transponder sub-leased from Star TV for US$6.8 million a year, ZeeTV became a major catalyst for change in Indian subcontinent television. It circumvented India's law banning commercial channels by uplinking from Hong Kong to AsiaSat1, the same satellite platform as StarTV. Although News Corporation acquired 49.9 per cent of its holding company Asia Today based in Hong Kong in December 1993, the remaining 50.1 per cent of its equity was still held by the founding consortium of non-resident Indians (NRIs). Capitalising on the rapid growth of unlicensed cable networks in India, ZeeTV penetration expanded from 3.8 million homes in February 1993 to over 13 million by mid-1995, though this was still a fraction of Doordarshan's reach [Dziadul 1994]. About 45 per cent of its programming was then commissioned in India and another 40 per cent produced in-house by Zee Telefilms. On acquiring a mutual shareholder in News Corporation in the mid-1990s, ZeeTV and StarTV had been bound by an agreement to cooperate on marketing, subscription management, new channel launches and programme production. In conjunction with StarTV, a general entertainment channel EL-TV was inaugurated in late 1994 and a pay-TV Hindi movie channel Zee Cinema was established in 1995. Regional language channels and further expansion into South Asia and West Asia were subsequently embarked on [APTC&S 1995: 111–12]. In the late 1990s ZeeTV parted ways with News Corporation and after a turbulent period operating on its own, teamed up with another media conglomerate, AOL Time Warner, in the early 2000s. Such developments are discussed in further detail in Chapter 5 which focuses on regional television of the Indian subcontinent.

TVBI

In late 1993 Hong Kong's Television Broadcasters International (TVBI) launched its first satellite service, Superchannel or TVBS, directed at the Taiwan cable market utilising the Palapa B2P satellite. The programming consisted of traditional drama, movies, local news, current affairs, music, light entertainment and sports, all dubbed or subtitled in Mandarin, 60 per cent of them sourced externally and 40 per cent produced in-house. The three TVBI channels distributed in Taiwan soon achieved a penetration of 3 million households or 60 per cent of all TV households [TVB 1994]. Given its aim to tap the potential of the Chinese television market and to make this market accessible to advertisers, TVBI produced a 40-hour light entertainment package specifically for syndication to 22 cable networks in that country [Green 1994]. TVB also reached agreements with terrestrial Chinese stations in Beijing, Shanghai, Guangdong and Fujian to provide them with programming from its library, regarded the world's largest. By the mid-1990s TVBS was available on SkyCable in the Philippines, Singapore Cable Vision and Universal CableTV (UTV) in Thailand [TVB 1995b]. TVBI then acquired a 52 per cent interest in The Chinese Channel that broadcast Chinese language programmes to ethnic Chinese in Europe via satellite and cable and had exclusive broadcasting rights to TVBI programmes in Europe [TVB 1995a]. In the late 1990s TVBI launched a Cantonese service called Jade Satellite Channel on Australia's east coast, providing the 400,000 ethnic Chinese minority with a 24-hour selection of TVBI news and entertainment programming [Adweek Asia 1998]. In the early 2000s TVBI added a Mandarin channel specifically targeted at the estimated one million Chinese-speakers in Japan [Brown 2001e]. It has since become the first foreign broadcaster to have two of its channels distributed in China by the state-owned CCTV in exchange for TVBI distributing four CCTV channels via satellite to Southeast Asia, Australia, Europe and North America. Thus TVBI illustrates how the lines between commercial and public, transnational and domestic broadcasters are being blurred within Greater China.

StarTV

The satellite broadcaster StarTV was initially wholly-owned by Hutchinson Whampoa, controlled by the family of Hong Kong billionaire Li Ka-Shing. Between August and December 1991 StarTV launched all its five channels on a pan-Asian basis broadcasting from AsiaSat1: StarPlus, Star Mandarin, Prime Sports, BBC World Service and MTV Asia. Star Plus, the English-language entertainment channel, broadcast 24 hours a day, reaching its target audiences across its footprint through different prime-times. Its "western" programming fare included dramas, comedies, soap-operas, talk shows, documentaries, cartoons and awards shows. Its counterpart was the Star Chinese channel which offered the only non-English programming on transnational satellite television when it was launched [StarTV 1992]. Its Mandarin programming was sourced initially from Taiwan, though audience preferences in Taiwan, China and to a lesser extent Hong Kong and diasporic Chinese saw expansion of its sourcing to Hong Kong especially.

In 1993 News Corporation, Rupert Murdoch's global media conglomerate, bought a controlling 63.6 per cent interest in StarTV [*Straits Times* 1993b]. StarTV began differentiating its channel offerings on the two AsiaSat1 footprints, the northern one covering China, Taiwan and the Philippines primarily, and the southern one mainly covering Indonesia, India and the Middle-East. In late 1994 StarTV increased its collaboration in India with ZeeTV and UTV, both of which News Corporation bought shares in. StarTV also developed a joint-venture with the Chinese government and private companies, Phoenix Satellite

TV which broadcasts Phoenix Chinese Channel and Phoenix Movie Channel [International Cable 1999b]. Having migrated 80 per cent of its channels to digital format, StarTV was able by the late 1990s to offer country-specific channel packages such as to India, Indonesia, the Middle East, Taiwan and China, among others.

National Public Channels

A number of channels beamed from Asian satellites were national and government-owned, utilising the satellite to reach remote pockets of its own territory cost effectively. Sharing the pioneering AsiaSat1 satellite with StarTV was China Central Television (CCTV) whose first three domestic channels were beamed at China's own cities while its fourth channel was directed at Macau, Hong Kong and Taiwan, territories over which it laid claim. On AsiaSat1's northern beam was Mongolian TV, while the southern beam carried Myanmar TV and Pakistan TV as well, though these are primarily for domestic broadcast. Palapa, designed to be a domestic satellite for Indonesia, became a *de facto* regional satellite for Southeast Asia because, since the late 1980s, it carried channels from Malaysia, Australia, Vietnam, France, USA, Papua New Guinea and Hong Kong [Setiawan 1994]. Over the 1990s a number of countries in the region launched international versions of their domestic channels, both to reach their expatriates and promote their culture and ideology on a regional basis.

TCSI

In October 1995 Singapore launched an all-Mandarin commercial satellite channel, Xinshi, catering primarily to the Taiwanese market. More commonly known as Television Corporation of Singapore International (TCSI), this regional arm of the country's domestic public broadcaster draws on the 7,000-hour TCS library of Chinese drama, news and other programming and was considering co-productions with Taiwanese partners. Another motivation for broadcasting via satellite was showcasing Singapore-produced programmes in order to market them to China's television stations and so the latter were provided with complimentary decoders [International Cable 1995]. The Singapore government was also keen to put forward its point of view on domestic and international political issues and market its economic interests in a mix of public relations and diplomacy. Despite claiming 2 million households in the region as early as 1996, owner Media Corporation of Singapore closed the channel unobtrusively in 2000 after five years on air [Lahiri 2001], leaving Channel News Asia as its standard bearer.

ABC Asia-Pacific

Australia's regional television service, first known as Australia Television International (ATVI), was launched in early 1993 by the public broadcaster Australian Broadcasting Corporation (ABC) and transmitted via the Indonesian satellite Palapa B2P [White 1994]. Despite being free-to-air, made available to any cable or domestic network to rebroadcast parts or the whole freely, and even approved by national governments in the region for retransmission domestically, ATVI had few takers. By the mid-1990s it negotiated rebroadcast agreements with 300 hotels throughout Asia and with cable networks in Taiwan, Thailand, Vietnam and Sri Lanka [Australia Television 1996a]. But it failed to achieve any significant viewership, apart perhaps from Australian expatriates in the region, due to its minimalist budget which placed considerable constraints on its programming. Despite publishing high figures of penetration potential such as 11 million households in the Asia-Pacific region [Australia Television 1996b], it failed to persuade advertisers. Unwilling to underwrite ATVI indefinitely, a new conservative Australian government sold it to the domestic, commercial Seven Network in 1996 which failed to turn it around, even at the time of the Sydney Olympics. The government then offered a subsidy and called for tenders, but Seven Network switched off the service by early 2001 [Lahiri 2001]. The station was re-launched in late 2001 as ABC Asia-Pacific, once again with direct financial support from the Australian government in pursuit of its foreign policy interests in the continent.

DD-India

Launched in 1995, this international service of the public broadcaster Doordarshan (DD) was meant to showcase India to the world in general and establish links with the Indian diaspora in particular. But by 2000 DD-India had not achieved its objectives and instead of closing it, Doordarshan embarked on a major redesign and relaunch. It repackaged 120 half-hour entertainment programmes and sourced

40 hours from the Ministry of External Affairs to put forward India's national and international policies. This meant US$3 million for quality programming and a further US$2 million for tele-films. As an example of growing global alliances in media, a Sri Lankan-based company won the right to distribute DD-India in Europe, a United Arab Emirates (UAE) company for the Middle East and a US company for the whole of North America (ibid.).

CCTV-4 and 9

The first regional channel, CCTV-4 broadcasting mostly in Mandarin, was so successful that in late 2000, the Chinese public broadcaster launched its second international channel, CCTV-9, this time in English. Both channels create some of their own programming as well as dubbing other programmes from the CCTV library, and are expected to acquire programming from outside the PRC. These regional CCTV channels are also available beyond Asia in the US, Europe, South Africa and Australia [Stein 2001]. As an indication of the links within Greater China, such international retransmissions of China's public broadcaster are usually in conjunction with commercial broadcasters from Hong Kong and Taiwan, or diasporic Chinese business interests.

SATELLITE PROVIDERS

Ever since AsiaSat1 helped StarTV pioneer transnational television broadcasting in Asia, several other satellites have entered the region with ambitions to tap into this fast-growing market. With the growing convergence of media and communications technologies, many satellites launched over the 1990s have been multi-purpose. There are now numerous satellites operating in the region which provide also telephony, data communications, navigation, geographic survey, meteorological studies and other such services. The Asian economic crisis in 1997 was seen as merely a temporary setback for the satellite industry with full recovery predicted for the early 2000s. Still there were over 90 geostationary satellites serving the Asia-Pacific region, located between 30 degrees East and 186 degrees East longitude [Verlini 1999]. Given the purpose of this book, its survey will be confined to those satellite platforms utilised by major television channels that covered the Asian continent over the period of the early 1990s to early 2000s, and seek to classify them in terms of their ownership and coverage.

International Satellites

Satellite systems have historically been the province of IGOs such as Intelsat and Intersputnik, sponsored by the capitalist West and the communist Eastern bloc respectively. Although they were public interest organisations catering to all nation-states, they represented efforts at political and economic hegemony by the two sides of the Cold War in this surrogate arena of space. These organisations sought to place satellite technology in the service of national development in developing countries in the 1960s and 1970s, an age when the commercialisation of that technology was relatively unknown. Both have since had to face up to the challenges of the market to their duopoly, and are now just two competitors among many such as PanAmSat in the new market for global satellite systems (Table 2.3).

Intelsat
This consortium of 133 nation-states had 12 satellites with large footprints over the Indian Ocean and Asia-Pacific region in the 1990s. These satellites carried such channels as Nippon TV, Deutsche Welle TV, ESPN, RFO Tahiti, Channel 7 Thailand, PTS Taiwan, Canal France, TNT, all the Australian networks and TVNZ. Faced with commercial competition, Intelsat replaced its aging satellites with Intelsat 7-series and Intelsat 8-series satellites, positioned over the Pacific Ocean [Via Satellite 1994b]. Then in 2001, responding to competitive pressures, Intelsat was converted from a treaty organisation of cooperating countries into a private corporation with 200 leading communications companies as its shareholders. As of the early 2000s it had 21 geo-stationary satellites globally and eight more on order. Despite its more recent economic woes, Asia remains a key market as indicated by the launch of two Intelsat satellites over the region in 2000–01 [Asia Pacific Satellite 2001].

Table 2.3
Selected International Satellites and their Major Television Stations Over Asia

Satellite	Intel 704	Intel 701	Pas-2	Pas-4
Location	66°E	180°E	169°E	68.5°E
TV Channels	Vijay TV	CNN	CCTV	BBC
	Sky News	Ten Network	Discovery	Canal
	MTB (Mongolia)	Nine Network	MTV	Animal Planet
	STV	TVNZ	ESPN	CNN
	TV5 Asia	NHK	TNT/Cartoon Network	DD India
	Gemini TV	ABC/CBS	National Geographic	Discovery
	Eenadu	Canal	CNN	ESPN-India
	CNBC Asia	Saudi Ch.1	Deutsche W.	Hallmark
	MCM	Abu Dhabi	BBC	MTV
			NHK	ZeeTV
			TVB	M-Net
				SonyET
				TNT/Cartoon Network

Sources: Asia Cable & Satellite World [2000c]; Cable & Satellite Asia [2000].

Intersputnik

An international satellite network rivalling Intelsat since 1971, the Intersputnik consortium comprised the former USSR and its allies in Europe and Asia. Operated by the Russian Ministry of Postal Services and Telecommunications, it had a range of aging Gorizont, Ekran and Raguda satellites covering the Asia region. In a sign of post-Cold War rapprochément, by the mid-1990s the US-owned Rimsat organisation operated two Russian-built satellites. One was an aging Gorizont used by one of the Indian commercial television channels. The other was a newer Rimsat1 covering a vast area from above the Pacific Ocean, stretching from Alaska in the east, Russia in the north, India in the west and Antarctica in the south. Then, the US-based aerospace manufacturer Lockheed Martin formed an alliance with Intersputnik to launch, insure, control and manage four satellites. The first was positioned over the Indian Ocean, while the others were over the Americas, Europe, Africa and the Pacific Rim [Lahiri 1999]. By the early 2000s, however, Intersputnik seemed no longer a major player in its own right as an intergovernmental consortium, certainly not in providing satellite platforms for Asia.

PanAmSat

A commercial rival to Intelsat, PanAmSat was owned by US and Mexican interests. It had two key satellites in the Asia-Pacific region as part of its global network of some 14 satellites covering 100 nations. Its Pas-2 and Pas-4 beamed channels into Asia such as ABN, Disney, NHK International (Japan), CCTV (China), SonyET, ABS-CBN (Philippines), TNT and Doordarshan International (India). The newer Pas-4 satellite has trans-Indian Ocean coverage, and carries further channels on its specific African and European beams. PanAmSat benefited from the shock failure of the Apstar2 launch when a number of the latter's clients opted to migrate to Pas-4, which also attracted Indian channels including public broadcaster Doordarshan [APTC&S 1995: 141]. In the late 1990s, PanAmSat launched its fourth satellite for the Asian region, Pas-8, which was also the eighteenth in its global fleet. Positioned over the Pacific Ocean it was also designed to complement Pas-2 in offering providing greater power and back-up to its existing customers [Asia Pacific Satellite 1998d]. In the early 2000s, PanAmSat sought to raise US$2 billion to repay and potentially takeover its parent company Hughes Electronics [Brown 2001e].

National Public Satellites

Originally, government-owned satellite operators aimed at their domestic markets, although progressively they provided platforms for neighbouring countries' public and commercial broadcasters as well as transnational broadcasters (Table 2.4). Furthermore, governments in Asia have been privatising their satellite operators which have in turn entered into strategic alliances with MNCs. Alternatively, these governments have been relegating national involvement in the satellite industry to joint ventures of domestic and foreign firms, the former often having connections directly or indirectly to the centres of political power in the country. Thus the line between domestic and transnational, public and commercial satellites in Asia has become increasingly difficult to draw.

Table 2.4
Selected Domestic-public Satellites and Television Stations Over Asia

Satellite	Insat 2E	Insat 2B/2C	Palapa C2	Cakrawarta-1
Location	83E	93.5E	113.0E	107.7E
TV Channels	DD-1 National	DD-4 Malayalam	TVRI	Animal Planet
	DD-2 Metro	DD-10 Marathi	RCTI	Cinemax
	DD-5	DD-5 Tamil	TPI	CMT
	DD-7	DD-9 Kannada	Indosiar	Discovery
	DD-8	DD-7 Bengali	TV Brunei	HBO
	Asianet	DD-8 Telugu	CTV	MTV
	ETV Bangla	DD-1 National	Discovery	TV5 France
	Vijay TV	DD-2 Metro	ESPN	Indovision
	Jaya TV	DD Gyandarshan	HBO	National
				Geographic
			CTS	RAI
			MTV Asia	TNT
			Channel V	SonyET
			Australia TV	BBC World
			Phoenix	CNN
			CNBC Asia	Bloomberg
			CNN	RCTI
			StarTV	SCTV
			C.News Asia	TPI

Sources: Cable Satellite Asia [1996b; 2000]; Cooperman [1995]; Indiantelevision.com [2001]; Nielsen SRG [1995]; Television Asia [1996c].

Insat

After experimenting with borrowed satellite transponders India began launching its own satellites in 1982–83 to carry Doordarshan, the domestic public television network. After years of little progress Insat received new impetus from the sudden expansion of Doordarshan into a multiple regional language service in response to competition from transnational satellite television [APTC&S 1995]. It launched three Insat2 series satellites between 1995 and 1997 to more than re-place earlier satellites [Cooperman 1995]. The Indian government then began gradually leasing spare transponders to commercial television, though to transnational rather than domestic commercial broadcasters. Vying for their use were channels such Discovery, Disney and TNT/ Cartoon Network, alongside DD-1 and other national, metropolitan and regional channels of Doordarshan [Television Asia 1996a]. From the late 1990s, in a departure from historic policy and practice, Insat satellites began accepting non-Doordarshan domestic channels for broadcast, particularly from the non-Hindi speaking South of the country. By the same token, Doordarshan also began utilising non-government satellites such as PanAmSats and Thaicoms, further blurring the lines between government and commercial, transnational and domestic entities.

Palapa

This Indonesian-owned satellite network, originally intended and long used for domestic broadcasting, has become a *de facto* transnational satellite platform. On its B2R satellite which carried the Indonesian national broadcaster TVRI, it also carried the domestic television services of Malaysia, the Philippines and Papua New Guinea. On its later satellite B2P, it carried Indonesian commercial channels as well as transnational channels such as CNN, ESPN, Discovery, HBO and MTV Asia, and regional channels originating in Australia and Hong Kong. Satelindo, the privatised operator of Indonesia's third-generation satellites, opted for wider coverage and higher capacity for its Palapa C series in order to meet broadcaster demand [Via Satellite 1994b]. In the late 1990s the new operator launched the 36-transponder Telkom 1 with a footprint that extends to Australia and New Zealand to replace the aging Palapa B2R and B4 satellites [Asia Pacific Satellite 1998b]. Further satellite launches seem to have slowed following the political and economic crises in Indonesia.

ChinaSat

Over the 1990s the China Telecommunications and Broadcast Satellite Corporation (CTBSC), a commercial arm of the PRC Ministry of Posts and Telecommunications, had four satellites in place: ChinaSats1, 2, 3 and 5. The first three were built and launched by the Chinese between 1988 and 1990, primarily for voice, data and television transmission by domestic television services [Cooperman 1995]. Chinasat5 was China's first foreign-built satellite though purchased second-hand in 1992. It was used by a number of national and provincial television stations for domestic broadcasting [Cable & Satellite Asia 1996b]. Although China has resorted to purchasing satellites from western sources, it insisted on launches via one of its own Long March rockets, perhaps to support that industry or simply out of national pride.

In 1997 it purchased ChinaSat8, its most powerful to date with 16 Ku-band and 36 C-band channels, which brought the total number of Chinese public satellites to 38. Its rivals, the semi-private China Orient Telecommunications and Sino Satellite Communications, planned launching three ChinaStar and two SinoSat satellites respectively for the early 2000s between themselves [Asia Pacific Satellite 1998a]. Once enjoying a monopoly, ChinaSat is increasingly facing commercial competition from within Greater China as well as beyond.

Regional-commercial Satellites

An increasing number of broadcast satellites over Asia were owned and utilised by commercial interests from within the region. However, the technology for the manufacture of these satellites and for their launch, with the possible exceptions of China and India, remained in the hands of MNCs or governments of the developed world. The pioneer commercial satellite owner on the continent was AsiaSat which helped establish the transnational television market and set the trend for the regional and global, public and commercial satellites to follow (Table 2.5). Subsequently there have been a number of satellites launched, often by domestic and regional corporations that have considerable equity and other financial assistance from national governments or politically well-connected businesspersons.

AsiaSat

The AsiaSat1 satellite on which StarTV began its operations was previously the Hughes Aircraft Westar VI that failed to achieve its geostationary orbit after launch in 1984. Retrieved by the US space shuttle Challenger, it was refurbished and then sold by the insurance company for a mere US$130 million to a consortium of Hong Kong's Hutchinson Telecommunications, the UK's Cable & Wireless, and the Chinese government's investment arm, China International Trust and Investment Corporation (CITIC). AsiaSat1 was launched successfully in April 1990 on one of China's Long March III rockets and positioned at an equatorial orbit slightly east of Singapore, in a slot assigned by the ITU to China [Asia Magazine 1990]. Hutchinson Telecommunications took control of a dozen transponders on it for the purpose of

Table 2.5
Selected Regional-commercial Satellites and Television Stations Over Asia

Satellite	AsiaSat3S	Apstar2R	Measat-2	Thaicom-3
Location	105.5E	76.5E	148E	78.5E
TV Channels	CCTV-4	CTS	HBO	DD channels
	CETV	CTV	TNT/Cartoon	Tara
	TNT/Cartoon Network	Formosa TV	MTV	ETC
	ESPN	TTV	NBC Asia	RajTV
	CNN Intl	GuandongTV	CNBC Asia	ATN
	CNBC	Fujian TV	CNN Intl	Jain
	Phoenix	Tibet TV	Hallmark	
	StarTV	TVB	MGMGold	
	ZeeTV	Hallmark	Star Movies	
	Sky News	HBO Asia	Star World	
		Raj	TVBS	
		Disney	TVB 8	

Sources: Asia Cable & Satellite World [2000c]; Cable & Satellite Asia [2000].

running a pan-Asian television service, namely StarTV. Most of the remaining transponders were leased by Bangladesh, Myanmar, Mongolia, Nepal and Pakistan, countries that could not have afforded a satellite of their own. Major shareholder CITIC was instrumental in signing up China's Ministry of Posts and Telecommunications as well as number of domestic channels [Asia-Pacific Broadcasting 1992]. About 60 per cent of the transponder capacity of AsiaSat1 was utilised for television, mostly transnational. The trend towards commercial television rather than telephony on Asian satellites followed closely that of Europe and North America. This rapid transponder take-up rate for AsiaSat1 gave its owners confidence to begin planning as early as 1992 for AsiaSat2.

Despite using identical Long March rockets which had exploded in recent years while launching two other satellites, the technologically more advanced AsiaSat2 was launched successfully in November 1995 [Television Asia 1996a]. With a larger footprint than AsiaSat1, it covered much of Central Asia and Russia in the north, stretching to Australia in the south, Japan in the east, and East Africa and Turkey in the west. It had 24 C-band transponders and nine Ku-band transponders, the latter focused on China, Korea, Southeast Asia and Indo-China. StarTV signed a US$200 million contract for exclusive access to 20 transponders across both AsiaSat1 and AsiaSat2 over 12 years

[APTC&S 1995: 137], thereby demonstrating its commitment to a long-term presence in the Asian television market. Despite industry concerns about a glut of transponder capacity, the AsiaSat3 satellite was launched in 1997 to replace AsiaSat1 and provide digital television across Asia, including the Indian subcontinent, the Middle East and Australia. In 1999, SES/Astra of Europe acquired 50 per cent of the AsiaSat corporation at a cost of US$331 million from its founding shareholders Hutchinson Whampoa of Hong Kong, Cable & Wireless of the UK and CITIC of China. This gave SES/Astra a reach of 335 million households or about 74 per cent of the world's population [Forrester 1999]. At the time of the sale, AsiaSat operated two satellites serving 53 countries with two replacement satellites planned. It had stable clients like StarTV and CNBC, but transponder uptake on its satellites was low [Hughes and Soh 1999]. Yet in the early 2000s, it announced intentions of investing US$2.5 billion in another new satellite, its fifth launch, to cope with demand [Leung 2000a].

Apstar

A close rival of AsiaSat was another China-funded company called APT Satellite Company, a consortium mainly owned by three Chinese government agencies: the Ministry of Posts and Telecommunications, China Aerospace Industry Corporation and a military science commission [Walsh 1994] as well as minority Hong Kong, Taiwan and Macau investors. Apstar planned for its satellites to carry a mix of global and regional channels, the latter largely Hong Kong, Taiwanese and Chinese. US-based satellite television such as CNN, Discovery, ESPN, HBO and TNT, comprising the proverbial "Gang of Five" channels, as well as other major transnational broadcasters migrated from other satellite platforms to its Apstar1 satellite in 1994. Regional broadcasters such as TVBI, CETV and several Chinese domestic channels also leased transponders on this first Apstar satellite [APTC&S 1995: 133]. Even before Apstar1 was launched a group of seven international broadcasters, including some of the "Gang of Five" plus Viacom Inc., Paramount Communications Inc. and Hong Kong's TVB signed an agreement to lease a further 16 transponders on their second satellite ApStar2 [AWSJ 1993a]. When ApStar2 exploded on launching in January 1995, all this competition to StarTV was postponed briefly till the replacement satellite Apstar 2R was launched in early 1997. Though its 16 Ku-band transponders were focused on Greater China, its 28 C-band transponders had a footprint covering most of Europe and Africa, and all of Asia including the Middle East and Australia [APT Satellite 1996]. While Apstar1A, launched around the same time, had a footprint over East, Central, North and Southeast Asia, it appeared to carry Chinese domestic channels almost exclusively [Tele-Satellite 2002].

Thaicom

The giant Shinawatra Group of Thailand, owned by a businessman who became prime minister subsequently in 2000, launched its three Thaicom satellites between 1993 and 1996. Though Thaicom1 and Thaicom2 provided coverage across Thailand and the Asia-Pacific and were utilised predominantly by domestic television of the Indo-China subregion, they were soon accepting transnational channels. Hence the next satellite Thaicom3 had 24 C-band transponders spanning Asia, Europe, Australia and Africa, and 14 Ku-band transponders had spot-beams aimed at Thailand and India [Boeke 1997]. Similarly Thaicom 4, launched in the early 2000s, covered 120 countries on the same four continents via its C-band transponders while targeting South Asia and Southeast Asia, specifically Indo-China with its Ku-band transponders [Asia Pacific Satellite 1998e]. Thus this originally domestic satellite platform soon developed regional and almost global ambitions.

Measat

An early user of Intelsat and Palapa satellites, Malaysia had its own Measat1 satellite built by Hughes and launched by Arianne in December 1995. Owned not by the Malaysian government but a private corporation it licensed, Binariang, Measat1 has footprints centred on Southeast Asia [Via Satellite 1995b]. In addition to telecommunications services it carried a 40-channel pay-TV service, Astro, on which both transnational and domestic channels were available. A second satellite Measat2 launched in November 1996 had a larger footprint stretching from Australia to South Asia, allowing it to expand the Astro DTH service it carried to Taiwan and the Philippines. In the late 1990s Binariang gained special status and grants from the Malaysian government to be the sole satellite provider for the nation's Multimedia Super Corridor [Asia Pacific Satellite 1998c]. In the early 2000s Measat invested in a 40 per cent share in the Galaxy satellite system, the majority of which was owned by TVB of Hong Kong, thus adopting a regional alliance strategy instead of expanding its own fleet of satellites.

Other Satellites Over Asia

Since the formation of its national space agency in 1969, Japan has been active in satellite manufacture and launches. As of the late 1990s it had four different satellite systems: JCSAT, N-Star, Superbird and BS/Bsat [APT Yearbook 1998]. In the mid-1990s Korea, a relative latecomer to the national satellite stakes, launched two satellites within six months of each other believed to be primarily for the domestic market [Via Satellite 1996]. Towards West Asia, the Arab Satellite Communications Organisation, a consortium founded by the Arab League in 1976, operated Arabsat 1C and ID. These were utilised for both telephony and broadcasting by West Asian states as well as transnational television such as CNN, Canal France International (CFI), Middle-East Broadcasting Center (MBC), Orbit Communications and Future Vision [Via Satellite 1995a]. Another satellite player at that western end of the Asian continent was Israel Aircraft Industries Ltd which launched the Amos1 and subsequent satellites (ibid. 1994a). Though having smaller footprints largely over Europe and the Mediterranean, its inclusion here is in the interests of impartiality in Middle East politics and not for bearing the name of this author. At the start of the twenty-first century European satellite operators such as SES/Astra, Eutelsat, EuroStar and Eurasiasat were also expanding into the growing Asian market, particularly India and China [Asia Pacific Satellite 2001]. The growing number of satellite platforms over West and Central Asia, and Oceania often sharing footprints with North Africa, Europe, North America and Australasia, are beyond the scope of the present book.

As of the late 1990s there were a total of 530 satellites of all kinds worldwide, about 180 of which were commercial communications satellites in geo-synchronous orbit. Another 1,700 satellites, mostly low-to-medium earth orbit, were planned for the first decade of the new millennium (Dan Schiller 2000: 66–68). By the late-1990s there were already 34 satellites serving Asia with an additional 21 satellites providing trans-Pacific Ocean and trans-Indian Ocean coverage. The skies above Asia were certainly getting congested with satellites (Table 2.6), illustrated also by incidents of jockeying for orbital slots. Yet the outlook for the Asian transnational television broadcasters was not altogether positive since the growth of domestic commercial television channels in Asia had spawned stiff competition among all broadcasters for viewer markets (Table 2.7). After the massive expansion of the 1990s, a glut of channels resulted and consequently a shake-out of satellite platforms was anticipated. But this did not turn out to be the case because many transnational broadcasters began utilising more than one satellite platform each, in their determination to tailor their channel offerings to different regional markets. Furthermore, there seems to be no correlation between ownership of channels and their preference to be located on satellite platforms owned similarly, the only criterion seemingly being the markets reached by the latter's footprints and the prices offered.

Table 2.6
Launches of Satellite Platforms Over Asia, 1991–2000

1991–92	1993–94	1995–96	1997–98		1999–2000
8 sats	14 sats	16 sats	31 sats		14 sats
		Gals-2	Insat 2D		
		Stationar-12	Rimsat Exp2	Telkom1	
	Thaicom	Stationar-20	Rimsat Exp3	LMI 1	Intelsat 902
	PanAmSat	Insat 2C	Measat-1	Chinasat 8	Astra 1K
	China/DFH	AsiaSat2	Measat 2	Agila 3	Thaicom-4
	Apstar1	Rimsat Exp1	Apstar-1A	Orion 3	Intelsat 901
	Rimsat 2	Nstar-a	Apstar-2R	Pas 8	AsiaSat4
	Gorizont-42	NStar-b	Intelsat 709	Pas 7	Astra 2B
Stationar-21	Express-2	Gals-1	DFH-3A2	Intelsat 801	Koreasat3
Optus B1	Stationar-3	Intelsat 703	Intelsat 802	ST-1	Turksat 2A
Palapa B4	Gorizont-41	Intelsat 704	Intelsat 803	Insat 2E	Apstar 3D
Insat 2A	Insat 2B	Insat2C	Thaicom-3	Nilesat 101	Eutelsat W4
Stationar-13	Intelsat 703	Pas-4	Palapa C1	Chinastar 1	Arabsat 3A
Intelsat 511	Rimsat 1	JCSat-3	Palapa C2	Intelsat 806	Yamal 200
PalapaB2R	Chinasat 3	Koreasat-1	Indostar-1	JCSAT 6	Intelsat K-TV
AsiaSat1	Palapa Pcfk	Koreasat-2	Mabuhay	Yamal 101	AsiaStar

Sources: Asia Pacific Satellite [1998a]; Cable Satellite Asia [2000]; Cooperman [1995]; Euroconsult [1995]; Television Asia [1996c].

Table 2.7
Household Penetration Projections for Asia Pacific Satellite and Cable Television

	1997	1998	1999	2000	2001
Digital DTH					
Digital dish households '000	790	1,845	3,169	4,386	5,509
Dish/TV households	0.2%	0.4%	0.6%	0.9%	1.1%
DTH revenues US$m	218	607	1,166	1,771	2,337
Cable/MMDS					
Cable & sat hh '000	89,792	101,045	111,245	119,780	128,285
Cable & satellite/					
TV households	18.5%	20.4%	22.0%	23.3%	24.6%
TV households '000	486,190	495,813	504,734	513,513	521,918

Source: Baskerville Communications, as cited in International Cable [1999a].

Over the 1990s, entertainment media and personal communication became the largest users of satellites in Asia, no longer government and big business, as subsequent chapters on regional television will demonstrate. Thus here as worldwide, there is a clear trend towards the commercialisation of space that is no longer considered a global public domain. The launching of satellites and channels is dictated not by national prestige but commercial expedience. There is also a decline of national loyalties in the decision by television channels of which satellites to use. Convergence of communications technologies is demonstrated in the many mergers between satellite, telephony, internet, cable and television firms. This has taken place amongst western firms, among Asian firms as well as between western and Asian firms. There is also increasing evidence of a partial reversal in flows of programming and information from West-East to East-West. Finally, in Asia it appears that internet use and e-commerce via broadband could be the key beneficiaries of the growth of satellite and cable technologies that is being driven for now by the diffusion of transnational and regional television.

CONTEXTUALISING GLOBALISATION

With the relentless integration of nation-states into a global capitalist economy, the growing perception of a shrinking world through communications technology, and the seeming spread of western culture via the mass media, the concept of globalisation gained mileage in the late twentieth century. Certainly this awareness of the interdependence of nations and societies within a world system is reflected in the widespread use of the term "globalisation" in business and media circles currently. Yet the concept remains unclear because both the academic use of the term across different disciplines and the popular usage of the term in various professional fields have resulted in a plurality of meanings.

ECONOMY AND POLITY

Depending on their point of view, the systematic growth of globalisation has been dated by some theorists either from European adventurism beginning in the middle of this millennium, or from industrialisation and colonialisation between the seventeenth and nineteenth centuries. Others have dated it from modernisation and development following the First and Second World Wars, more recently from the demise of the Cold War in the late 1980s, or even from the advent of post-industrial phenomena in the late twentieth century. Neglected in most of these accounts of nascent globalisation has been the explorations, imperialism and cultural hegemony within Asia by empires in China, India and later Japan over the same historical periods. Perhaps this is because globalisation has almost always been taken to imply a "westernising" process. Whatever its history, the present understanding of globalisation seems to be that it represents an acceleration of the spread of "western-style" modernisation. It is with this concept that this review of the academic literature begins.

Modernisation Theories

If one accepts the view that globalisation is not a new process, then it must be possible to trace its roots in the discussion of modernisation across various disciplines. Although modernisation theorists recognised that social change was a complex multicausal process, under Keynesian influences there was still a tendency to see economic factors as the pre-eminently determinant ones. For instance, Rostow (1960) claimed that with adequate preparation an economy would take off into a period of self-sustained growth. The newly independent countries of the so-called Third World in the post-World War II era were very interested in this viewpoint but soon came to realise that an influx of capital was not a sufficient factor in and of itself. There was positive social change in some of these countries as a result of capital investments but not in others; Hoselitz (1957) argued that this was due to the latter's lack of appropriate institutions, human resource development and proper attitudes.

The predominant structural-functionalist theory of the day analysed how functions adapted to maintain a stable structure comprising of mutually dependent subsystems, or failed to adapt resulting in dysfunction. Still, one of the most influential structural-functionalists of the twentieth century, Parsons (1973) believed in the inevitability of modernisation resulting in economic growth, universal education and political democratisation worldwide. While this initial paradigm espoused certain sociodemographic and structural prerequisites for modernisation globally, research in developing countries actually undermined these notions and demonstrated the ahistoricity, paternalism and ethnocentricity of such functionalism and thus modernisation theories. As Waters (1995) demonstrated, for one thing, capitalism grew out of the peculiar European monarchal/feudal system of the sixteenth to the nineteenth centuries, and for another, the path of modernisation in the West subsequently has not been without social and economic crises. According to Eisenstadt (1973), each national society was composed of multiple subsystems of social, cultural and economic organisations that differentiated one society from another; such differences extend or limit the choices that a society has in relation to the process of modernisation.

Thus Lauer (1991) claimed that social change at the global, societal and institutional levels might not guarantee that similar changes would have an impact at the community or individual levels. Likewise, Giddens (1990) conceived of globalisation as influenced by four factors: capitalism, the interstate system, militarism and industrialism. For him, globalisation was a process arising out of the differentiated interaction of these factors in various parts of the world, and not a steady, homogenising diffusion of a western political-economic structure across the world. Thus Giddens saw globalisation as a natural outgrowth of modernisation when traditional social institutions were "dis-embedded" or superseded by global ones. Achieved through better communications, this phenomenon resulted in a greater sense of world citizenry or of interdependence on a global basis among individuals. Whether politically, economically, socially or culturally, the Third World then is simply not comprised of homogeneous developing nation-states as modernisation theorists presupposed, let alone as clones of the developed world prior to industrialisation.

Dependency Perspectives

Taking a more radical or critical approach, dependency theorists argued that underdevelopment was caused not by sociocultural factors but by politico-economic ones, namely the exploitation of developing countries by capitalist developed ones. This view originated with Marx who explained historical transformation of societies through the growth of capitalism, which in turn was due to the exploitation of the working class. Lenin expanded this model to incorporate the relationship between imperial powers and their colonies. According to O'Connor (1970), the need to update this Marxist perspective led to the dependency model which asserted that persistent underdevelopment of any society was symptomatic of its place within an exploitative world-capitalist system. Even though many developing countries may have become politically independent from their colonisers and seemed to have national sovereignty, they were still subject to neocolonialism, a form of economic and political dependency. Chase-Dunn (1975) demarcated three aspects of this dependency: (*a*) exploitation of the developing countries, namely through developed country investments, (*b*) infrastructure distortion of the developing economies, (*c*) and suppression of autonomous policies by the developing world. As such, any effort to achieve economic development such as import substitution was fraught with difficulty, and even aid from the developed world served to perpetuate the exploitation.

The only alternatives left open to every developing country were to isolate itself from the capitalist world system, or to seek to have the terms of international trade radically revised. Amin (1982) pointed out that the former alternative was tested by some countries, such as those of the former Second World which sought to set up a socialist-communist world system, and found wanting. The latter solution was pursued via the General Agreement on Tariffs and Trade (GATT) and resultant World Trade Organisation (WTO) with greater impetus since the end of the Cold War in the 1990s. But dependency theorists are sceptical of the value of GATT for developing countries, especially those in financial strife and increasingly controlled by the World Bank and International Monetary Fund (IMF) which are themselves influenced by their donors' foreign policies. After all, the Third World's lobbying during the 1970s and early 1980s for a New International Economic Order (NIEO) through the United Nations was impeded by the US and other First World countries that preferred GATT as their platform since developing countries were not a collectivity in it. Thus Raghavan (1991) considered the Uruguay Round of GATT to be an attempt by the First World countries to control world trade and provide opportunities for their MNCs to dominate Third World markets. In what might well be described as re-colonisation, he anticipated Third World countries forfeiting their already limited economic sovereignty in their desire for integration into the capitalist global economy controlled by First World countries.

As critics of structural-functionalism, dependency theorists tend to err in the opposite direction by propounding theories emphasising the forces of conflict and disruption, and often failing to acknowledge the forces for social order and stability. Like many others before and since, Berger (1991) made a determined defence of capitalism against dependency theories. He sought to persuade that the efficient productive power and high standard of living in advanced industrial nations of the First World were being replicated in those Third World nations which were well incorporated into the global capitalist system. Berger contrasted these developments of Third World countries replicating First World ones through economic integration with his control case of the then Second World, a questionable choice. Revealing clear ideological bias, he postulated that there was an intrinsic link between industrial socialism and inefficient economic and authoritarian political systems. In contrast, in the First World, capitalism promoted a class system that permitted social mobility, individual autonomy and democratic processes, though he acknowledged that these were slow processes in the Third World given its traditional culture and society. Of particular interest to this book was Berger's emphasis on East Asia's newly industrialising countries which, he believed, demonstrated that genuine economic growth could occur despite state intervention in the economy and their relative dependency on the global capitalist system. But his views certainly need revising in the light of the so-called Asian meltdown and subsequent economic woes around the turn of the twentieth century.

World-systems Theories

Through his study of modernisation in Africa, Wallerstein (1979) became convinced that the state was not the valid unit of analysis when the economic system spanned the world. Thus he formulated "world-system" theory, a variation of dependency theories which stated that there exists a global economic system through which capitalist developed, or core countries, and their MNCs exploit developing, or periphery countries, through low prices for raw material and high prices for finished goods. As part of the system, semi-periphery countries were both dependent on the core countries and co-exploitative of the periphery ones. In his prognosis, the global integration of this system in favour of the inequitable status quo between nation-states would have resulted in resistance, fragmentation and its ultimate collapse, but for the buffer of semi-peripheral states (ibid. 1991). However, in postulating that capitalism perpetuated a global economy or what he termed as a "world-system" comprising nation-states of unequal power and wealth, Wallerstein adopted a uni-causal analysis of globalisation which naturally had its limitations.

Criticisms of "world-systems" theory have revolved around its simplistic one-dimension analysis of causality, namely economic exploitation. Bergensen (1990) criticised Wallerstein for the assumption that the world-system was formed by developed and developing nation-states in an unequal relationship. He argued the opposite view, namely that the world-system preceded the existence of these nation-states and was even instrumental in the latter's formation. Some critics have put forward alternative models of geopolitical factors, primarily citing political power rivalry between nation-states. Robertson (1992) saw "world-systems" theory as merely a reaction to the inadequacy of modernisation theory which had used developed nations as the basis of comparison for developing countries, but which failed to demonstrate political and economic relations between the two systematically. Critics from the classical economics school such as Shannon (1989) would argue instead for the theory of comparative advantage, which holds that all countries involved are better off through unrestricted trade than if they did not trade at all. Therefore peripheral countries chose to trade with the core because it was to their advantage to do so, core countries did not need to coerce them, and peripheral countries were not necessarily exploited when core countries progressed, stated Chirot and Hall (1982).

Perhaps in response to these criticisms, other theorists adopted a more multicausal perspective of the political economy. In contrast to Wallerstein's view of monolithic global capitalism and in lieu of Marxist and non-Marxist periodisations, Lash and Urry (1987) offered a three-stage model of the development of capitalist economies: liberal, organised and disorganised. They attribute the present "disorganisation" of capitalism in the industrialised nations to three globalising processes. First, those processes from above included MNCs and international financial markets. Second, decentralising processes from below included the decline of mass industries, devolution of government and dispersion of the population. Finally, transformation from within included the growth of the "service class", their quaint description of white collar professionals. Through their analysis of the major western economies of the late twentieth century at varying stages of capitalist development, Lash and Urry demonstrated that collectively they were all well on the road to producing globalised post-modern cultures. But what significance this perspective holds for the prospects of developing countries is unclear.

Interdependence and Fragmentation

Globalisation has been conceived in contemporary literature as a process of linking individuals and organisations that transcends the boundaries of the system of nation-states which comprise the manifest world political-economic system. More specifically, McGrew (1992a) contended that it was "a process through which events, decisions in one part of the world can come to have significant consequences for individuals and communities in quite distant parts of the globe". He sketched three paradigms in the analysis of globalisation: realism/neo-realism, liberal-pluralism and neo-Marxism. Realism/neo-realism saw nation-states as still the dominant actors and perceived order as attained by balance of power, largely military, between hegemonic states. Liberal-pluralism acknowledged the rise of MNCs, international organisations and other forms of transnational relations or movements, and the decline of nation-states as primary actors. It considered technological and economic interdependence to be aiding globalisation, with communications especially responsible for the erosion of national boundaries. Neo-Marxism perceived the capitalist world system as dominant and thus constraining nation-states, MNCs and other transnational organisations to act in the interests of the dominant capitalist classes. McGrew (1992b) also argued that power was based neither on military might nor on political interdependence, but rather on economic integration into the capitalist system of global production and exchange.

Other thinkers have grappled similarly with the issue of what constitute the lynchpins of economic and political globalisation today, though less succinctly. Referring to the three major ideologies as economic nationalism, liberalism and Marxism, Gilpin (1987) traced all controversies of political economy to their differing conceptions of the relationships between state, society and market. For him, globalisation was closely tied to the worldwide growth of capitalism with its accompanying processes of commodification and marketisation. With an international relations perspective, he also identified the rise and decline of a liberal hegemonic power, namely the US, as the catalyst nonetheless for a somewhat democratic world order and global marketplace that encouraged interchange and interdependence. More relevant to this book was another multicausal thinker, Rosenau (1990), who attributed globalisation largely to newer communication technologies. With the onset of the post-industrial age, he saw also nation-states being co-players along with MNCs, NGOs and other IGOs on the world political stage. Coming from business academia, Porter (1990) took the contrary viewpoint that economic globalisation did not undermine the role of the nation-state in fostering international competitiveness of particular industries and their constituent corporations. Perhaps supranational constraints were less prominent in the 1980s and so Porter's research then focused on the status quo of corporations and national governments.

To Friedman (2000), globalisation was an integrated political and economic system that succeeded the divisive Cold War, and carries with it the risk of Americanisation of cultures worldwide. Yet, it balanced the sole "superpower" the USA against all other nations, the nation-states against the "supermarket" of MNCs, and "super-empowered" individuals against nation-states. On the one hand, globalisation was obsessed with market efficiencies and technological innovation. On the other it was beset by historical and almost irrational struggles over culture and geography. Friedman considered the new communications technologies, particularly the internet, to be a force for economic growth for those nations and corporations with the foresight to capitalise on it. At the same time, such people-to-people communication empowered them to influence governments and corporations on social, economic and environmental matters for instance. In contrast to thinkers like Sassen and Greider, he considered the global capital markets as a benign mechanism for rewarding sound business judgement and penalising poor ones, almost as a faster version of the proverbial "unseen hand of the market".

Sustainability and Governance

Worldwide changes in technology, education and mass communications have affected social issues, conflict and political institutions in the capitalist West, liberalising communist world and developing countries alike. One particular consequence pointed out by Inglehart (1990: 5–14) and widely acknowledged by other thinkers was the declining political interest in nationalism and increasing popular support for supranational entities and ethnic identities. Haverkamp and Smelser (1992) argued that increasing globalisation seemed to make a mockery of domestic economic policy in the West because the latter generally failed to consider developments in other countries, particularly in the Third World. This was quite evident in the intransigence of the economies in the developed world to domestic policies over the 1990s designed to create growth and employment. These policies failed simply because they did not recognise the changed global political and economic environment of which the nation-state is a part.

Sceptical of the self-interest that underlines capitalism leading to unsatisfactory social outcomes, Handy (1997) commended a spiritual quest for a higher purpose than profit and shareholder value for both organisations and their employees. Gray (1998) was less sanguine about the prospects of global capitalism, suggesting that it would duplicate all the social, political and economic upheavals that accompanied industrialisation in Europe in the nineteenth and early twentieth centuries. In the face of increasingly powerful players in the global market, Greider (1997) advocated that national governments needed to assert their power to regulate them, both in the interests of the nation as well as the increasingly interdependent global community. He placed the onus on governments, particularly of the affluent developed world, to support the pioneering of new technologies and modes of production that reduced and recycled waste through a regime of economic incentives and discentives. While the General Agreement on Trade in Services (GATS) may represent the victory of the free market in services and thus global media corporations over cultural industries, French and Richards (1996) had their doubts whether such formal rules would overcome the resilience of domestic cultural products against global competition. So, the global free market in services might turn out to be a non-event, if each Second or Third World country chose to maintain its own brand of culture rather than adhere to the First World model.

Nonetheless, the territorial sovereignty of the modern nation-state is being significantly eroded by the likes of global capital markets, the WTO, geographically dispersed production, labour migration, offshoring of back-room services, rating agencies, international commercial arbitration and the growth of electronic commerce. Hence Sassen (1996: 24–28) argued that when the nation-state participated in the transnational governance of such economic activity often through involvement in supranational organisations, it was itself transformed. This may even mean having to overturn its own national, state and municipal laws to comply with the international ones it was now obligated to regulate. Siochrú et al. (2002: 163–81) highlighted the trend towards a decreasing role for governments and the UN and the increasing role of private sector and civil society in media governance, even in developing countries. Consequently, they put forward a "wish list" of media and communications governance that would aim for social, economic and cultural well-being, transparency and participation, diversity of content and ownership, among other ideals. But they were also realistic in implying that trade liberalisation rather than multilateral cooperation was the likely outcome of current trends. Thus Melkote (2002) rightly underscored the demise of objective standards of modernist national development in the post-modern era that was far more concerned with economic sustainability and social justice of smaller communities.

The understanding of economic and political globalisation has progressed beyond prescriptive modernisation theories and critical dependency perspectives, perhaps towards a more pragmatic approach in understanding the interrelated processes of political, economic, cultural and technological change worldwide. A major contribution of world-systems theory was that it compelled social thinkers to move beyond societal level analysis and perceive global factors which had an impact on social change within nation-states. Certainly, in recent years governments of diverse ideological persuasions have been instrumental in promoting the global integration of their national economies in return for anticipated or real economic benefits and thus their own political longevity. This results in their participation in regional, transnational and intergovernmental organisations, their collaboration with MNCs, and their use of improved global communication technologies. In the process governments, such as those of the nation-states used as case studies in the following chapters of this book, seem to unwittingly lose some measure of control over their economy, ideology, culture and information and risk political fragmentation along lines of geography and ethnicity. This is because the capitalist political and economic system foregrounds global markets in goods and services, but ignores public investment in education, health, land reform, local government and the like which would help eradicate inequity and poverty. Thus while developed countries and their MNCs may thrive, the cultural and societal consequences for governments and citizens of developing countries may be dubious at best.

CULTURE AND SOCIETY

Ambivalence about the massive sociocultural change that follows economic development in developing countries often causes their more nationalistic citizens to blame developed countries for the imposition of foreign cultures. Yet this apparent global homogenisation process need not necessarily be seen as deliberate cultural imperialism by developed countries of developing countries, but simply as a correlate of modernisation which developed countries themselves have experienced and incorporated into their cultures, albeit much earlier. While globalisation leads to some measure of homogenisation of cultures, there has been often a concurrent counter-movement towards heterogeneity through the rediscovery and reassertion of the local, as seen in the ethnic renaissance and conflicts which have characterised the late twentieth century. This section of the literature review will examine critically the dynamics of the widely perceived and much vaunted globalisation of culture and society.

Media and Social Change

As theorised by functionalists, the role of media was to democratise access to cultural products and facilitate gradual change without threatening the social system. In fact, modernisation was seen as a process by which empathy with the idea of social mobility was fostered through the mass media. Modernisation theorists have long advocated precipitating dissatisfaction with traditional life as a means of stimulating aspirations for the material benefits of modern society. Notably, Lerner (1958) claimed that the mass media was a key accelerator of the take-off into modernisation along with urbanisation, literacy and political participation. On commission by the United Nations Educational, Scientific, and Cultural Organization (UNESCO), Schramm (1964) had prescribed specific media policies for developing countries as a means of achieving modernisation and its benefits. He asserted that the mass media aided in widening horizons, focusing attention on development, raising expectations, and changing attitudes and values, among other positive effects. Thus many governments in the developing world introduced television as a means of promoting modernisation, either directly through development programming or indirectly through "westernised" entertainment programming.

Influential as structural-functionalism was in media development, research on its hypotheses in the developing world bore equivocal results. Indeed, when Rogers (1962) investigated the diffusion of innovations, he found that the media were important to the earliest stage of awareness of innovations but it was interpersonal communication that was critical to the final stage of their adoption. This dependence on opinion leadership confirmed the two-step flow model of communication pioneered by Katz and Lazarsfeld (1955), which was often ignored in negative views about the social impact of new media. Investigating the effect of modern institutions in developing countries, Inkeles and Smith (1974) found that while schools were more influential upon personal modernity than the workplace and media, the latter two were quite powerful nonetheless. Advertising, in particular, was also seen as benefiting modernisation by encouraging competition, production efficiency, product innovations/variety and lower prices, as well as subsidising the media. This assumed the national dominance of a commercial media system which gave viewers the right of choice, and content that was produced domestically to reflect values of the social system, as is generally true of the US. Thus development communications as propounded by theorists such as Lerner, McClelland, Pool and Schramm did not take into consideration the context of US hegemony of the world market, media industries, and international relations in the Cold War era (Sussman and Lent 1991).

Critics charged that a structural-functionalist approach was deficient in explaining social change because it emphasised the elements that keep societies stable (Dahrendorf 1973). But a risk of using the media to promote social change was that it may also cause rising expectations and intolerable frustration within a society, with the possible dysfunctional outcome of a populist revolution, as alleged in some developing countries. On the other hand, structural-functionalists might argue that such "western" media content had value as a form of escapist distraction or sedation for the masses, and was therefore functional in reducing social tension and political dissent in developing countries (Tunstall 1977: 212). However, it was the introduction of media over which governments could exercise little control, such as transnational television via satellite, which heightened fears that the steady development of their countries and their political hold could be undermined. This was because its programming might promote consumerist

lifestyles and advertise products to their citizens well before other cor-
relates of economic development and could be at odds with national
cultural policies.

Marginalised Identities

It was the communication of new ideas via print in vernacular or
trade languages rather than esoteric foreign languages or very localised
dialects which helped form nation-states out of more traditional
sociopolitical entities. Anderson (1983) detailed how the modern
nation-state had its origins in the arrival of print which coincided
with the growth of capitalism. Through a phenomenon he called
"print-capitalism", people who participated in a sociolinguistic market
for print media such as books and newspapers began to feel connected
with all others who did, leading to the formation of nation-states on
the basis of a common language. Similarly, post-colonial nations of
the Third World were defined either by an inherited colonial language
or a revived "national" language. Citizenship was an artificial construct, inasmuch as the nation-state is, which detached people from
more real localised identities and formed a new pseudo-community
of strangers. Cultural authenticity was often based on xenophobia
for, as Hobsbawm (1990) indicated, ideas of primordial ethnic identity
have dubious roots and nationalistic self-determination seeks to recover
irrecoverable history. Thus national culture was quite an unproblem-
atic concept and taken for granted in the 1960s and 1970s, but it became increasingly questioned and problematised as a sociocultural
construct in the 1980s and 1990s.

Other social thinkers were less interested in analysing the obvious
economic and political factors contributing to cultural globalisation
than in mapping the cultural consequences on individuals, society,
nation-states, even humanity as a whole. Spybey (1996), for one, seemed
concerned particularly with how the globalisation of political, economic and cultural institutions affected participants in every social
system in a process he termed "reflexive modernity". He thought that
the individuals exposed to information through these globalising
processes had greater expectations of lifestyle choices and personal
fulfilment. The ready availability of transnational satellite television
enhances such exposure to cultural globalisation, of both consumerism

as well as social causes. Morley and Robins (1995) addressed the difficulty of defining cultural identity in an era of post-modern geography, where spaces were defined increasingly by electronic connectedness rather than physical proximity. Pertinent to this thesis was their evidence of young people being the heaviest users of transnational television in Europe. But Ferguson (1993) cautioned cultural thinkers and industry practitioners alike to differentiate between "surface" identities, which may reflect global consumerist trends, and "deep" identities, which reflect the persistence of ethnicity, religion, gender and the like. Quite accurately she deemed the dominant myth in cultural industries of global cultural homogenisation to be as simplistic as the concept of national cultural purity.

The politics of cultural identity, according to Foucault (1978: 66–73), has been concerned with marginalised groups such as women, homosexuals and ethnic minorities finding a voice and being able to move centerstage in the wider culture and society they are a part of. This has led to the problem of speaking positions, or whether only those who inhabit the marginalised groups have the right experience to speak from and the only ones worthy to be listened to when speaking on behalf of the groups. Speaking positions was also an issue on a global level, one which Tomlinson (1991) grappled with, of whether thinkers in the developed world could speak for those in the developing world. While attempting to redress past silencing of minorities, this attitude taken unthinkingly to the extreme could mean little true dialogue over cultural conflicts. Far more pessimistic of the prospects for cultural engagement, Huntington (1998) warns instead that global conflicts in the post-Cold War era will be neither political nor economic but cultural. The compression that globalisation made possible has meant that interactions between the historical civilisations would increase but cause friction rather than amalgam. Unsecularisation, particularly by religious fundamentalists, was claimed to be filling the void left by differences in political ideology. But his nomenclature of the eight civilisations as Western, Confucian, Japanese, Islamic, Hindu, Slavic-Orthodox, Latin American and African betrays a superficial grasp of both world culture and world history.

Using culture as a basis for furthering or curtailing economic ties would only perpetuate the inequities that cause international conflicts. By contrast, Fukuyama (1992) announced the arrival of a global culture based on the capitalist economic world-system undergirded by advanced technologies. Rather superficially and prematurely, he pronounced the "end of history" upon the collapse of the Soviet Union. Far more realistic was Tehranian (1999) in arguing that newer, more accessible communications technologies could enable a dialogue between civilisations or at least its citizens who seem to be forming new global communities. Towards that end, he believed the structures of international relations such as nation-states, IGOs, MNCs, NGOs and others needed to be geared towards reforming global governance. Tehranian's analysis of historical civilisations, current political spectra and their implications for media, communications and cultural policy is insightful. Still, Huntington's ideas may have gained greater credence in the traumatised post-11 September 2001 US, but they would remain unconvincing in much of the world where its western-based ethnocentrism would be quite evident. In its small way, this present book attempts to give voice to those in the developing world as well as those in the developed world who are equally concerned with issues of cultural globalisation, in order to facilitate engagement, even honest debate between them.

Cultural Hegemony

The concept of cultural hegemony can be traced to the Marxist perspective of Gramsci (1978) who saw the capitalist class convincing the working class to accept being ruled. But by the same token, a working class-led revolution would first have to free itself from the hegemony of the capitalist class and then to legitimise itself by dominating all institutions of society with its ideology and moral authority. So keen was Gramsci for Marxist ideology to be demonstrated in practice that he emphasised cultural rather than economic factors in his analysis of social change. According to this influential school of thought that grew into critical or cultural theory, "culture" is to be seen not as something one absorbs unconsciously but as an arena for the struggle against hegemony and towards authenticity. However, the process of a dominant social group winning the marginal groups' consent without overt coercion has an inherent instability about it because cultural power has always to be negotiated and so is conflict-prone. A similar situation of cultural hegemony existed also between colonists and their overseas subjects, and might be said to exist between neo-colonial developed countries and their MNCs and economically-dependent developing countries today.

Critical theory holds that the media induces passivity as well as addiction in audiences, thus making them amenable to domination by the political and economic elite in society who often controlled the media. In its view, with industrialisation mass culture became a product for a mass market or audience, produced by a cultural industry. The central thesis of this theory, propounded by the Frankfurt School in pre-World War II Germany, was that this commercialised mass culture was the means by which the capitalist system of production and consumption sustained itself. In their seminal essay, Adorno and Horkheimer (1972) criticised what they termed the cultural industry for mass-producing cultural products in the service of capitalist economies. As such, they claimed these products were unartistic and generic, pandering to the mass taste and discouraging of intellectual response and that all forms of popular culture, including the mass media, traced their roots to the rise of the middle class in Europe. Being rather elitist, they saw the media both as the means to subjugate the masses as well as the undoing of civilisation as they idealised it rather belatedly in the industrial age. Government leaders and the social-political elite of developing countries today tend to share the critical theorists' disdain of mass culture, particularly of foreign origin or of a hybrid foreign/local nature. Yet, paradoxically, they seem keen to harness the tools of media to manage the political and economic choices of their masses through promoting a subservient national culture.

Tele-visual Literacy

The impact of the medium of television on societies with a long tradition of print media has intrigued many social thinkers. In McLuhan's (1964) view, oral and instant communication which characterised the new electronic media was re-tribalising human society, emphasising touch and sound over vision. As a leading technological determinist, he would rebut Gerbner's view on the cultivation effects of media with the categorical claim for which he was famed, that "the medium was the message". Another dictum of McLuhan was that "the media was the massage", a more colourful expression for his argument that the medium impressed its own message on the audience, subordinating the actual content it was carrying (ibid.: 268–94). Through television the world had become an electronic global village where there was extreme awareness and curiosity about other cultures. But it has remained unclear whether McLuhan was implying that television was globalising culture since, among other things, the process has not been accompanied by greater social harmony and tolerance. Perhaps he only meant that all viewers of television were participants in a televised culture, regardless of what they watched or where they were located around the world.

In Ellul's view, television images were inimical to interpersonal discourse, intellectual reflection and social action, thus implying that the world can never become a global village. While by no means targeting McLuhan directly, he (1985: 113–53) contended that personal communication for human relationships could not be achieved through the media. Taking a different tack, Esslin (1982) expressed the concern that accepting the dictum that the medium was the message neglected the other messages carried by television. In any case, McLuhan has had no shortage of critics who have accused him of coining clever metaphors, overstating the case and developing unprovable theories (Stearn 1968). Yet in the intuitive appeal of his ideas to the wider public, policy makers and media practitioners, even if not to social scientists and media theorists, lay the root of McLuhan's success. To this day, purveyors of satellite communications are fond of citing his "global village" and "medium is the message" metaphors in promoting the benefits of their technologies while ignoring the more negative connotations he implied by them. Certainly McLuhan made no overt comment about ownership of the media and control of the technology, and could be assumed to have imbibed an uncritical right wing view towards economic development and social change.

Rejecting both optimistic and pessimistic views of media impact, Baudrillard (1988) expounded the view that the mass media do not simply distort reality but were in fact a new social reality. Television images which distort time and space cause our culture to consist primarily of simulations. As a post-structuralist/post-modernist, he defined simulation as not only presenting the imaginary as real, but also presenting objects and discourses as having neither origin, referent or standard (ibid.: 209–19). Consumer lifestyles provide people with their identity in society rather than their role in the economic production system and thus people are being incorporated into the "simulacra" they surrounded themselves with. In a style reminiscent of McLuhan and Ellul, he proclaimed that the media, especially television, overwhelms with information and renders impossible any true feedback from its audience even by polls, and thus are a form of pseudo-communication. The only way that the masses could avoid the influence of the media, according to Baudrillard, would be to avoid watching it themselves or to be shielded from it by authorities. The former is an unlikely scenario since the masses worldwide seem to find the media an irresistible form of entertainment and information, while the latter is what some governments in Asia have endeavoured to do with transnational television with dubious success.

Post-modern Society

Like globalisation, post-modernity is a phenomenon over which there has been little consensus of definition in part because it is discussed in art, architecture, history, literature and sociology among other disciplines. Lyotard (1984) characterised post-modernism as a new era marked by scepticism towards meta-narratives or those ideological systems that give bearing, purpose and meaning to life in the past. Thus all aspects of life can have no objective reality or meta-code by which to be judged, only the "hyperreality" of meanings relative to each other. On the other hand, Jameson (1984) portrayed post-modern society primarily as a consumer society characterised by pastiche and schizophrenia, eroding distinctions between reality and imagination. In his view, post-modernism was in continuity with modernism and simply the cultural logic of late capitalism, a mere shift from imperialistic and market capitalism towards social heterogeneity without a collective project and lacking any norms. Similarly, Harvey (1989) considered post-modernism to be characterised by fragmentation and chaos, making it impossible to attempt a comprehensive worldview. He noted a collapsing of time-horizons and a propensity to spectacle in post-modern culture, as demonstrated by trends in popular culture from fashion and architecture to advertising and television. Culture was seen as a random series of freely intersecting texts, the total meaning of which is relative to each participant. Notably for this book, Harvey attributed a shaping role to television, a medium quintessentially post-modern in its collation of images past and present, from far and near into an endless, uniform stream of spectacle piped into homes.

In the post-modern societies as with globalised cultures, time and space are re-ordered such that events that are far away and at a different time intrude on the experience of people and seem more significant than their local situation, often through the "mediation" of the media. One of the leading thinkers on globalisation, Giddens (1990: 18–21) understood the concept as the "interlacing of social events and social relations 'at a distance' with local contextualities". Augmenting this viewpoint was another major theorist on globalisation, Robertson (1992: 8) who believed that it "refers to both the compression of the world and the intensification of consciousness of the world as a whole ... both concrete global interdependence and consciousness of the global whole in the twentieth century". He claimed that societies were converging in economic and technological aspects yet diverging especially in social relational aspects, while staying constant in other aspects. Yet another conceptualisation of the relationship of the parts and the whole was Braman and Sreberny-Mohammadi's (1996) "inter-penetrated globalisation" by which they claimed that there was plainly no local not infected by the global, nor no global not present also in the local. They introduced the notion of tertiary locality, or the increasing participation in hyper-real or virtual communities via the internet, as a signpost of our post-modern condition. If one were able to interpret Wilson and Dissanayake (1996) adequately, they appear to be championing the same paradoxical experience of becoming more globalised and more localised concurrently, or of pluralisation within a world-system. Antagonistic towards post-modernism, post-colonialism and multiculturalism as being too accommodating to global capital, they promote instead the notion of a "transnational imaginary" in tracking the global-local nexus across geopolitical sites.

Cloning and Hybridity

The concept of "glocalisation", or the localisation of global issues as well as the globalisation of local issues, is first attributed to Robertson (1992). Disbelieving that global-local issues, whether these concern politics, ecology, human rights or the media, should be thought of as a macro-micro dichotomy, he kept company with a growing number of contemporary thinkers who saw the global embedded in the local and vice versa. Featherstone (1990), for one, questioned the conventional idea of a global culture as "national culture writ large", and stressed instead the need to move away from the bipolar dichotomies such as homogeneity/heterogeneity in regard to culture. Therefore he perceived globalisation not as cultural imperialism but as symptomatic of the openness of post-modern societies to cultural eclecticism. Subsequently, he described globalisation as a process of showcasing discordant world cultures within the home (ibid. 1995). Presumably this was achieved via the productivity of global media industries and local business franchises in the post-modern world. Rather than thinking of globalisation as a late form of modernisation or "westernisation", Pieterse (1994) similarly preferred to describe it as post-modern hybridity. Hybrid social structures encompassed both supranational and subnational regionalism within an understanding of a "world society", in his view, while cultural hybridity could take a range of forms from mimicry, syncretism and creolisation to global mélange and counter-hegemony. Lent (1995) documented this phenomenon in Asia across the arenas of television, music, theatre, sport, food, movies and a range of popular culture, but singled out television for blame or credit for introducing the westernisation element. Thus hybridity might indeed be a useful key for understanding the development of television-based cultures in the developing world.

The seminal work of Appadurai (1990) has been responsible for delineating the cultural flows which accompany globalisation. First, these were "ethnoscapes" of business travellers, expatriates, immigrants and refugees. Second, there were the "technoscapes" of machinery, technology and software, and third the "finanscapes" of capital and securities. Fourth came the "mediascapes" of images and information via print, television and film, and finally the "ideoscapes" of democracy, human rights and other western ideologies. Though globalisation was not simply sociocultural homogenisation, it used various homogenising agents, advertising being a key one, which then incorporated the global into local culture and politics. The phenomenon of cultural globalisation has certainly been accelerated through new electronic communications, including television broadcasting. The electronic distribution of images worldwide or what Appadurai termed "mediascapes" could well be agents for the spread of "ideoscapes" or ideologies of western nation-states, political movements or corporations. Lash and Urry (1994) attempted to analyse such flows within the context of post-modern economies and societies, advising that pessimism over the future was caused unnecessarily by overly structuralist conceptualisations. They argued that all these "scapes" are de-territorialised, with "mediascapes" becoming increasingly global in character, dominant over "ideoscapes" and undermining notions of citizenship in favour of both global consumer identity and local re-constructed ethnicity (ibid.: 305–13). Whether transnational television might be a constituent of one such "mediascape" which taps also into "ethnoscapes", is something this book will seek to uncover in the Asian context.

While the print medium may have contributed to the development of the modern nation-state, the television medium seems to be taking this process much further towards the formation of post-modern globalised societies, through bypassing the need for literacy to inform and using visual images to entertain instead. Perhaps via transnational satellites, the social and cultural impact of television may be coming full circle by uniting disparate ethnic communities in different nation-states, whether geographically close or distant, thus creating "global villages" of quasi-homogeneous cultures. Since such electronic communication media make possible or heighten transnational networks of individuals and groups which then become dependent on them, one issue that needs to be addressed is whether they are a cause or an effect of globalisation. The next chapter will explore national responses within the various Asian subregions to the advent of the transnational medium of satellite television.

M ost countries in Asia were once colonised or dominated by one or more of the European powers. Over the 1950s and 1960s all of them gained independence and, like other countries of the post-colonial world, embarked on programmes of nation building, modern-isation and development. Regardless of whether the political and economic models adopted were more socialist, capitalist or a hybrid, the national media, particularly television, was seen as a means of in-tegrating the nation as well as promoting social and economic change. Concern among these developing countries over neo-colonial cultural imperialism by the growing number of satellites broadcasting trans-national television caused their governments to respond with policies and regulations, either proactively or reactively. Increasingly, countries are devising laws and regulatory bodies that recognise the convergence of communications technologies. But an evaluation of the laws will be confined to television in this book as their application to other media is beyond its scope.

REGULATING TRANSNATIONAL BROADCASTS

While regulatory policies seem at first glance to be incredibly diverse, it is possible to discern certain categories. In analysing the situation in Asia in the early 1990s, Chan (1994) offered four ideal types of na-tional responses to the advent of transnational television: (*a*) "virtual suppression", (*b*) "suppressive openness", (*c*) "illegal openness" and (*d*) "regulated openness". Inspired by that typology, I propose a six-point continuum of government policies (Figure 4.1) deemed more pertinent to regulating the increasingly complex transnational television scene in Asia. But unlike the earlier typology, it will also demonstrate policy shifts of national governments in the region over the first decade of transnational television. The extreme stage in this continuum is represented as "active suppression" of transnational television viewing, rather than Chan's more ambiguous term "virtual suppression". Since his term "suppressive openness" seems almost a contradiction in terms, "latent suppression" is used in this book to better define a policy of not enforcing existing prohibitions.

Figure 4.1
Typology of Government Policies Towards Transnational Media

Policy	Explanation
Active suppression	Severe restrictions on access to transnational media which are rigorously enforced
Latent suppression	Policies generally against access to transnational media which are either not enforced or irregularly enforced
Complacent inaction	Lack of specific laws concerning access to transnational media due to government disinterest, incapacity or negligence
Prudent inaction	Interim legal void concerning access to transnational media as the government analyses developments and considers its options
Controlled access	Access to some transnational media allowed subject to government regulation or industry self-regulation of content
Liberal access	Access to all transnational media without any regulation or with explicit legal rights and protection to consumers and providers

In the typology adopted for this book the term "complacent inaction" is used to encapsulate the broad category of situations where there is a lack of government policy, even a lack of urgency to rectify the situation. By default then, there is a legal void concerning transnational satellite and cable television which invariably allows the medium to flourish. On the other hand, "prudent inaction" refers to the case where the government deliberately opts not to act in the interim, pending further analysis of media developments and perhaps observation of the effectiveness of neighbouring countries' policies. Furthermore, there is a need to differentiate between policies of access to transnational television. A policy of "controlled access" is one where a government proceeds to limit viewers' access to certain transnational channels via domestic pay-TV or licensed satellite dishes, or via terrestrial re-broadcast, often duly censored. By contrast, a government which grants its citizens "liberal access" is one where the latter have the right to watch as they please, whether by installing their own satellite dishes or via unregulated cable providers. This typology of policies towards transnational television applies well to the countries within key regions of Asia, as well as an indication of policies towards other new electronic media such as the Internet.

SOUTH ASIAN POLICIES

The seven nations analysed here form the South Asian Association for Regional Cooperation (SAARC) which aims at fostering regional integration. But in fact the unresolved conflict between the two largest members India and Pakistan since partition at independence some 50 years prior is a continuing impediment to its progress. Within the region India, by its very geographical size, has been dominant economically, culturally, politically, even militarily, and therefore treated with some suspicion given regional history. In terms of the media this may be illustrated by the fact that India's public television service, Doordarshan, has long been available via spill-over or satellite in neighbouring states and hence considered a *de facto* transnational broadcaster by them. Despite shared history, geography and culture, the policies of the various nation-states towards transnational television are only marginally convergent (Figure 4.2).

Figure 4.2
Government Policies in South Asia Towards Transnational Media, 1991–2001

	Active Suppression	Latent Suppression	Complacent Inaction	Prudent Inaction	Controlled Access	Liberal Access
Pakistan			1992–99		2000–	
Bangladesh			1992–96		1996–	
Sri Lanka				1992–94	1994–96	1996–
Nepal				1991–93		1994–
Bhutan	1991–95	1996–				
Maldives				1991–		
India			1991–95		1995–98	1998–

Pakistan

In 1991 the first semi-private channel, Shalimar Television Network (STN) began operations by re-broadcasting the transnational CNN around-the-clock, initially in Islamabad, Karachi and Lahore. Subsequently, this free-to-air terrestrial channel included the news bulletins of BBC and the local public broadcaster PTV as well since it was not permitted to produce its own news. Due to censorship disputes with different governments and financial difficulties Shalimar was occasionally off-air in later years (Ali and Gunaratne 2000: 171). In 1992 with Japanese funding the government launched a second public channel, PTV2, and leased an AsiaSat1 transponder to transmit programming to satellite dishes in 26 centres around the country. Though the only South Asian country then with a transponder on AsiaSat1, Pakistan used it initially for educational television broadcasts, telephony, news-gathering and radio transmission and not for pan-Asian television broadcasts [World Broadcast News 1993: 63]. By late 1992, satellite dishes in Pakistan for the reception of transnational television such as StarTV and ZeeTV were permitted on the payment of a fee to the government and there were an estimated 2,500 such dishes in Karachi alone [Zuberi 1993].

Cable systems had pre-dated the arrival of satellite television because they were a means of watching Indian movies at home. Religious groups have continued to lobby against transnational broadcasts, anticipating someday to benefit from a conservative backlash as in some other Islamic nations (Barraclough 2001). Nonetheless, cable systems expanded from Karachi to Lahore and Islamabad but were not as popular as direct reception via satellite dishes or microwave-delivered pay-TV. Although there was a licence fee for having a satellite dish, few paid it (Page and Crawley 2001: 97–98). Only in 2000 was there an attempt by the new military government to license cable operators, who had previously existed under a legal vacuum till then because there were no specific cable laws or regulatory body. Then in 2001 the telecommunications authority granted the very first pay-TV licence in Pakistan to the transnational broadcaster StarTV [Leung 2001a]. Thus the policy of the government of Pakistan towards transnational television over the years has been a consistent one of "complacent inaction" for its citizenry till quite recently when it has attempted to initiate "controlled access", as with the decision not to proceed with pay-TV. The only exception seems to be outright banning of the relaying of Indian and StarTV channels by Pakistan cable operators following the diplomatic or military crises with India over Kashmir, such as in the late 1990s and early 2000s.

Bangladesh

In the early 1990s the public broadcaster Bangladesh Television (BTV), the sole domestic channel in Bangladesh, also re-broadcast some programmes from the transnational news channels, BBC and CNN. Subsequently there were demands for alternative television channels and the government feared that these would be funded by opposition political parties. So it approved the renewal of the CNN contract with BTV and permitted satellite dishes for the reception of transnational television (Anwar 1993). In 1996, the government first decided to launch a second channel which would broadcast both terrestrially and via satellite, and offer slots for sale to private broadcasters [AMCB 1996a]. Finally in 1999 the government granted a 15-year license to Ekushey Television (ETV) as a Bengali language terrestrial and satellite channel to reach audiences in West Bengal (India), South Asia, Southeast Asia, the Middle East, Europe and North America (Bhuiyan and Gunaratne 2000).

Cable television in Bangladesh began in 1992 with Translinks, a local franchise of the StarTV group which had a number of affiliated cable operators. This firm also dominated the manufacture of satellite dishes, import of reception equipment and production of programming. Despite negotiations between government and cable operators since 1994, there were still no laws governing their operations in Bangladesh which were consequently neither legal or illegal. The process was undermined both by Translink's strategy of dominating the market and the government's disinterest since cable operators were broadcasting primarily entertainment, not domestic news or views critical of it (Page and Crawley 2001: 93–95). From the early 1990s cable television grew in popularity; by the end of the decade there were estimated to be about 2,000 cable operators serving some 1 million households, with the capital Dhaka and port city Chittagong having the highest penetration. These cable operators offered about

20 transnational satellite television channels and were licensed for an annual fee by BTV on behalf of the government (Bhuiyan and Gunaratne 2000). Thus the policy in Bangladesh, not unlike that of Pakistan of which it was once a part, may be described as shifting from "complacent inaction" to one of "controlled access" though for different reasons of political expedience and economic constraint.

Sri Lanka

This country has the distinction of being the permanent residence of Arthur C. Clarke who originated the idea of geostationary satellites and through whose satellite dishes CNN reports on the Gulf War were relayed to the national TV network. Subsequently enterprising Sri Lankans constructed satellite dishes out of chicken wire and formed informal cable networks [Weerackody 1993]. In the early 1990s the popular private station, Extra Terrestrial Vision, re-transmitted sports, hourly news, educational programmes and documentaries of StarTV 24-hours per day to the capital and surrounding areas [World Broadcast News 1993–94: 30]. By 1996 some 16 entities including foreign joint ventures, local firms and NGOs had applied for licences to set up radio and television stations under a newly established broadcasting authority [Television Asia 1996b: 4]. In 1999 the government licensed two other private channels, Comet Cable TV and Channel 9, a direct-to-home pay-TV service owned jointly with an Australian broadcaster, which rebroadcasts StarTV, ESPN and other pan-Asian channels.

By the late 1990s, most terrestrial broadcasters in Sri Lanka were re-transmitting programmes from transnational and regional satellite broadcasters. Rupavahini relayed Discovery Channel and ITN relayed Deutsche Welle, while Sirasa TV relayed SunTV and Swarnavahini relayed RajTV and ATN, the last three being of Indian origin (Gunaratne and Wattegama 2000). The Sri Lankan government's policy of diversifying its domestic television industry was instrumental in suppressing local interest in cable operations and satellite dishes. With its five terrestrial channels re-broadcasting selected programmes of the transnational broadcasters, most citizens enjoyed access at no further cost. There has also been less debate about cultural invasion, sex, violence or politically-sensitive issues on satellite or cable television in Sri Lanka than elsewhere in the region (Page and Crawley

2001: 99–100). Thus "prudent inaction" gave way unobtrusively to "controlled access" and now to "liberal access", policies which have paid off for Sri Lanka over the first decade of transnational television.

Nepal

Even prior to having its own television station in 1985, the Nepalese had access to India's Doordarshan programming through first a national booster antennae and then via satellite dishes. By 1990 there were 8,000 sets in the country for both television and video watching [DECORE 1991]. Such satellite television reception received further impetus from CNN's coverage of the Gulf War and the subsequent launch of StarTV. In Nepal satellite dishes for the reception of transnational television were legal, though they needed to be licensed regardless of whether they were installed prior to the National Communication Policy of 1992. By the early 1990s there were five major satellite-dish manufacturers in the capital Kathmandu, the total number installed was estimated as exceeding 1,000 and there were 13 satellite channels accessible through household cable-sharing [Panday 1993]. In 1994 the government of Nepal licensed a cable network in the Kathmandu valley and a satellite television service. In 1996 the latter service was authorised to broadcast in Nepali when previously it was only allowed to down-link and distribute foreign language programming [AMCB 1997a]. Space-Time Network cabled several thousand subscribers in Kathmandu and several towns, while Shangri-la Channel relayed satellite channels via terrestrial broadcast (Rao and Koirala 2000). Given its circumstances as a small neighbour of India both geographically and economically, Nepal had always pursued a policy of "prudent inaction" towards transnational broadcasts which has shifted gradually to one of "liberal access" without political debate or obvious policy decision making.

Bhutan

Having no national television till 1999, watching broadcasts by spill-over from India and Bangladesh might have been a temptation in Bhutan, except that the mountainous terrain prevented this except in its southern lowlands. Transnational broadcasts via satellite even prior to StarTV changed all this, and in 1989 the king banned privately-owned satellite dishes, ordering the removal of existing ones (Pek 1998). Yet in 1998, the king presented satellite dishes to three tertiary education institutions and permitted a large screen in a sports ground of the capital for its population to watch World Cup soccer via Indian television. In the absence of choice in television apart from the development programming-oriented domestic broadcaster, there was a thriving trade in videos for foreign movies from India, Hong Kong and Thailand [Conlon 2000], many of them pirated and possibly from satellite television broadcasts. Having banned satellite dishes on grounds of cultural sustainability, Bhutan's policy towards transnational television was initially one of "active suppression". But the demand for access by the educated urban elite and the ready availability of satellite television in border regions suggest that from the mid-1990s onwards the national policy has tended to be one of "latent suppression".

Maldives

There is relatively little information on media in this small nation in the Indian Ocean which has just one domestic television station. However, from reports that Doordarshan of India, CNN, CFI and various Arab satellite broadcasters had provided technical assistance (Ahmed 1993), it might be inferred that there was some access to transnational television via the domestic broadcaster. It is difficult then to establish the current policy of the Maldives government towards transnational television, though given its strict control of domestic media since the 1990s (Karan and Viswanath 2000) it would seem at best to be one of "prudent inaction", at worst, one of "latent suppression".

India

When StarTV began broadcasting Asia-wide in 1991, its four English language channels were soon available on the extensive unregulated cable networks in India which had developed to provide alternative programming to the sole public broadcaster Doordarshan. In 1992

ZeeTV, a Hindi language channel catering to both urban and rural areas of India, was launched utilising the same AsiaSat1 satellite as StarTV. Their success and growth was a spur to other transnational and regional broadcasters to target the Indian market. India's broadcasting policies then dictated government control of broadcasting, through legislation dating from 1885 and 1933 which pre-dated even radio, let alone television, satellite and cable technologies. Ironically this restriction has spurred the use of satellite broadcasting to circumvent restrictions on commercial broadcasting within India, while the legislative vacuum facilitated the growth of domestic cable networks. In 1994, legislation was enacted to regulate the cable industry while a broadcasting bill continued to be shelved by successive unstable governments. Thus India's initial response to StarTV and other transnational television may be summed up as "complacent inaction", which around 1995 changed to "controlled access" and headed towards being one of "liberal access". In the late 1990s, the Indian government further liberalised its policies on broadcasting, allowing for instance uplinking of domestic commercial channels and giving the public broadcasters greater autonomy. The complex situation within South Asia vis-à-vis satellite, cable and terrestrial television, both transnational and domestic, will be analysed fully in Chapter 5.

SOUTHEAST ASIAN POLICIES

All nations of this region lie under the footprint of pioneering transnational satellites in Asia, most notably the AsiaSats and Palapas. Seven of them are members of the Association of South East Asian Nations (ASEAN), a political, economic and cultural forum which is becoming a free trade area. Singapore, Malaysia and Thailand are among the newly industrialising countries of Asia, which may be equated with semi-periphery countries in the dependency perspective or world-systems theory. Till economic woes in the late 1990s raised doubts about some, they were variously proclaimed as "economic miracles", "tiger economies" or "mini-dragons" by modernisation theorists. Indonesia and Philippines were probably at earlier stages of similarly rapid economic growth, while oil-rich Brunei has long been prosperous. Vietnam, Laos, Cambodia and Myanmar (formerly

Burma) are the newest member nations of ASEAN but being relatively poorer are not significant markets for transnational media. So despite belonging to one regional politico-economic association, each country has adopted a different response to the onset of transnational television (Figure 4.3).

Figure 4.3
Government Policies in Southeast Asia Towards Transnational Media, 1991–2000

	Active Suppression	Latent Suppression	Complacent Inaction	Prudent Inaction	Controlled Access	Liberal Access
Singapore	1992–94				1995–	
Thailand				1992–94		1995–
Philippines			1990–93			1994–
Vietnam		1996–		1992–95		
Brunei		1997–	1991–96			
Indonesia						1990–
Malaysia	1992–97 (west)	1992–97 (east)			1998–	

Singapore

Satellite dishes require special permission in Singapore and this has been granted only to certain government departments, educational institutions, the financial market and world class hotels. The early response of the Singapore government to transnational satellite television, despite grass roots demand for the service from its affluent English and Chinese literate populace, could be described as one of "virtual suppression" (Chan 1994). Ironically, Singapore began utilising a satellite in 1994 to broadcast an 18-hour all-Mandarin satellite channel utilising PanAmSat2 as a means of raising the country's regional and international profile. Later, in recognition of market demand, three channels of downlinked satellite programming, namely HBO, CNN and Mandarin Entertainment, were made available by subscription from Singapore Cable Vision, a subsidiary of the public broadcaster Singapore Broadcasting Corporation or SBC [Hukill 1993]. In the mid-1990s, the government-owned Singapore Telecom began experimenting with a video-on-demand service to the country's 3.2 million residents [World Broadcast News 1995]. By the late 1990s, the government had semi-privatised the television industry, though there is much cross-ownership by domestic media conglomerates. Some channels, notably Channel News Asia, have sought a regional rather than domestic audience. In its bid to become the regional broadcasting hub, Singapore has attracted about a dozen transnational broadcasters to set up their Asian operations in the country. Paradoxically, the state restricts the flow of all mass-mediated and information commodities operating otherwise in market economy (Wong 2001). Still the situation in Singapore has become one of "controlled access" to a growing number of transnational channels via the government-approved cable network.

Thailand

This nation was the pioneer within ASEAN in introducing pay-TV and cable-TV in 1990, following a recommendation of the regulatory body to deregulate the industry. By the early 1990s there were two providers of pay-TV: International Broadcasting Corporation (IBC), owned by the Shinawatra group, and Thai Sky TV. All programmes on the four IBC channels were imported, mostly from the US, and either dubbed or subtitled in Thai to cater to the vast majority of the population which was not English literate [Hamid 1991]. Thai Sky TV offered three channels, all dubbed in Thai and subtitled in English, and sourced programming from ITN, BBC, NBC and NHK for its news channel, and MTV, Virgin, MGM and Paramount among others for its entertainment channel [Siriyuvasak 1993]. During the years of economic boom, new licences were awarded by the government, including UTV (Thai Cable Vision). Due to the economic troubles of the late 1990s, Thai Sky went out of business, while UTV and Thai Sky TV merged in February 1998. The following year, popular pressures for reform over price hikes, the military's ownership of media and the demand for freer news culminated in two new regulatory bodies. These included representation from government as well as civil society groups, particularly media academics who have spearheaded the push for reform (Lewis 2000). Ever since the arrival of transnational television, Thailand has been a country with "liberal access", though the language barrier meant that the appeal of its programming was confined to an educated and affluent minority and expatriates.

The Philippines

Ever since the 1986 toppling of the Marcos dictatorship and its crony capitalism by "people power", the Philippines had liberal laws governing ownership of cable networks, content and satellite dish licensing which would explain the relatively high viewership of transnational television (Figure 4.4). Three Manila TV stations have historically utilised Palapa satellites for nationwide broadcast of their programmes. But many of the 400 original dishes were believed to be picking up other signals from Palapa, IntelSat, AsiaSat and Japan's DBS satellites, some of them for unauthorised re-transmission via cable, terrestrial TV and videotape [Stuart 1993]. The arrival of transnational television such as CNN, StarTV and ESPN in the 1990s was a major impetus to the phenomenal growth of the cable industry that had existed as a regulated monopoly in the 1970s and 1980s. Of the 11 million TV households in the Philippines, 250,000 were connected by 300 cable operators, most of them small family businesses though they had forged alliances with key multisystem operators and invested an estimated US$60 million in the industry by 1995 [Broadcast Asia 1994]. By the mid-1990s the cable operator Sky Cable was offering over 55 transnational channels including StarTV, ABN, AusTV, MTV, TVBS, CTN, as well as French, Russian and local programming [Kwang 1995]. Soon after, plans were announced for Philippines' own

Figure 4.4
Reception of Satellite and Cable Television at Home, June 1999–July 2000

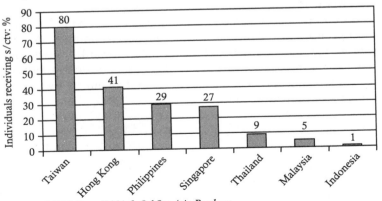

Source: AC Neilsen [2001a] *CabSat Asia Brochure*

broadcast satellite to be owned by its long-distance telephone company. By the early 2000s there were indications that the Philippines government and industry were drafting a media convergence law which would allow uniformity of limits concerning foreign investment [Brown 2001h]. In keeping with its commitment to civil society and political freedom, the Philippines' policy towards transnational television may best be described as one of "complacent inaction" long since turned towards "liberal access".

Vietnam

Having embarked on a programme of economic liberalisation, Vietnam has received considerable commercial investment from Thailand. In 1993, a Thai firm supplied 30 satellite dishes to offices, hotels and embassies in Hanoi and Ho Chi Minh City [Asian Communications 1993: 23–26]. A year later Vietnam Television (VTV) was the first foreign broadcaster to use Thaicom2, a satellite which was expected to attract French broadcasters to the former colonies [World Broadcast News 1994]. However, being under communist party control much of its broadcast relayed information on government decisions and events, spawning a video rental industry as an alternative for entertainment (Shoesmith 1994). Later VTV operated a limited mocrowave re-distribution service, while other access to satellite television was prohibited in 1996 [AMCB 1997b]. In the late 1990s, it offered nine channels such as CNN, the French TV5, Discovery, OPT, NBC, MTV, TNT/Cartoon Network, Star Sports and its own VTV1, but the cost of installation and subscription was prohibitive to most citizens (Forrester 1998). True to its ideological commitment to communism, the Vietnamese government's policy towards transnational broadcasts seems to have reverted to "latent suppression" after some years of seeming "prudent inaction", before economic growth made access by consumers a reality.

Malaysia

While Malaysia banned the use of dishes for the reception of satellite broadcasts in the early 1990s, in its state of Sarawak on the island of

Borneo, some 2,000 illegally installed satellite dishes were reported to exist [Noordin 1992]. It licensed satellite dishes only for hotels enabling their guests to watch CNN and two StarTV channels. Thus a situation of "active suppression" towards transnational television existed in West Malaysia while "latent suppression" existed in East Malaysia. Then the government granted its first licence to Satellite Network Systems (SNS), a consortium of the public broadcaster RTM and commercial interests controlled by the ruling coalition, to provide up to eight pay-TV channels by 1995 [Via Satellite 1995b]. MegaTV was established in late 1995 in peninsular Malaysia and provided transnational channels such as CNN, Cartoon Network, Discovery, ESPN and HBO. Since Malaysia launched its own domestic satellite named Measat-1, it has permitted a 22-channel DTH pay-TV service called Astro [Hughes and Masters 1996]. While it offered a range of transnational and in-house channels, the former were first downlinked and subjected to government-supervised censorship at the Astro facilities, and then uplinked for re-broadcast to subscriber homes (Safar et al. 2000). In 1998, a new Multimedia and Telecommunications Act was enacted which embodied both greater privatisation in the pursuit of rapid economic development and government control in the name of "Asian values" (Nain 2002). So Malaysia could be said to have made a cautious move towards "controlled access" to transnational television through its own pay-TV services.

Brunei

Being a relatively small country, Brunei received Malaysian channels easily by spillover, notably the government-owned RTM1 and RTM2 and the commercial TV3. Regional and transnational networks such as Astro and StarTV were also accessible via subscription. Government regulations proscribed the viewing of foreign channels whose quality and content are deemed unacceptable (Safar and Ladi 2000). Hence Brunei's policy towards transnational television stayed relatively unchanged over the first half-decade as one of "complacent inaction". Since 1997 it seems to be verging on "latent suppression" in keeping with a national trend towards Islamisation and thus resembling more conservative policies usually found in West Asia.

Indonesia

In comparison with other Southeast Asian nations, Indonesia adopted a seemingly enlightened attitude to commercial television, including transnational satellite broadcasting. Using the typology adopted in this book, it may be said to have a response of "liberal access", since the technology for receiving satellite broadcasts had been in place for decades for domestic television purposes. Although a licence was required to own a satellite dish even for domestic reception, there were estimated to be five times as many illegal ones and each was widely shared. The policy of licensing domestic commercial television stations from the late 1980s represented a significant move by the government away from its past fear of commercialism and political subversion via the media. But it was also fortuitous in winning the loyalty of Indonesian viewers to domestic television over transnational television, which arrived in the 1990s. Throughout the repressive Soeharto regime and the post-reformation governments of Habibie, Wahid and Soekarnoputri, the policies towards transnational television have remained relatively untouched. As the most liberal country in this subregion towards trans-national satellite television, the case of Indonesia together with culturally-similar Malaysia will be discussed in greater detail in Chapter 6.

NORTHEAST ASIAN POLICIES

This region is dominated geographically by China though Japan is still the dominant economic power, and these two nations provide an axis on which to divide it. Although China was never fully colonised, it endured control of its ports by various European powers till the Japanese overran them and large parts of the country in the Second World War. Hong Kong and Macau were colonies of Britain and Portugal respectively till the late 1990s and are now administered as semi-autonomous parts of China, while Taiwan has been estranged since the former nationalist Chinese government retreated there over 50 years ago. Still there is increasing acceptance of the notion of Greater China which treats China (PRC), Taiwan (ROC), Hong Kong and Macau as a single entity both economically and culturally, even if it is less integrated politically. Japan itself was never colonised but was a coloniser of some nations for centuries and conqueror of much of East Asia during the Second World War. South Korea and Taiwan were once colonies of Japan and so retain some cultural ties with the latter. Previously under the ambit of the former USSR, Mongolia has come to re-assert its national identity only in recent years, while North Korea remains a closed Stalinist state. Far from having similar histories despite the political interactions, the countries of Northeast Asia display considerable diversity in their national policy responses towards transnational television.

Japan

Though the launch of StarTV surprised Japanese broadcasters and policy makers, it was even then only one of numerous satellite television services accessible in Japan. In addition to the transnational

Figure 4.5
Government Policies in Northeast Asia Towards Transnational Media, 1991–2001

	Active Suppression	Latent Suppression	Complacent Inaction	Prudent Inaction	Controlled Access	Liberal Access
Japan					1989–95	1995–
S. Korea		1997–	1991–93	1993–96		
N. Korea	1991–					
Mongolia			1991–97			1998–
China		1994–99	1991–93		2000–	
Taiwan				1990–93	1994–98	1999–
Macau			1991–			
Hong Kong					1991–97	1998–

broadcasters such as StarTV, CNN, ESPN, HBO, CFI, China's CCTV4 and India's ATN, there were international relays by US and Australian networks using Intelsat satellites. There were also domestic television relays by Russia and China, even domestic broadcasting such as those by India on Insat and Indonesia on Palapa [Shimizu 1993]. In Japan private reception of transnational satellite television was not restricted although re-transmission by cable networks was, and therefore it was a country that practised "controlled access". But transnational television services have had little effect on Japanese households because they have access to as many as seven free-to-air domestic channels in metropolitan areas, and up to 30 cable channels in larger cities like Tokyo.

Apart from the domestic television alternatives available, there was also the language barrier for the Japanese. Thus in the early 1990s, less than 500 households in all Japan were believed to be receiving StarTV using the three-metre satellite dish required for AsiaSat1 (ibid.). Since the government officially granted "liberal access" to transnational broadcasters in 1995, the latter have been tailoring their programming and directing specific channels towards Japanese viewers in conjunction with domestic communications firms. In 1997 the JSkyB, a joint venture of News Corporation and three major Japanese corporations, launched a 12-channel service [Hughes 1997]. It later merged with PerfecTV, a locally-owned service which offered 100 television channels, and the resultant Sky PerfecTV had about 1.7 million subscribers (Saito 2000).

_____ **South Korea**

Although South Korea had long received broadcasts via satellite and spillover, the early government policy on transnational television seemed to be one of "complacent inaction" as there was neither restriction on nor regulation of reception (Vanden Heuvel and Dennis 1994). In 1993 the government liberalised the domestic television industry by licensing cable channels to broadcast sports, Korean and foreign movies and other programmes, in a move which seemed like "controlled access" [Clifford 1993]. A Gallup survey reported that 230,000 households or 2 per cent of all South Korean households had satellite dishes. Yet dish manufacturers estimated that only 10,000 households used it to watch StarTV while an overwhelming 200,000 preferred to watch JBS, a Japanese satellite broadcaster. Rather belatedly, the Korean government decided to launch a domestic broadcast satellite of its own, Moogunghwa or Koreasat 1, to wean its populace off transnational television, but emphasising public broadcasting and education [Won 1993].

In late 1995, four new cable channels were launched, specialising in a Korean game, cartoons, Christian issues and culture respectively, catering to about 370,000 subscribers [AMCB 1996b]. However, in

1997 the government banned the relay of transnational television by South Korean cable networks, while not interfering in their private reception by households [Asian A&M 1997b], in a move which might be characterised as "latent suppression". The strong guidance of the government has also been quite accurately described as a combination of economic "carrots" and political "sticks" (Park et al. 2000). Thus although there were 20 cable networks offering 30 channels in 1999, these were exclusively Korean in origin (Heo et al. 2000).

North Korea

In keeping with its strict Stalinist form of communism, North Korea sees broadcasting as an ideological weapon and so bans reception of transnational broadcast media except by a few senior party leaders. This policy goes to the extent of fixing personal radio and television sets to receive only domestic broadcasts so as to prevent reception of transborder broadcasts from South Korea and even communist China, and subjecting even suspected violators to severe punishment (Gunaratne and Kim 2000). Ironically, its Kaesong TV channel deliberately uses the NTSC system to broadcast propaganda programmes targeted specifically at South Korean audiences. Thus the national policy of North Korea over the five decades since its formation has been a relentless case of "active suppression", though given the rapprochement with South Korea in recent years there might be some relenting towards "latent suppression" in the future.

Mongolia

Like North Korea, Mongolia was under the influence of the former Soviet Union rather than China, though this influence was even earlier, dating from the 1920s. In the 1990s, as with the Soviet bloc nations in Eastern Europe, its socialist and later democratic government implemented free market reforms. This meant a shift from state ownership of broadcasting to encouragement of commercial participation, including foreign ownership, amidst a lack of laws throughout most of the 1990s to finally dissolution of state broadcasting in 1999 (Lowe and Gunaratne 2000). Only in 1998, after eight years of deliberation, was a law passed freeing the media from government interference and censorship. Mongolian TV has incorporated programming from foreign channels such as Canal France International, MTV and StarTV, which though popular enjoy less popularity than Russian programmes on RTR and ORT (due to language barriers). Since the mid-1990s cable networks allowed citizens in the capital to receive an additional 20 to 30 international channels (Myagmar 2000).

Mongolia has utilised satellites technology both to uplink domestic television to its more remote regions as well as to downlink transnational television for rebroadcast in the capital Ulaanbaatar [APT Yearbook 1998]. Kazakhstan television was received for the Kazakh minority in Mongolia's far western province while Russian programmes were also received via satellite in Ulaanbaatar. Transnational channels such as StarTV appear confined to selected sites such as top hotels and large apartment complexes [Williams 2000]. While the Mongolian constitution guaranteed freedom of information, only in 1998 was a media law promulgated which prohibited censorship (Myagmar and Nielsen 2001). Therefore like many former Soviet bloc countries in Eastern Europe, Mongolia's policy on transnational television seems to have made the quantum leap from "active suppression" to "complacent inaction" virtually overnight in the early 1990s, before eventually being formalised as "liberal access".

China (PRC)

Only in the early 1990s with the launch of AsiaSat1 and StarTV did satellite dish sales soar in China. By the end of 1993 there were estimated to be 600,000 to 1 million dishes in use giving 30 to 70 million Chinese access to transnational satellite television [Ciotti 1994], believed to be more in the south than north of the country. Galvanised by News Corporation's purchase of StarTV, the Chinese government acted in March 1994 to restrict satellite dish ownership to public institutions such as financial, media and educational organisations, tourist hotels rated two-star and above, and residential buildings built for foreigners [AWSJ 1994]. However, AsiaSat1 was used by certain provincial television stations to reach remote areas, giving residents there and elsewhere within the country an excuse to possess satellite dishes. The Chinese response in the early 1990s to transnational television could be seen as an example of "latent suppression". For while the national government might have wished to ban transnational broadcasts, it either lacked the political will, given some provincial and municipal-level party, military and government investment in the satellite and cable industry, or the logistical ability to do so in a large nation. In 2001, the PRC government sought to merge city and provincial television and cable stations into regional media conglomerates as a means of tightening government control of broadcasting and fending off foreign competition [Leung 2001e]. Yet the continued economic liberalisation of the country appears to be leading China inexorably back towards "complacent inaction" or even "controlled access" as far as its policy on transnational television is concerned.

Taiwan (ROC)

Poor quality and politically conservative programming on the government-controlled domestic channels spurred the growth of an illegal cable television industry offering over 100 channels, which caused the reduction of combined prime time ratings of the terrestrial broadcasters from 100 per cent to just 65–70 per cent by 1995 [ASIAcom 1995b]. New legislation in 1993 legalised the status of its 300 cable TV operators, but banned foreign ownership of them and required that 20 per cent of all programming be local. In early 1999, a new cable broadcasting law allowed cable operators to own and manage related telecommunications businesses with minimal restrictions. Furthermore, the government allowed foreign investment in cable systems of up to a 20 per cent stake, which resulted in mergers and various strategic alliances [International Cable 1999b]. This would explain Taiwan's enduring leadership in the transnational television penetration stakes in Asia (Figure 4.4), which will be analysed in a latter chapter. In its determination to be a digital broadband-linked island and regional broadcasting hub, Taiwan's policy towards transnational satellite television has shifted steadily from one of "prudent inaction" through "regulated access" to virtually "liberal access" in recent years.

Hong Kong (SAR)

In December 1990, the then colonial Hong Kong government licensed StarTV to operate a pan-Asian satellite television service for 12 years, though it was not allowed to broadcast in Cantonese, the dominant language of the colony. Thus by 1993 StarTV had achieved a penetration in the colony of only 5 per cent or a daily reach of 253,000 viewers. The station was allowed to offer a pay-TV service from October 1993 provided these channels were made available in Hong Kong through the sole licensed cable provider. Though known to be a laissezfaire economy, Hong Kong has nonetheless adopted a cautious form of "controlled access" towards transnational satellite broadcasting in Asia, balancing its desire to promote the colony as a communications hub whilst concerned not to offend its dominant neighbour and ultimate political master, China.

As at the end of the 1990s and despite becoming a Special Administrative Region (SAR) of China, Hong Kong had no restriction on the reception of transnational television except for some technical specifications. As an uplinking centre for transnational broadcasts, it imposed similar standards on content as it did for domestic broadcasts but initially prohibited any broadcasts in Cantonese so as to protect its domestic channels' revenues (Lee 1998). In late 1998, the government liberalised its broadcasting policy, allowing satellite broadcasters to offer pay-TV services in Hong Kong and requiring Cable TV (previously Wharf Cable) to open its broadband network to other television and telecommunications services. The policy also lifted restrictions on cross-ownership of telecommunications and broadcasting to enhance convergence and competition (So et al. 2000b). In a further attempt to stem the flow of global broadcasters which have relocated their regional base to Singapore, the government also lifted the 49 per cent cap on foreign ownership of broadcasters allowed to uplink from Hong Kong.

Macau (SAR)

The other Chinese SAR, Macau does not restrict access to transnational television and seems not to have any regulation of cable networks, characteristic of "complacent inaction". In fact Hong Kong channels dominate the local television scene by spillover, as they do

Figure 4.6
Recency of Viewing any Satellite/Cable Channel, June 1999–July 2000

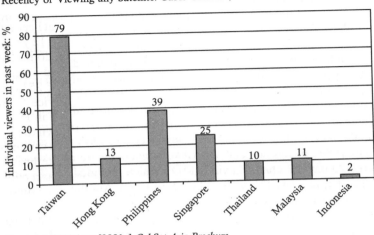

Source: AC Nielsen [2001a] *CabSat Asia Brochure*

also in the coastal parts of Quandong province in China. Macau's attempt in 1997 to boost its television broadcast signals to cover Hong Kong were thwarted by the latter's broadcasters lobbying their government to threaten retaliatory action which would have crippled Macau's tourism and casino industry (ibid. 2000a). Apart from Hong Kong's domestic channels, few other broadcasters show any concern in Macau's broadcast regulations because, with a population of less than half a million, its market is of little economic interest. Only in 1998 was the first pay-TV service established for Macau. As a sign of the impending change of sovereignty, in the same year Teledifusao de Macau's Chinese channel began carrying China's CCTV-4 news in Cantonese, even if this happened past midnight. The variegated case of Greater China, specifically China (PRC), Taiwan (ROC) and Hong Kong, will be discussed in detail in Chapter 7.

WEST ASIAN POLICIES

In West Asia, often referred to as the Middle East, satellite dishes were legal in the Gulf states of UAE, Kuwait and Oman for most of the 1990s. In addition to a commercial station in UAE's Dubai and

Abu Dhabi, there were cable networks operating there early in the decade [World Broadcast News 1993]. Since there was an estimated two expatriate employees for every local Arab in the UAE, most from other West Asian as well as South and Southeast Asian countries, this audience became of interest to transnational television stations [Via Satellite 1995a]. The Omani government debated the cultural impact of transnational television when it was first introduced in 1991 but approved satellite dishes, believing that systematic Islamic teaching would immunise its 1.5 million citizens from the more adverse effects. Despite an official ban on satellite dishes in Bahrain, 6 per cent of its 230,000 television households had some access to DBS television by the late 1990s. In addition to its own five channels, the state broadcaster offered 23 pay-TV channels via MMDS which included StarTV and ZeeTV channels (Al-Thawadi and Callard 1997). Another Gulf state, Qatar, initially imposed a ban on satellite dishes and later opted to install a cable network to carry selected and censored programming from the transnational television channels [*Straits Times* 1994]. Quite unexpectedly in 1995, Qatar lifted restrictions on all media and introduced a satellite television channel called Al-Jazeera which revolutionised news and information programming for the whole region (Al-Hail 2000). The liberalism and professionalism of the channel brought it to international prominence following the terrorist attacks on the US in September 2001 and the consequent war in Afghanistan.

Although watching transnational television was never approved of officially in Saudi Arabia, estimates of up to 400,000 satellite dishes and 2 million viewers were made as early as the mid-1990s. Owners hid them behind brick walls or under tarpaulins, while prices of satellite dishes and receivers doubled with official crackdowns (Al-Makaty 1995). However, some members of the Saudi royal family had considerable investments in Arabic satellite television broadcasting from Europe and elsewhere in the Middle East. Later a micro-transmission system was installed in the country to re-distribute regional and international channels monitored to ensure programming in line with the country's religious and cultural values. But the consequent media isolation of Saudi citizens may explain ironically their motivation for seeking access to television via direct broadcast satellite instead (Boyd 1999).

Although religion was a major factor in the development of television in West Asia, a major stimulus in the demand for transnational television was the start of the Gulf War in 1991. As in the rest of Asia, it compelled domestic television and restricted pay-TV to compete with new free-to-air transnational broadcasters via satellite (Kumar 2000). In discussing the development of a new satellite channel in the UAE, Boyd-Barrett (2000) pointed out that the motivations for such ventures in the region were not only economic, but included promoting the country internationally as well as political interests domestically. Gher and Amin (1999) classifed some Arab nations as having a "national mobilisation philosophy" exercising tight control, while others have a "bureaucratic laissez-faire philosophy". While Iran is not an Arab nation, given its theocratic Shia-Muslim form of government, it would maintain quite restrictive official policies towards transnational television, though little research has been published on these. On the other hand Israel, the other non-Arab nation in the region, identifies rather with Europe and adopts quite liberal policies. According to this book's typology of government policies towards transnational broadcasters such as StarTV, most West Asian states finally adopted one of "controlled access", while Qatar later opted for "liberal access" and Saudi Arabia shifted slightly from "active" to "latent suppression". Thus policies towards transnational television in West Asia display much diversity and on-going change (Figure 4.7).

Figure 4.7
Government Policies in West Asia Towards Transnational Media, 1991–2001

	Active Suppression	Latent Suppression	Complacent Inaction	Prudent Inaction	Controlled Access	Liberal Access
Bahrain				1991–		
U.A.E			1991–			
Qatar		1991–92			1993–94	1995–
Saudi Arabia	1991–95	1996–				

There are yet other regions within Asia, notably Central Asia and Oceania, but generally they represent peripheral markets for the leading transnational satellite/cable television broadcasters investigated in this book. Till the past decade, the nations of Central Asia were part of the former Soviet Union and to this day their television is dominated by Russian commercial broadcasts and programming, despite much nationalism. However, there are suggestions that the Muslim-majority nations in that region may learn from the experience of similar nations in Southeast Asia such as Malaysia (Saidkasimov and Tukhtabayev 1998). Media in this general region will warrant further attention given the questionable US "global war on terror" in Afghanistan and in Iraq post-11 September 2001. Less strategic are the islands of Oceania since the moratorium on nuclear testing by the West. The nations there are quite minute in geographic size, population and economy, if one discounts Australia and New Zealand as not culturally identified with Asia in any case. This survey covers primarily the politico-economic contexts of major regional markets of Asia in which transnational broadcasters operate. Regardless of whether one concurs with every country's classification in the typology, it is evident that new communications technologies and government policies alone do not seem to dictate the success of any transnational medium. The interaction of other factors such as terrestrial versus satellite programming, cultural and linguistic barriers and economic affluence in each country prove critical, as subsequent chapters demonstrate.

5

TELEVISION ON THE INDIAN SUBCONTINENT

Soon after its arrival, transnational television was an urban elite phenomenon on the Indian subcontinent with estimates of a quarter of all StarTV households in Asia located in affluent suburbs of the metropolitan cities of Bombay, Dhaka, Delhi, Calcutta, Karachi and Madras. But it was ZeeTV and its quasi-domestic competitors who revolutionised the television market in the region. Governments had initially proposed laws to restrict what they defined as cultural invasion by satellite television, but later their own public broadcasters resigned themselves to competing, even collaborating with commercial satellite broadcasters, transnational and domestic. Over the decade, the television market in South Asia has been totally transformed from single dominant public broadcasters having virtual monopolies of each nation-state, to one in which there are over 100 transnational and regional channels available across borders. Given the size and complexity within the region, this chapter focuses on dominant transnational television broadcasters in northern and southern India while correlating them with developments in other South Asian national diasporic markets.

PUBLIC BROADCASTERS

India's Doordarshan

Public broadcast television in India had its origins as a socio-economic education project for villagers in 1959. With the advice of major US corporations, India then experimented with a number of foreign satellites to support more such projects before launching its own satellites in 1982–83, equipped to transmit television, radio, telephony and data [Pendakur 1991]. While its television programming over the 1970 and 1980s may have sought to meld the rural and urban, traditional and modern segments of India into one nation, the advertising it carried seemed targeted at the socio-economic elite.

Commercial Entertainment Phase (1982–91)

The gradual shift of successive Indian governments from an earlier commitment to socialism, together with the hosting of the Asian Games in 1986, prompted the massive growth of television in the country. By the late 1980s its terrestrial transmitters covered 70 per cent of its population (Hudson 1990: 202–05). About that time, DD switched to colour transmission and shifted its emphasis from social-educational to commercial-entertainment programming. In 1984, a second channel was commissioned for the Delhi metropolitan area and over the next four years for Bombay, Calcutta and Madras metropolitan areas in which local language/ethnic preferences in programming were catered to partially, though the primary motivation might have been to target the urban elite for advertisers. Apart from minor changes in programming and distribution there were few developments in DD till the arrival of transnational television in 1991. DD continued to be a government bureaucracy and exercised monopoly despite parliamentary inquiries during the 1960s and 1970s, such as the Chandra and Verghese Committees, which advocated greater diversity of providers and autonomy from political manipulation (Thomas 1990: 4–13).

Television was seen as a catalyst of social change and national development, sensitising society about social justice, educating the population and developing its human resource (Acharya 1987: 90, 117). However, a programme-flow study found that in all television centres, local drama/movie programmes accounted for almost a quarter of transmission time (Joshi and Parmar 1992), unsurprising given the fact that India is the world's largest producer of feature films. Information programmes dealing with health and agriculture occupied another quarter while education took up 12 per cent, with sports and news following closely. Despite programming inadequacies DD penetration continued to grow, because between 1982 and 1992 the number of government television transmitters increased from 39 to 531. This emphasis on hardware was criticised for having led to dependence on advertising revenue and neglect of programming quality (Bhargava 1991: 6). Over the same period the number of television sets also increased significantly from 2.1 million to an estimated 34.9 million sets, making for a maximum Indian audience of potentially over 200 million individuals. Video parlours provided the poorer classes who could not afford a VCR with an entertainment alternative to the dismal programming on DD, and were estimated to number around 50,000 by 1988 [Noble 1989].

The success of a Mexican tele-novela in promoting social-educational themes such as family planning and women's rights in Latin America was replicated in India in 1984 with an indigenous soap opera (Singhal and Rogers 1989: 88–121). Although it had a social development agenda, *Hum Log* was also the first sponsored programme of DD, spawning numerous other soap operas created by India's film industry and co-opted by its advertising industry. Another television genre found to be popular in India was that of historical epics. But on analysing the text of the televised epic *Mahabharat*, Mitra [1993a] found DD perpetrating a Hindu religion/Hindi language cultural hegemony of multicultural and multireligious India, in defiance of the constitutional commitment to state secularism. In recounting the religious significance given to watching a related epic *Ramayana*, Vilanilam [1996: 83] alleged that such broadcasts were responsible for the rise of Hindu fundamentalism in the Indian political sphere. Religion has been a key element of national cultural identity in India, given its role in the post-colonial partition from Pakistan and Bangladesh.

Ethnic Diversification Phase (c. 1993–97)

With economic liberalisation within the country and globalisation pressures from without, India's political system had been more willing to accept change in its broadcast policy. The de facto "open sky" policy which came about with StarTV and ZeeTV spelt the slow decline of DD, especially in urban areas though rural areas still had little choice (Sinclair and Hemphill 1997: 13–21). The change was exemplified by the drop in ratings of popular programmes such as Hindi films on Doordarshan's primary channel DD1 from over 80 per cent down to 49 per cent [Karnik 1993]. Doordarshan reacted strategically to transnational television by re-launching all the metropolitan-based DD2 channels as a single nationwide Metro channel in January 1992 to cater to an urban, middle class, young, upwardly mobile audience similar to ZeeTV's. Initially this was offered terrestrially to a few major cities but by 1994 was available via satellite to 15 cities [Interview Ind 02.05]. In order to attract sponsors or audiences, DD re-organised itself in the early 1990s with DD1 as its primary channel, DD2 as its Metro entertainment channel, DD3 as an upmarket channel in English, with DD4, DD5 and DD6 as subregional language/ethnic channels (Bhatt 1994: 96–102).

In the mid-1990s, Doordarshan went into satellite broadcasting itself with DD1 being made available on Insat 1D, broadcasting partially in Bengali, Oriya and Telugu, and on Insat 2A partially in Assamese, Kashmiri, Malayalam, Tamil, Marathi, Kannada and Gujarati. A further five-channel package of entertainment, music, business and current affairs, sports and enrichment was broadcast terrestrially to 6 million television households in the four metropolitan areas of Bombay, Delhi, Calcutta and Madras from December 1993, and available via Insat 2B to another 4.9 million cable television households. These new channels experimented with semi-privatisation by leasing time to private production houses which would create programmes without DD preview and sell commercial time to advertisers [HTA 1993a]. By August 1994 in a determined bid to combat the growing subregional ethnic language satellite channels such as Asianet, JainTV, UdayaTV and SunTV, Doordarshan re-organised itself once again, this time into 10 ethnic language channels in addition to three national channels, each uplinked from the subregional station where that language was dominant and made available via satellite throughout the country [HTA 1994].

Thus it became possible for Indians to watch television of their own ethnic culture regardless of their location in the country. Entertainment on DD Metro expanded in response to its rising popularity and with the manifest intent of giving stiff competition to the StarTV channels. A broad range of programmes was put together including the 300-episode *Dallas*, a Hindi serial *Mirch Masala*, a multistar *Junoon*, a detective serial *Gehrai*, and many Bombay film industry based programmes [Interview Ind 02.05]. It also screened popular Hindi movies, privately produced quizzes, film and chat shows that were clones of the StarTV and ZeeTV programming genre. Positioned as an upmarket English language channel, DD3 was re-launched by Doordarshan in November 1995 to compete head-on with the transnationals like StarTV, TNT/Cartoon Network and others [International Cable

1996]. Broadcast free-to-air from Insat 2-C, India's newest satellite, it was available via cable throughout the country plus terrestrially in the four major cities of Bombay, Delhi, Calcutta and Madras. The strategy of Doordarshan was to allow the cannibalising of DD1 audiences by its own DD2 to DD15 channels rather than to lose them to ZeeTV, StarTV channels and other transnational and regional channels.

When the Indian government proposed a law to restrict the "cultural invasion" by satellite and cable television, StarTV countered with an offer of a transponder on its satellite, as a means of saving one of its larger markets [AWSJ 1993b], which was not taken up. Instead Doordarshan embarked on a Rs 7,000 million (US$233 million) expansion of the television network, to achieve 95 per cent coverage of the country's population by 1994. Doordarshan was compelled by competition not only to give voice to the country's many ethnic groups but also provide programming that resembled what was on offer on the transnational channels (Table 5.1). It broadcast imported soap operas such as *Dallas* and *Dynasty*, incorporated MTV programming into its schedule and pursued rights to international sports competitions such as Wimbledon. Its aggressive wooing of advertisers also meant changes to its own standing rules with regard to the use of foreign models and locales, and permitting advertising by foreign banks and airlines. But DD had also gone to the extent of denying use of its satellite uplink facilities

Table 5.1
Doordarshan Channels in the Late 1990s

International Channel	National Channels	Subregional Language Satellite Channels	State Networks
DD India	DD 1 National DD 2 Metro DD Sports DD News	DD 4 Malayalam DD 5 Tamil DD 6 Oriya DD 7 Bengali DD 8 Telugu DD 9 Kannada DD 10 Marathi DD 11 Gujarati DD 12 Kashimiri DD 13 Assamese and Northeastern languages DD 18 Punjabi	DD 14 Rajasthan DD 16 Uttar Pradesh DD 15 Madhya Pradesh DD 17 Bihar

Source: Adapted from DD-ARU [1999].

for the transmission of an Indian cricket series by StarTV to which it had lost the domestic telecast rights [Pathania 1996]. In its determination to upgrade, Doordarshan had tied up with CNN for staff training and technical assistance [Interview Ind 02.07]. Furthermore, the Indian cabinet approved CNN's utilisation of a transponder on Insat 2B [Rai 1994]. The deal, worth US$1.5 million annually to Doordarshan, faced calls from opposition parties for its cancellation and objections from other transnational and regional commercial broadcasters denied uplinking rights from within India.

Regionalisation-diasporic Market Phase (c. 1998 early—2000s)

By the late 1990s DD was delivering its national channels round-the-clock via satellite, with some signals in digital format on the domestic-public Insat-2E and the global-commercial Pas-4. However, given the constraints of the audience market, all channels were also available in analogue format. In 1999 it inaugurated a dedicated sports channel which also had exclusive telecast rights to all major cricket matches played in India, catering to fans of what comes closest to being a national sport. In addition it featured major events like World Cup soccer, Grand Slam tennis, Summer and Winter Olympics and Commonwealth Games. It also added a news and current affairs channel, which incorporated business, sports, gender issues and interactive programmes. It produced news bulletins thrice a day in Hindi and English and news headlines on the hour for DD 1, news in Urdu for DD 2, and sub-regional news bulletins for DD state and language channels. Together with the international channel DD India, DD Sports and DD News were also made available to diasporic audiences via satellites Pas-4 and Pas-1 in the Middle East, East, West and Central Africa, CIS/Central Asia, Southeast Asia, Europe and North America [DD-ARU 1999].

At the start of the 2000s, DD had 47 programme production centres producing 1,400 hours of original programming each week, 19 satellite transponders, 1,056 terrestrial transmitters and 19 channels. It is watched by 300 million people in their homes and by another 150 million at community sets or neighbours' homes, representing a reach of 87 per cent of the population which was well ahead of the commercial satellite and cable channels [Ambez Media and Market Research 1999]. In 2001 there were further restructures afoot at DD after the dedicated DD News channel failed to generate sufficient advertising revenue. It was clear that this attempt to emulate the success of

BBC World, CNN, CNBC Asia-Pacific and other dedicated news channels had failed. News resources were shifted into DD1, with a new "cultural channel" replacing DD News and DD2 being converted into a channel run on commercial imperatives (Brown 2001h). All of DD's strategic moves throughout the 1990s suggested that, due to its dependence on advertising revenues, DD no longer saw itself having a special role as a public broadcaster, no matter what the political rhetoric claimed. In the early 2000s DD could still claim to have the highest rating programmes in all-TV households, even if it could not compete in cable and satellite households (Table 5.2).

Table 5.2
Top 10 Television Programmes in India in Early 2000

All TV Homes				Cable and Satellite TV Homes			
Rank	Channel	Programme	TVR	Rank	Channel	Programme	TVR
1.	DD1	Suraag	9.4	1.	Star Plus	Kyunki Saas Bhi	10.0
2.	DD1	HFF-Aflatoon	9.3	2.	Star Plus	Kahaani Ghar	8.7
3.	DD1	Aap Beeti	9.1	3.	Star Plus	Kaahin Kissii Roz	5.6
4.	DD1	Shaktimaan	7.5	4.	Star Plus	Kasauti Zindagi Kay	5.5
5.	DD1	Kudrat	7.5	5.	Star Plus	Sanjivani	4.4
6.	DD1	Dishayen	7.2	6.	Star Plus	Son Pari	4.3
7.	DD1	Junior G	7.0	7.	SonyET	Kkusum	4.2
8.	DD1	HFF-Yaarana	6.8	8.	Star Plus	Kismey Kitnaa	4.1
9.	DD1	Manzilein	6.8	9.	Star Plus	Des Mein Nikla	4.1
10.	Star Plus	Kyunki Saas Bhi	6.4	10.	Star Plus	Kyunki Saas Bhi	3.7

Source: ORG-Marg Intam, cited in Indiantelevision.com [2002].

As a public broadcaster Doordarshan had constraints on its development initially, such as the policies on cultural integration and political unity of the Indian nation. National integration was paramount on the Indian political agenda 20 years ago. Yet even in the 1970s and 1980s there was evidence that television broadcasting in India was furthering the agenda of its political and economic elite. Observing the influence of the media on political reform movements in Eastern Europe in the late 1980s and early 1990s may have caused some concern to governments in Asia and helped motivate their leaders to learn how to be able to manage social change. Thus with politico-economic liberalisation and globalisation of the world system, the Indian political structure has been prepared to accept further change in broadcasting policies not envisaged before the 1990s. Symbiotic diversity is the new catchphrase in cultural policy in India as in many developing countries, but this appears to be in the pursuit of advertising revenue rather than any social, political or economic development which undergirded previous strategies.

Pakistan Television (PTV)

Pakistan Television (PTV) had begun in 1963 as joint venture between the government and NEC of Japan, and expanded gradually over the next two decades. In 1974 the last of its five stations was inaugurated at Peshawar, adding to earlier ones at Islamabad, the political capital, Quetta, Lahore and Karachi, the commercial capital. Its programming was said initially to have had some intellectual appeal but succumbed to commercial pressures. In 1992, 56 per cent of its programming was entertainment, and only 25 per cent news and educational, about 54 per cent of which was in the national language of Urdu, 16 per cent in English and the rest in local dialects (Gilani and Zuberi 1993). Throughout the 1970s and 1980s, PTV was the sole provider of television in Pakistan and was supported by advertising as were most public broadcasters in Asia. Under Pakistan's military ruler Ayub Khan, PTV was perceived as a major means of national integration. The secession of East Pakistan as Bangladesh meant continued strict controls over PTV, even under the democratically elected government of Zulfiqar Ali Bhutto which followed (Page and Crawley 2001: 54–55).

Perhaps in response to the challenge of the Pakistani private channel Shalimar and Indian public television, PTV launched a deliberately transnational service in 1992. Named Pakistan International Television (PITV) it was beamed via AsiaSat1 and targeted Urdu-speaking audiences in India, Bangladesh, the Persian Gulf as well as parts of Pakistan not reached by terrestrial television [King 1996]. In 1998 another satellite channel called PTV World was started to reach Pakistanis elsewhere in Asia, and Prime TV was set up to transmit PTV programmes to migrant Pakistanis in Europe. Then in 1999 the PTV Mid-East Channel was launched, further acknowledging the target market of expatriate Pakistanis particularly in the Persian Gulf region. Despite receiving all the necessary government approvals PTV abruptly shelved plans to inaugurate a cable network comprising 100 channels in 2001.

Though it cited financial costs of laying cable, some believe that it was under pressure from conservative religious groups not to expand foreign programming [Brown 2001f].

While audience statistics are not readily available, journalistic accounts confirmed that the viewership for ZeeTV in particular and other Indian channels was very high. Urdu is similar to Hindi except in the written script and most Pakistanis therefore understand programmes on northern Indian broadcasters. The only complaint seemed to be the bias of news and current affairs programmes especially over the Kashmir question, but the only real alternative for Pakistani viewers was the state-run PTV which was equally propagandist. There has been concern expressed about the "Zee-ification" or "Hindi cultural invasion" of Pakistani society by political leaders and some social taboos against admitting to viewing of Indian television [Rout 2000]. Ironically, Pakistani opposition leaders sometimes appeared on ZeeTV and exhorted supporters to watch it instead of the government-controlled PTV (Sonwalkar 2001). On the other hand, PTV has long been readily available across the border in the Indian state of Punjab, though there are doubts whether its earlier largely development programming drew much of an audience.

Given the obvious popularity of game shows, drama serials, music and other entertainment programmes on ZeeTV, Channel V, SonyET and other northern Indian channels, ShalimarTV and even PTV cloned such programme formats in Urdu for domestic audiences. Barraclough (2001) documented the dilemma faced by Pakistani policy makers over the attraction of permissive programming of transnational television and liberal programming by national television on gender issues during Benazir Bhutto's rule, versus the objections of Islamic conservatives then in the political opposition. Under the Nawaz Sharif government from 1997 anti-western cultural guidelines and strict censorship were imposed on both programming and advertising on PTV. In late 2000, PTV lost is 36-year monopoly on news when the government of General Musharraf launched Pakistan News Network (PNN). Broadcasting intially in Hindi, Bangla and Chinese, PNN seemed designed to counteract the regional dominance of Indian news channels [Brown 2000a]. In the following sections we look at some of the commercial players in the regional and national television environment which prompted South Asia's political and economic elite to re-examine their policies and cultural strategies.

COMMERCIAL BROADCASTERS

Northern Channels

Zee TV

In October 1992 a group of domestic and NRI investors launched
ZeeTV, utilising the same AsiaSat1 satellite as StarTV. It was a Hindi
language channel catering to both urban and rural areas of India, the
latter relatively untouched by StarTV. Though Doordarshan had long
reached that segment, ZeeTV was free of the former's restrictive programming policies. ZeeTV represented diversification into the
entertainment industry by the Essel Group of Indian entrepreneur
Subhash Chandra. To launch this channel Chandra formed a joint
venture in Hong Kong called Asia Today Limited (ATL) in partnership
with StarTV and unnamed NRI investors. While Essel was responsible
through a firm called Zee Telefilms Ltd for producing the programming, ATL was responsible for the uplinking of the channel from
Hong Kong (Nadkarni 1993: 24–25). ZeeTV was broadcast across
three time zones, targeting the Indian domestic market as well as NRIs
in the Middle East, and was said to have become profitable after just
six months on air. In December 1993 News Corporation purchased a
49.9 per cent stake in ATL, acceptance of the minority position explained as a means to avoid an adverse reaction by the Indian
government [Dubey 1993b].

The ZeeTV programme staples of Hindi films, variety games and
talk shows provided Indian viewers with a refreshing alternative to
the staid programming on DD, most of them made by its own subsidiary Zee Telefilms. Following equity participation by News Corporation, plans were announced by ZeeTV to double its broadcasting
hours to 24 per day by mid-1994, to launch a second channel on the
next satellite AsiaSat2, and to explore potential markets for Hindi
language programmes in Europe, North America and Africa (ibid.).
To cope with the increased demand for programming, ZeeTV turned
to independent production houses. Towards the end of 1994, ZeeTV
unexpectedly terminated its long-term production agreement with
UTV after losing its bid to purchase a 49 per cent stake in it to News
Corporation [Mullick 1994a]. In diversifying its production sourcing,

ZeeTV formed a production company in Sharjah in the Persian Gulf, considered joint productions with Pakistani companies, and began purchases of programming in other Indian languages [Dziadul 1994]. As early as 1996 ZeeTV was reported to have explored the possibility of dubbing some of its Hindi programmes into subregional Indian languages to reach new audience segments, as well as dubbing subregional programming into Hindi for its prime market [AMCB 1996f]. In response to a highly diversified market that followed the launching of several satellites and new rival channels, it began operating as a multichannel broadcaster called Zee Network [Wanvari 1996a].

By early 1996, ZeeTV had a penetration of 15 million out of the estimated 40 million TV households in India, not counting other audiences abroad. In Europe where it broadcast 17 hours a day as a payTV channel via the Astra 1D satellite and used SkyTV's channels for direct-to-home broadcasting, ZeeTV claimed 83,000 subscribers and a viewership of some 350,000 viewers in Britain alone among expatriate Indians, Pakistanis, Bangladeshis and Sri Lankans. About 30 per cent of its European programming was made locally at its London studios, while the rest was supplied by Zee Telefilms [Sidhu 1996]. ZeeTV was also carried for 1.5 hours daily on the pay-TV International Channel which reached 7.2 million Asian-origin homes though not all of them are ethnically South Asian. Since the early 1990s it has been available in Mauritius, which has an ethnic Indian majority, via an arrangement with a domestic broadcaster there. It was also launched in Fiji in mid-1996 as a pay-TV service in conjunction with TVNZ, catering to a sizeable ethnic Indian population there. From 1996 ZeeTV was also available as a premium tier channel on the South African pay-TV service, Multichoice, targeting the estimated 500,000 Indian households throughout Africa. By the early 2000s, ZeeTV was available via cable or DTH dishes in an estimated 170,000 UK homes, 54,000 US homes, 1.24 million homes in the UAE and 45,000 African homes. Within South Asia itself it was in 4 million Pakistani homes and 1 million Bangladeshi homes, while there were no figures for Nepal (Sonwalkar 2001).

Over the late 1990s ZeeTV created new channels such as Zee English, Zee Movies, Music Asia, ZED, its educational channel, as well as subregional language channels such as Alpha Marathi, Alpha Punjabi and Alpha Bengali. It has also diversified into learning systems (Zee International Learning Systems), cable networks (Siticable), Internet (Zee Interactive Multimedia), music publishing (Zee Music) and feature films (Essel Vision). In 2000 ZeeTV entered into an agreement with Nickelodeon for the latter to provide a sizeable proportion of its daily children's programming dubbed into Hindi. In 1999 all these media-related firms were consolidated into Zee Telefilms Limited and the corporation reached an amicable separation from News Corporation. As a consequence ZeeTV began broadcasting in English and StarTV in Hindi, competing for similar audience markets. Despite some programming setbacks and strong competition, ZeeTV remained the market leader among cable and satellite channels targeting Indian households (Table 5.3). In 2001, it entered into a strategic alliance with the global media conglomerate AOL Time Warner as the latter's representative broadcaster in the region.

Table 5.3
Television Penetration in India in the Early 2000s (in million households)

Channel	National Total	Total C & S*	Total non-C & S*	Urban Total	Urban C & S*	Urban non-C & S*
DD1	68.3	29.0	39.3	38.6	21.4	17.2
DD2	29.3	17.3	12.0	22.7	15.1	7.6
ZeeTV	21.7	21.7	0.0	18.7	18.7	0.0
SonyET	18.7	18.7	0.0	15.8	15.8	0.0
Star Plus	16.2	16.2	0.0	15.1	15.1	0.0

Source: Channel 9 Gold [2000].
Note: C & S* = Cable and Satellite.

SonyET

The Japanese entered the market quietly on the Pas-4 satellite with the Sony Entertainment Television (SET) channel, 60 per cent of which was owned by Sony and 40 per cent by Argos Communications Entertainment, a Singapore firm. Drawing initially on soap operas, serials, game shows and movies from Sony's Columbia Tristar and Indian movies from the Argos 400-title library, the channel commissioned 1,000 hours of Hindi programmes in its first year [APT-C 1995: 102]. It would add two more channels, one in Tamil and the other a music and movies channel [Narang 1996]. In 1998 it launched AXN, featuring action-oriented American movies, live shows and animated programmes, but it did not prove as popular due to its predominantly foreign programming. In 1999 the company launched Sony Max, featuring cricket and movies. However, SonyET had difficulty creating a bouquet of channels to dominate the prime band on television sets in India, and this was compounded by its lack of a strategic alliance or corporate affiliation with any cable network MSO (Ambez Media and Market Research 1999). In 2001, it took the radical step of making its entry into the Australia and New Zealand market as a channel on the Zee Link bouquet of rival South Asian channels there. SonyET was a relative latecomer to Indian television and represented the first foray by the Japanese media conglomerate into managing a television channel. Given its considerable global resources, it was soon one of the market leaders in the Indian television market strongly challenging ZeeTV and StarTV.

Early Hindi Broadcasters

Asia Television Network (ATN) was inaugurated in August 1992, ahead of ZeeTV, with much publicity as the world's first Hindi satellite television channel. But ATN failed to take off since its reception required cable operators to install a second satellite dish at some expense to receive just a few hours of programming per night. It was overtaken by ZeeTV which commenced two months later and was available along with the StarTV channels from AsiaSat satellite. Later ATN, broadcasting two channels via the Russian Statsionar satellite, managed to reach 8 million viewers or 6 per cent of all Indian TV households by January 1994. The ATN One channel had programming links with other satellite television channels, carrying Reuters, the American ABC and Thames TV, while the ATN Gold channel programming majored on Hindi movies and general entertainment [APT-C&S 1995]. ATN ceased transmission in 1995 and recommenced in mid-1996. By migrating to the PanAmSat satellite Pas-4 from Gorizont, it was able to reach 77 per cent of Indian audiences which was comparable to ZeeTV at 85 per cent and StarTV at 82 per cent [Narang 1996]. By the late 1990s it was certainly no longer a major player in the Indian market.

In operation since January 1994 and transmitting from the Russian Statsionar satellite, JainTV was the first 24-hour channel and soon penetrated 66 per cent of all cable operators in India. Since the Statsionar21 satellite was located at 103 degrees, and AsiaNet was on 105 degrees, the same satellite dish could be used to receive both, with only an additional low-noise block needed [Interview Ind 02.06]. Circumventing Indian laws by uplinking from near Moscow, JainTV innovated the real time broadcast of Bombay Stock Exchange prices, late night adult movies and "live" coverage of state elections. In a desperate attempt to increase its penetration, JainTV floated a proposal to form a cable forum with cable operators to assist in the procurement of quality programming in return for sharing the advertising revenue [Cable Quest 1994a]. It also outfitted its fleet of 125 video vans with satellite dishes to bring JainTV to India's rural market [Karp 1994]. However, by 1996 it was off air pending a public shares issue to raise Rs 180 million (US$5.2 million) to upgrade its studio and software library [Masters 1996a]. In 1999 it returned in the form of an education and information channel, offering programmes on medical advice and financial analysis for instance. It was also expanding into digital news channels, webcasting, e-commerce and internet services. One of the few Indian-owned and registered companies providing commercial television to the domestic market, Jain TV seemed poised at the start of the 2000s to take advantage of new laws allowing uplinking by such firms [Bamzai 2000]. Nonetheless, it does appear that JainTV, ATN and other national Hindi language channels have lagged significantly behind their competitiors (Table 5.4).

Table 5.4

Top 10 Television Channels by Audience Share in India, Late 1990s

Channel/Rank	Time Spent per Person (min.)	Audience Share %
1. Cable	173	15
2. Sony	139	12
3. SunTV	94	8
4. ZeeTV	83	7
5. Zee Cinema	71	6
6. Eenadu	53	5
7. DD1	47	4
8. DD2	32	3
9. Siti Cable	32	3
10. Gemini	32	3

Source: TAM Media Research, cited in Asia Cable & Satellite World [1999b].

Other Northern Channels

Launched as far back as 1989, the first private free-to-air channel in Pakistan, Shalimar Television reached 10 major cities within the country. By the late 1990s, Shalimar and PTV were watched avidly in the neighbouring Indian states of Punjab, Rajasthan, Himachal Pradesh as well as Delhi via spillover or where cable operators were persuaded to offer it. A major draw for these cross-border audiences was Urdu dramas, a respected cultural form throughout South Asia [Interview Ind 04.09]. Launched in 1998, Reminiscent Television Network (RTV) developed two channels, Lashkara and Gurjari which addressed the cultural needs of the Punjabi and Gujarati communities. Punjab and Gujarat in India border Pakistan (in which there is also a Punjab state) and are the homelands for large diasporic communities abroad. Understandably, in 2001 the two channels were launched along with six other subregional language channels in the UK to cater to the South Asian community there [Reminiscent TV Network 2002].

In a reversal of the usual trend, B4U was launched in 1999 initially for expatriate Indians or NRIs residing in Europe, USA and the Middle East, and then subsequently expanded to India. B4U, supposedly to represent "Bollywood for you", has two channels, a music channel and a movie channel, both intially free-to-air but eventually to be encrypted. A latter entrant into the Indian television market was SABe TV which was launched in 2000 by a programme production house Sri Adhikari Brothers Television Network Limited which previously produced for DD, ZeeTV and others. A former chief executive of DD and later of StarTV India, Ratikant Basu launched the Tara network in 2000 with multiple channels in subregional languages [Cable Quest 2000a]. ZeeTV itself launched its own stable of subregional language channels under the brand name Alpha, and by the end of 2000 had four separate channels in Marathi, Gujarati, Punjabi and Bengali. Perhaps emboldened by its alliance with AOL Time-Warner, in 2002 ZeeTV also acquired stakes in a new rival ETC only three years after the latter was launched as a music and Punjabi language network. Other channels were planned, such as Raag, a musical channel, BanglaTV for the Bengali community, Anjuman for the Urdu-speaking community, which extends from India into Pakistan, and Asia1 for the Hindi-speaking [Cable Quest 2000b]. Most of these channels have gained relatively small market shares and were niche broadcasters to particular cities, subregions or ethnic groups within India and in some cases cross-border audiences.

Southern Channels

Although DD and ZeeTV dominated northern India for the first half of the 1990s, the non-Hindi-speaking southern part of the country was relatively untouched by them. When broadcast and advertising industry executives in Bombay and Delhi were first interviewed for this research in the mid-1990s, they were aware of channels in the south but it was considered a niche market of little import. By the early 2000s the industry had come to recognise that the next stage in the development of satellite and cable television in India was a major shift from countrywide Hindi language programming to state-based ethnic language programming, as exemplified by the southern channels led by SunTV.

SunTV

The world's first Tamil language satellite television service was provided by SunTV which transmitted from the Russian satellite, Gorizont, and reached 8 per cent of all Indian TV households by January 1994 [APT-C&S 1995] with programming which was mainly blockbuster Tamil and Hindi movies. It was only with the advent of subregional channels such as SunTV in early 1993 that cable began to grow in Tamil Nadu [Interview Ind 01.04]. Still, the penetration of SunTV at the end of 1993 was low in Madras, at only 4 per cent of all TV households due to the low penetration of satellite television in general. But it was higher in the rest of Tamil Nadu at 14 per cent and even higher at 21 per cent in the cosmopolitan city of Bangalore in neighbouring Karnataka [HTA 1993b]. However, by 1996 SunTV had achieved advertising revenues of Rs 450 million (US$12.9 million), a 200 per cent increase over revenues of the previous year (AMCB 1996f). With a penetration of 86 per cent of Tamil Nadu, it was the only satellite network in India other than ZeeTV to turn profitable, which was enough to be wooed by StarTV in vain. In its primary market, the state of Tamil Nadu where Tamil is predominantly spoken, SunTV had three channels, SunTV, Sun Music and Sun Movies, out of a total of seven competing channels [Wanvari 1996b]. Over the late 1990s, SunTV began aggressive expansion into other southern markets, often through acquisitions.

In another southern state of Karnataka, where the Kannada language is spoken, Udaya TV began broadcasting in 1994 as part of the SunTV stable. It subsequently took over Gemini which broadcast in Telegu primarily in the state of Andhra Pradesh. The only southern state in which SunTV had no television channel as of the mid-1990s was Kerala where Malayalam is spoken. Even though Asianet had a considerable headstart with its integrated satellite and cable operation, SunTV decided to enter that market with SuryaTV [Interview Ind 02.10]. By the late-1990s SunTV was being retransmitted both by Singapore CableVision with which it shared the cable subscriptions and by Sri Lanka's private Maharaja Television with whom it shared advertising revenue [Narang 1996]. Although it faced competition from other channels, SunTV was the undisputed market leader by the late 1990s (Table 5.5), able to claim nine out 10 top rating programmes in southern India and the top five programmes in Chennai, the capital of Tamil Nadu [Interview Ind 01.13]. Yet, recognising the limited market and competitive environment of its home state and perhaps within India, SunTV was simultaneously targeting wealthier, diasporic southern Indian communities around the world.

Table 5.5
Top Five Television Programmes in Indian Cable and Satellite Households, Late 1990s

City	Rank	Channel	Programme	Rating
Mumbai	1.	SonyET	CID	11.4
	2.	SonyET	Aahat	8.6
	3.	ZeeTV	Closeup Antakshari	8.2
	4.	SonyET	Hum Sub Ek Hai	8.2
	5.	ZeeTV	Hum Paanch	8.2
Delhi	1.	ZeeTV	India's Most Wanted	12.3
	2.	ZeeTV	Aashirwad	11.9
	3.	ZeeTV	Amaanat	11.2
	4.	SonyET	Bhanwar	8.2
	5.	ZeeTV	Jaan	7.9
Chennai	1.	SunTV	Marma Desam	11.1
	2.	SunTV	Sun News	10.2
	3.	SunTV	TFF Ranuva Vee	10.1
	4.	VijayTV	My Choice	9.6
	5.	SunTV	Panchami	9.7

Source: Indian Market Research Bureau [1998].

Other Tamil Channels

There were three other broadcasters in Tamil: Vijay TV, Raj TV and JJ TV, the last of these owned by a politician and current chief minister of Tamil Nadu state, Jayalalitha, but closed due to corruption alleged by the government that toppled hers [Interview Ind 03.11]. Political rivalry continued into the early 2000s between SunTV which was owned by a former government minister and Jaya TV owned by a nephew of the former chief minister, Karunanidhi [Brown 2001f]. It was noteworthy that the subregional language channels existed only in the five languages in which 80 per cent of Indian movies were made. A large proportion of programming on all commercial satellite channels is movie or movie-based, and so the film industry is indispensable to the Indian television industry [Sekhar 1999]. In a surprising move in 2001, the transnational broadcaster StarTV took over control of programming, content, distribution and air-time sales of the locally-oriented Vijay TV, though not ownership, from the Indian production house UTV. Whether this represents a further stage in globalisation of the Indian television industry has yet to be confirmed.

Asianet

This first Malayalam language channel was beamed via the Russian satellite Ekran-M which did not require a satellite dish, just a helical one. Since Kerala did not have a pre-existing cable network, Asianet inaugurated 15 satellite dish "farms" across the state where signals from the various satellites such as AsiaSat and Ekran-M were downlinked and re-distributed to as many as 100,000 neighbouring households. This cable system was set up with the technical support of the state's electricity board enabling the use of its poles for cabling [HTA 1993b]. This satellite channel received a boost when the US cable network, Falcons Communications, bought a 40 per cent stake subsequently and it has since expanded into a variety of multimedia services [The Hindu 1994]. By the mid-1990s Asianet was achieving advertising revenue earnings of Rs 70 to 80 million (US$2.6 million) by targeting Malayalee viewers, both residents in their native Kerala and expatriates in the Middle East [Wanvari 1996b]. Asianet was the precursor of many multiservice providers which came to dominate the Indian satellite and cable television industry. By the early 2000s it offered a web portal, internet services, interactive gaming, voice/data transmission, and educational, music and other channels. Despite facing competition from two other Malayalam channels, SuryaTV (owned by SunTV) and Kairali, by the late 1990s it was claiming to be the largest in Kerala. In 2000 Asianet entered into a strategic alliance with ZeeTV to expand into Kannada, Telegu and Tamil programme production and channels [ZeeTV 2000]. Soon a major portion of this southern channel was owned by the dominant northern Indian channel, which in turn had an alliance with the global media conglomerate AOL Time Warner.

Telugu Channels

In the neighbouring southern state of Andra Pradesh, where Telugu is spoken by its 70 million people, two competing channels began in 1995. Eenadu TV had links with the leading Telugu newspaper of the same name, and by 1996 there were reports that Eenadu TV had achieved a viewership of 3.3 million [AMCB 1996f]. Founded in partnership with SunTV and other Madras-based film studios, Gemini TV was eventually bought out by SunTV. Although Gemini TV broadcast in Telugu for only 12 hours a day, it was leading in advertising revenues over Eenadu TV which broadcast for 18 hours [Wanvari 1996b]. The Gemini strategy for competing successfully with the market leader Eenadu was localisation by districts, and by 1999 it covered about 25 districts besides catering for Telegus in the neighbouring states of Tamil Nadu, Karnataka and Orissa [Interview Ind 03.11].

Most northern broadcasters began as Hindi language channels and expanded into regional or state-based language broadcasting, in response to newer niche broadcasters. On the other hand, southern broadcasters began as state-based language channels and expanded into neighbouring states, first in pursuit of same language audiences and then into other southern languages. Although normalisation of political and economic links with Pakistan may be a far off aspiration and Nepal seems gripped by civil strife, Sri Lanka (following peace initiatives with the Tamil insurgents) and Bangladesh offer opportunities for cross-border television markets. India may be thought of less as a single unified nation-state such as the US and more as a federation of culturally diverse states resembling the European Union. If so, its television development highlights the consequences of a poverty of media policies in response to the aggressive market driven strategies of global, regional and subregional broadcasters.

SATELLITE/CABLE TELEVISION

India had cable services long before transnational satellite television arrived because entertainment programming on DD channels was limited and predominantly in Hindi. These were popular as they were less expensive than borrowing from video libraries and more convenient than using video parlours. Video news was also on offer as an alternative to DD's more politically innocuous version. The leading news magazine, *India Today,* produced *Newstrack*, while the Hindustan Group produced *India View*, and both sold these programmes to individuals and cable operators [Interview Ind 02.02]. Beginning in 1984 in Bombay and spreading to Gujarat and Maharashtra, it took another six years to reach Delhi and was then largely an urban phenomenon. Thus the cable industry had been around for almost a decade, taking advantage of the lack of laws governing their operations to wire apartment blocks and urban neighbourhoods (Rahim 1994).

Cable *wallahs*

Neighbourhood cable operators, known locally as "cablewallahs", provided Hindi and English movies along with soap operas like *Dynasty*. When the Gulf War began, these cable operators took to buying satellite dishes in order to relay CNN's "live" coverage of it. Having invested in the hardware they sought new uses after the War. Initially all satellite dishes were tuned to CNN but after the Gulf War were re-directed to AsiaSat1 for StarTV and ZeeTV channels. Since satellite dishes cost Rs 20,000–25,000 (US$650–800) each, most consumers chose to have access to satellite television via cable subscriptions. Thus StarTV's reach in the Indian subcontinent benefited from the pre-existence of cable television in the region, and the cable industry received a further boost in consumer demand in late 1991 from the advent of transnational and regional satellite television.

India

Cable operators had created the market for StarTV and ZeeTV and were considered able to ruin their market if the satellite broadcasters did not accede to the cable operators' demands [Interview Ind 02.08]. Each cable operator wielded considerable control over the programmes watched, although he or she needed to take into account the majority opinion of the neighbourhood. In the mid-1990s it was not possible for a cable operator to provide all 20 channels available because of the costs of purchasing multiple satellite dishes and a receiver for each channel transmitted to homes. So they practised channel sharing, showing ZeeTV all day on one channel while all other satellite stations shared the remaining 10 to 12 channels provided to homes among themselves or with cable operator-selected movies, often two stations per channel over a 24-hour period. For instance, Bombay which drew its residents from all over India had suburbs which were segmented ethnically and so cable operators provided whatever ethnic language programming was preferred in their particular neighbourhoods. The subscription charge was about Rs 100 to 150 (US$3 to 5) per household for a 12-channel package. Through being available conveniently on neighbourhood cable, StarTV and ZeeTV had superceded the popularity of local video rental shops, even if some of their programmes had been seen before on video [Interview Ind 01.11].

Cable operators came from varied backgrounds though unaccountably video library owners had not diversified into this industry. Due to the relatively low set-up costs of using the family television set and VCR, unemployed sons, housewives, students and the less-educated tended to get into this business. The average *cablewallah* operated from a small room in an apartment block on the roof of which there were two or three satellite dish antennae. Along one or more walls would be a bank of VCRs which taped satellite broadcasts for later transmission or played movie videotapes. Along with a divider, receiver, frequency modulator and booster, the total investment was about Rs 50,000 (US$1,700). Each cable operation covered a radius of half to one kilometre and every neighbourhood had about four operators, each differentiating itself by service and programme offerings [Interview Ind 01.06]. Since competition was fierce, many offered free installation and more programming, such as up to 16 television channels and two movie channels. Back in the 1980s cable operators had started by just providing one DD channel and one video channel which screened three movies a day and they charged about the same subscription fee then.

The Cable Operators Federation of India (COFI) had sought regulation of the industry as they then had no legal recourse when cables were stolen or illegal tapping occurred. Cable operations in a number of cities were alleged to be controlled by organised crime or under the protection rackets of corrupt local police [Interview Ind 02.08]. There had also been moves towards cooperative operations such as establishing single control rooms, through cable operators' associations. Around the mid-1990s between 25,000 and 35,000 cable networks and SMATV systems were estimated to be relaying free-to-air satellite channels into one in three Indian television households. Cooperation between operators was imperative if only to reduce costs since subscriptions had not increased in proportion to the amount of programming offered, and there was to be an entertainment tax imposed by the government at 35 to 40 per cent of subscription revenues. Added to this was the amendment to the copyright law which enforced copyright and prevented operators from illegally re-distributing encrypted channels [Cable and Satellite Europe 1994a]. COFI found its lobbying task difficult with the rapid changes of government and ministers, but nonetheless succeeded in preventing a DTH license being granted to News Corporation [Interview Ind 02.20].

The expectations of the broadcasting industry in the late 1990s were that cable networks would continue to be instrumental in the further growth of transnational television in India (Table 5.6). In the years to come pay-TV systems developed by existing and newer transnational and domestic commercial broadcasters would be used to deliver their channels, perhaps in conjunction with local cable operators. Most StarTV channels were expected to eventually become pay-TV channels since this would represent a major income source with minimal effort such as charging the cable operator a nominal fee per subscriber (ibid.). Out of the 12 million cable viewers, 8 million might accept their cable operator passing on the cost to them by asking for another Rs 10 or 20 (US$0.30 to 0.50) more each month in subscriptions [Interview Ind 01.10]. There was some dissent about the feasibility of the implementation of such a strategy in India. Given the relatively free or cheap access to transnational channels thus far, the concept of pay-TV and pay-per-view was considered unlikely to be popular with the general population in India in the near future [Interview Ind 01.03].

Table 5.6
Indian Cable and Satellite Television Growth Forecasts

	1998	1999	2000	2001	2002	2003
Households (millions)	194	197	200	203	206	209
TV households (millions)	62	65	69	73	77	81
Cable subscribers (millions)	22	26	30	34	37	41
DBS subscribers (millions)	0.3	0.7	1.1	1.6	2.3	3.2

Source: The Strategis Group, cited in International Cable [1999c].

Pakistan

Neighbourhood cable networks in the country were supposed to be under strict control but this was not exercised until the military government of General Musharraf took office in early 2000. Throughout the 1990s a legal situation similar to India's cable industry in the early part of that decade existed in Pakistan and there was no effort to legislate control over the cable networks. As of the late 1990s, an estimated 13 per cent of Pakistan's population was believed to have access to satellite television, a high proportion of them urban. Having the largest number of Urdu speaking migrants from India following the partition upon independence, Karachi had the most developed if informal cable networks. Many of these were set up to enable Pakistanis to view movies, in this case largely Hindi movies. By 2000 cable networks had spread to other major cities in Pakistan such as Lahore and Islamabad, though direct viewership via satellite dishes remained popular (Page and Crowley 2001: 97–98).

Major Cable Operations

With growing numbers of satellite channels for re-transmittal, India's cable operators were forced to upgrade their systems, making a strong case for mergers, including possible alliances with global media businesses. The lack of trust between cable operators in Bombay was a barrier, but the industry ultimately had to be run on a corporate basis with adequate infrastructure. Merging among themselves or accepting investment from outside the country may have been the only option, causing India to be one of the world's most lucrative markets for cable hardware [Malhotra 1994]. Together with the passing of the Cable Bill and other broadcast legislation, the estimated 50,000 cable operators were compelled to merge or else go out of business, as most of them had neither the expertise or finance to expand alone.

IN Cable Network

A subsidiary of the Hindujas Group, an NRI business concern, this was the first dedicated multiservice provider in the Indian market. It was involved in franchised distribution of multiple cable television

channels through IN Cablenet, in programme acquisition and production through IN Vision, in niche publications through IN Print,
and in the production and distribution of movies through IN Movies.
The company began with IN Mumbai comprising one interactive and
three movie channels distributed to 1.2 million homes through franchised cable operators. Eventually IN Network planned to serve 15
Indian cities with 99 channels each via a centralised source, as well as
providing other value-added services such as telephony, video con-
ferencing, computer networking, video-on-demand and pay-TV. To
compete against the market leader ZeeTV, IN Network opted to find
a niche as a city centric channel, providing programming specific to
each city it operated in as well as more generic channels such as Cable
Box Office and Cable Music [Lahiri 1995a]. In 1997, IN Cablenet
consented to distribute the NBC family channel and its sister business
channel CNBC into an estimated 2 million households in India [Asian
A&M 1997j]. Given the relatively high cost of cable subscriptions in
India and yet low returns to the operators, IN Cablenet lobbied for
further government regulation of the industry [Hingorani 2000]. By
the early 2000s it was generally believed that pay-TV and other interactive services such as those offered by IN Network would cater to a
different audience than the "free-to-air" channels provided for a
nominal fee by neighbourhood "cablewallahs".

SitiCable

Most notable among the many entrants into the market was SitiCable,
which concentrated on northern India and New Delhi in particular.
A major rival to IN Network and owned jointly by ZeeTV and StarTV,
it claimed over 2 million subscribers in 141 Indian cities by early 1997
[Wanvari 1997]. That same year both SitiCable and In Cablenet agreed
to collaborate by carrying each others' programming, instead of competing ruthlessly and even litigating against each other. It was believed,
however, that the real reason for the truce was because News Corporation
was interested in an equity stake in IN Cablenet, after disappointment
with SitiCable's poor distribution in Mumbai (previously known as
Bombay). By the late 1990s SitiCable became a wholly-owned subsidiary of ZeeTV, a channel and interactive services provider in its
own right, working closely with the *cablewallahs* in each district/sub-
urb. In Delhi, for instance, SitiCable had 15 wholly-owned headends

servicing about four joint venture partners who supplied cable programming to some 20 "cablewallahs" catering to 100 homes each [Interview Ind 02.19]. With such arrangements cable networks did not own the "last mile", without which it was not able to generate further revenues through interactivity, internet, VOD and so on from the growing Indian middle class. Yet the investment outlay for that would be considerable and cable networks were under threat from the eventual approval of DTH which already had an estimated 100,000 households. Nonetheless, by the early 2000s, SitiCable was the largest cable network in India with 4.5 million households across 43 cities and a 25 per cent share of the market [Leung 2001c].

RPG/UIH

Around Calcutta, another multiservice provider, RPG Group, entered into franchising arrangements with cable operators in the mid-1990s, producing programmes in the Bengali language and transmitting 32 channels in conjunction with the UK-based United International Holdings (UIH). The service delivered several Doordarshan channels, ZeeTV, ATN, StarTV channels, SunTV and Raj TV. The RPG Group, which also owned the left wing state's Electric Supply Board, was planning a value-added services network incorporating tele-shopping, video-conferencing and educational services [Lahiri 1996a]. UIH in turn teamed up with United Breweries of India, which also owned the Tamil language Golden Eagle TV and Kannada Udaya TV, to develop cable networks for Bangalore, Bombay, Hyderabad and New Delhi [Bailes and Hollister 1996: 98]. In 1998, UIH/RPG started a channel of its own, offering 18 hours per day of news and current affairs, interactive programming and entertainment [Television Asia 1998b] reflecting the ethos of Calcutta, the centre of Bengali language and culture which are quite distinct from Hindi.

Other Networks

Through establishing United Cable Network (UCN), BITV became a multiservice provider in three cities by leasing satellite dishes to or negotiating equity arrangements with existing cable operators, through which it achieved a subscriber base of 200,000 households [Vora 1997]. IITL, another joint venture of Falcon Cable of the US, this time with The Hindustan Times publishing group, claimed up to 20,000 subscriber homes [Asian A&M 1997j]. By 1996 a Gujarati channel was launched by Shristi Videotech in the hope of breaking even in its first year of operations since the state of Gujarat alone had 20 per cent of India's cable homes [AMCB 1996f]. In 2000, the global News Corporation's Asian network StarTV took a 26 per cent share in local business Hathway Cable and Datacom, which operated India's second largest cable network with 2.5 million households wired [Leung 2000e], another link between the global and the domestic media industries. Among other significant brand names in the cable industry of India are Cine Channel, CCN, Win Cable, CVO and SCV, some of them partly owned by the larger cable and satellite television networks. In Pakistan, the only pay-TV system was Shaheen TV, delivered by microwave and operated by a charity foundation run by retired airforce personnel.

All multiservice providers had subscribers in the hundreds of thosusands or millions each in marked contrast to the situation of independent neighbourhood cable operators in the tens or low thousands, at best. One complication though was that the latter were compelled to pay for a "slab" of channels or minimum number of assumed subscribers by all the multiservice providers. Even if they wished to utilise just one or none, cable operators paid up to avoid harassment, but the consequence then was gross over-reporting of audiences by all the channel providers [Interview Ind 02.20]. Thus none of subscriber figures supplied by the multiservice providers could be verified independently as of the early 2000s and so advertising agencies have had to utilise them with some scepticism in their media planning.

To overcome the problems of limited distribution of channels on the earlier neighbourhood-based cable networks in India, many newer and some older players in the cable market formed new multiservice providers who re-broadcast only satellite channels with which they were affiliated, produced programming for domestic channels and were often also local channel operators themselves. Major global and domestic electronic and communications firms entered the cable industry in India as investors and franchisors, and as a result a shake-out of the industry took place in the late 1990s. Still the cablewallah system was firmly entrenched in the Indian subcontinent because they provided the high level of personalised service sought within their neighbourhoods.

PROGRAMME INTERCHANGE

Unlike other countries there was little interaction between the prodigious Indian film industry and the television industry, till the success of the soap opera *Hum Log* and the growth of video parlours around the mid-1980s. Still domestic television programming in India remained largely an in-house affair of DD till transnational satellite and local cable television spurred demand for more and varied programming. Filling programme time on the 13 to 15 channels it created to combat the competition was a challenge to DD when its own production facilities and equipment were lacking. This demand had a considerable impact on the development and growth of independent production houses which, as we have noted earlier, served also as media brokers between DD and advertisers. There were said to be at least six to eight major television production houses, and numerous independent producers operating in India in the mid-1990s.

United Television (UTV)

Bombay-based UTV started in the early 1990s with entertainment programmes such as game shows, chat shows, before diversifying into soaps, serials and business programmes. Within a couple of years UTV had created 700 television episodes, 50 advertising commercials, 24 corporate video documentaries, 27 hours airline in-flight programming, not including the dubbing of 104 animated episodes. UTV produced TV programming ranging from soaps to sitcoms, quizzes to talk shows, children's programmes to travelogues for the Doordarshan metro channel, ZeeTV and other satellite broadcasters [UTV 1994]. It preferred doing movie-based programmes which had low production costs, and yet were quite certain of attaining high ratings. UTV either sold one-off programmes it produced to DD, or negotiated a price for production. ZeeTV purchased programmes from UTV but sold its own advertising spots as UTV was obliged under that contract only to produce programming [Interview Ind 01.03]. By the end of 1994, UTV was to have 10 separate programmes telecast regularly on ZeeTV alone. UTV was still managed by Indians and treated as independent from ZeeTV in which News Corp had a similar ownership interest. Subsequently UTV added studio complexes in Delhi and Madras to Bombay, and within three years had produced 500 hours of original programming for almost every channel on the South Asian region, in addition to dubbing and television commercials.

In 1996 UTV entered the Southeast Asian television market, setting up studio complexes in Singapore and Kuala Lumpur to produce multilanguage programming in English, Tamil, Malay, and Bahasa Indonesia [UTV 1996]. It has also developed another business line in dubbing programming into Indian languages for the major transnationals [Lahiri 1996b]. By 2000 it had purchased Vijay TV, a Tamil language channel in South Asia, and invested in film distribution, internet, animation and multimedia firms. It could claim to producing over 475 hours of programming, over 50 commercials and dubbing over 1,200 hours of television in a year, not just for Indian broadcasters but most major Asian broadcasters. Its programmes were being exported to 19 countries, including the US, UK, Canada, Singapore, Malaysia, Indonesia, Fiji and the Caribbean [UTV 2000]. Thus UTV was another example of an Indian firm that has globalised its operations over the 1990s, as a consequence of the growth of transnational television in the region and continent.

Nimbus Communications

This firm began in 1990 by airing on domestic television international sports tournaments in football and cricket. Nimbus then diversified into dubbing foreign programmes, particularly for children, and into acquiring movies for television and marketing them to advertisers. Since then Nimbus produced more than 150 programmes of its own which represent over 1,200 broadcast hours, in as many as nine different languages using its own in-house "creative directors" to oversee the work of freelance directors and crew. Nimbus claimed to have a turnover in excess of Rs 52 crore (US$17 million) though an industry source estimated that it sold US$25 million in advertising media alone. It had more than 200 clients across the country including such multinationals as Hindustan Lever, Pepsi, Cadburys, Procter and Gamble, Johnson and Johnson, Kelvinator, Brooke Bond and Gillette [Nimbus 1994]. Nimbus was the largest production house in Indian by sales, all of which was placed with DD. It did not work with ZeeTV for fear of political fall-out of being perceived by the Indian government as a partner of DD's chief rival. From the mid-1990s Nimbus produced, purchased and sold Indian programmes both for domestic television and for export, mostly to the UK and the US, some to the Middle East and former USSR, Southeast Asia, and even Japan [Interview Ind 02.04]. Thus Nimbus was a pioneer in the reverse flow of Indian programmes from the Third World to the First.

Other Production Houses

HTV, a New Delhi production house owned by the Birla family which also owned the *Hindustan Times* newspaper, signed an agreement with the British media conglomerate Pearson and Hong Kong's TVB for a US$48–65 million joint venture to produce programming and launch up to two satellite channels [Karp 1994]. Channel Eight, a Calcutta-based production company has achieved a cult following for its Bengali language soap opera *Jononi* on DD and has followed that up with chat shows, game shows and serials for ZeeTV, EL TV and JainTV as well [Lahiri 1996a]. Plus Channel, another production company, produced programming for DD as well as international clients like BBC, South African Broadcasting Corporation and Mauritius Broadcasting Corporations [Dziadul 1994]. Beginning with three video magazine programmes for DD in 1991, it rode on the expansion of DD2 Metro so that by 1995 it was producing a number of daily and weekly programmes ranging from business to soap operas [Ninan 1996: 171]. With the domestication of StarTV and its establishment of a 24-hour Indian news channel in the late 1990s, the production house New Delhi Television (NDTV) has been subcontracted to produce all news bulletins, breakfast shows, talk-back programmes in both English and Hindi. It also produces *Question Time*, Moneywise and other news related programmes for BBC World [Interview Ind 02.09].

Transnational television broadcasters such as ZeeTV, StarTV and BBC2 were negotiating with such production houses for serials, news-magazines and docu-dramas, as were Asian satellite and cable television networks in UK and the US. Thus this relatively new industry was estimated to be growing at more than 50 per cent per annum, with some production houses claiming to be growing even faster. Overall, the trend among production houses in India was to form either a strategic alliance or joint venture with a global media corporation, and to expand the markets for programming to countries in Europe, North America, Africa and the Asia-Pacific where there are diasporic South Asian communities.

The widely reported phenomenal growth of transnational television viewership on the Indian subcontinent was really of regional commercial television such as ZeeTV, SonyET, Asianet and SunTV which rode in on the coat tails of the transnational broadcasters such as StarTV and CNN. In addition the growth of viewership for all broadcasters via satellite was due to the pre-existence of cable operators in urban areas, a fact recognised by the more recent multiservice providers that have sought to franchise them. Such developments have stimulated the concurrent astronomic growth of domestic programme production, which in turn was undergirded by a prolific film industry. Thus, transnational television has moved from being perceived as an invasion to being an ally to Indian subcontinent commercial broadcasters, public broadcasters, cable operators and multichannel operators alike. This process of globalising domestic television and domesticating transnational television has been concurrent with its own political and economic transformation from a socialist oriented political economy to a quasi-capitalistic one. Similar marketisation of the economy has occurred in the Malay Archipelago and Greater China with somewhat different consequences as we shall see in the chapters that follow.

6

TELEVISION AROUND THE MALAY ARCHIPELAGO

In the Malay language subregion within Southeast Asia, Indonesia and Malaysia are the dominant players by virtue of audience reach and relative affluence of certain social groups. But the television of each country is largely national apart from some spillover in border regions where the dialects spoken are similar within the Malay Archipelago, to use an accurate geographical name, if presently a seldom used one, for this subregion. However, there are virtually no international, diasporic markets for Indonesian and Malaysian television, and the only cross-border markets are a minority in Singapore and southern Thailand and the small nations of Brunei and East Timor. Still, Indonesia and Malaysia are the key targets for transnational television in Asia by virtue of their population and/or growing affluent middle class, though the prior development of their domestic television markets helps explain the relatively minimal impact of the newer medium.

PUBLIC BROADCASTERS

Indonesia's TVRI

Television in Hong Kong began in 1957 as essentially a commercial service when Redifusion was licensed to provide a wired television service comprising two subscription channels. A decade later Television Broadcasters Ltd (TVB) began operating a wireless television service under an exclusive licence. When the government offered two more wireless licences after a broadcast policy review, Redifusion terminated its wired services to take up wireless broadcasting in 1973. This station subsequently changed owners and was renamed Asia Television (ATV). The other licence was granted to Commercial Television (CTV) which began transmissions in 1975 but ceased operations in 1978 having failed to cope with stiff competition from TVB and ATV. This led to the view that the Hong Kong market could support only two domestic television stations [Hong Kong Government 1994b].

Domestic Satellite Television Era (c. 1975–86)

The role of foreign MNCs in the development of the television medium in Indonesia has a long history. Though the idea of a national communications satellite had been rejected earlier by the policy body Bappenas, a Hughes Corporation representative was said to have met President Soeharto at an Intelsat launch and sold him on the idea as a means to integrate Indonesia's islands [Interview Mly 04.01]. The cost of installing the satellite-based television system for such a large territory and scattered population could not have been justified on a commercial basis alone, even if Indonesia had been a developed country. At the behest of President Soeharto the Indonesian government nonetheless took the radical step in 1975 of purchasing a communication satellite, the first developing country in the world to do so. Christened "Palapa", it was meant initially for telecommunications to link extractive industries in remote areas with their Jakarta offices and not for broadcasting. TVRI had planned originally to use microwave transmissions instead but it was estimated to take 50 years to provide television coverage for all the islands. Hence it decided to utilise the Palapa satellite for national broadcasts of TVRI and permit the use of satellite dishes by the populace in the name of economic development of Indonesia [Parapak 1990]. Consequently, by the 1980s second generation domestic satellites, Palapa 2A and 2B, were launched, while by the early 1990s the third generation Palapa C satellites were planned [Interview Mly 04.02].

The comprehensive longitudinal study between 1976 and 1982 conducted by Chu et al. (1991) in conjunction with the Indonesian government claimed that satellite delivery of TVRI to rural Indonesia had stimulated considerable social change, though possibly indirectly. Through its development programming the research found that TVRI had facilitated the adoption of "modern" agricultural practices such as high-yielding rice, chemical fertilisers, pesticides and intensive planting, promoted also via government-sponsored farmers' organisations. TVRI programmes were also attributed with changes of attitude towards government health clinics, "western" child birth practices and family planning, and towards education and vocational opportunities, while not undermining religious values. Perhaps particularly heartening to the government was the finding that TVRI had contributed to learning of the national language, a lynchpin in its programme of national integration. However, the responses of the sampled viewers may be somewhat biased given the survey had the "full cooperation of the Indonesian government at central, provincial, and local levels". (Chu et al. 1991: 28–29) and utilised local public servants. Nonetheless, of interest to the present book are the findings with regard to economic behaviour which would have elicited less concern by viewers about ideological rectitude. The research found that advertising on the public broadcaster had achieved statistically significant changes in the purchase of consumer goods. This is particularly significant since advertising had been banned a year prior to the research.

Commercial Television Era (c. 1987–96)

The ban on advertising was rescinded in 1987 when commercial television stations were licensed by TVRI which then received a percentage of their advertising revenue. Despite the introduction of commercial television, TVRI continued to have the highest penetration of all the television stations in Indonesia. Nonetheless the domestic commercial channels were formidable competitors to TVRI which had lost much market share to them, particularly RCTI. The Indonesian "open skies" policy was initiated because there were reception "blank spots" in the public broadcaster TVRI's national transmission. This resulted in Indonesian viewers having access to television from other transnational sources [Interview Mly 02.05]. Though by Indonesian regulations satellite dishes had to point to Palapa satellites to obtain domestic channels, this could not be easily monitored nor was it enforced.

The main national channel TVRI 1 had a policy of 80 per cent local programming, though in reality it was about only 50 per cent. It broadcast for 10 hours per day and its programming included drama, movies and variety shows as well as news, religious shows, information programming [Vista TV 1993–94]. The second channel TVRI 2 was available only in Jakarta, Bandung, Surabaya, Ujung Pandang and other major cities, was largely a local channel providing programming relevant to each area and ran for 6.5 hours each day [Interview Mly 04.02]. The Indonesian government became embroiled in a controversy over TVRI licence fees in the mid-1990s when then-President Soeharto authorised their collection by a private company, owned by his relatives and business associates. The company had undertaken to increase TVRI's revenues by more efficient collection and higher fees. But the widespread objections from citizens was uncharacteristically given much publicity in the press. Perhaps fears that it might affect upcoming elections led to an announcement that fees could be paid at post offices, though there was no stepping down on the fee hike (Kitley 1997).

Reform Era (1998–Present)

Under the reforms of the broadcasting bill that Soeharto signed into law prior to stepping down in 1997, TVRI was authorised to accept advertising in its own right. But it came immediately under attack from the commercial broadcasters who complained of TVRI's unfair advantage of government subsidy. While the commercial stations were required to contribute 12.5 per cent of their advertising revenues to TVRI, they were soon in arrears of about Rp. 30 billion (US$3 million) due to the economic crisis. In the early 2000s, the public broadcaster was gearing up to accept advertising itself and may therefore have to forgo its traditional cut of the advertising revenues of the commercial stations. Although TVRI was restructured under the Wahid administration as an autonomous body, there were concerns that its freedom from government influence was being quietly eroded under the subsequent Soekarnoputri and Yudhiyono administrations of the early 2000s.

Malaysia's RTM

An understanding of how the domestic television industry developed in Malaysia prior to the advent of transnational television provides some insight into its response to the new competitor. Television has had a 30-year history in Malaysia and, as with many countries newly independent from colonial rule, has been seen by the government as a tool of national integration and economic development. This continues to be the underlying ideological stance, even though there has been some deregulation of the medium in recent years. But in the mid-1980s, there was a decided shift in programming direction precipitated by the introduction of commercial television, even if the first entrant, TV3, was owned by political parties in the ruling coalition (Karthigesu 1994: 83–90). In order to compete for audiences and more pertinently advertising revenue, RTM began to import more recent, higher quality foreign programmes, catering via programme scheduling to ethnic minorities (notably the Chinese) with greater buying power, lowering restrictions to exempt tobacco brandnames being used to advertise other products and so on.

As of the mid-1990s RTM1 commanded 26.5 per cent of the national audience despite extending broadcast time to 18 hours daily. In keeping with government policies to promote unity through the national language three-quarters of its programming was in Malay, though that includes both dubbed and subtitled programming. The rest of the programmes were in English. News and documentaries comprise just 12 per cent of programming while the bulk of the remainder may be classified as entertainment. RTM2, which was meant to cater for the minority languages and imports 60 per cent of its programming, held 22.1 per cent of audience share. In fact English was the dominant language at 54 per cent of programming, Malay next at 21 per cent, while Mandarin commands only 14 per cent and Tamil 11 per cent. Together, RTM channels reached 2.7 million Malaysian households as well as most Singapore households by signal spillover (Baskerville Communications 1996: 161–62).

In the late 1990s viewership for RTM1 remained high among the Malay ethnic group associated with the leading political party (Table 6.1), and this was believed to be particularly so in the rural areas where it had a penetration of 45 per cent. This segment was significantly less for RTM2, and the commercial channels TV3 and Metrovision [Wong 1998]. RTM had endeavoured to improve both its channels to compete with the comercial channels, especially through programme acquisitions, but was believed to be constrained by bureaucratic procedures due to its being part of the government [Badarudin 1998]. In 1999, perhaps as an indication of waning appeal to Malaysian audiences RTM1 and RTM2 registered a decline in advertising revenue, while the TV3 and NTV-7 increased their share [Selva 2000].

Table 6.1
Viewership of Malaysian Terrestrial Channels by Ethnic Group, 1997

Ethnic Group	RTM1	RTM2	TV3	Metrovision
Malay	78.4%	55.9%	60.7%	35.4%
Chinese	13.1%	33.4%	29.3%	46.9%
Indian	7.8%	10.1%	9.4%	17.2%
Others	0.7%	0.6%	0.5%	0.4%
Total viewers '000	6,202	7,707	8,664	1,584

Source: Adapted from Wong [1998], citing '98 Media Guide.

COMMERCIAL BROADCASTERS

Indonesian Channels

RCTI

In 1987 the public broadcaster TVRI licensed Rajawali Citra Televisi Indonesia (RCTI) to broadcast and to advertise, purportedly only products conducive to national development, in return for a percentage of revenue to TVRI to be applied to the latter's own operations. It was two years before RCTI commenced broadcasting, in greater Jakarta to those who could afford to purchase a decoder and pay a monthly fee, and elsewhere in Indonesia to those who chose to own a satellite dish [Suparto 1993]. RCTI was established as the first privately-owned commercial television station in Indonesia and was jointly owned by two Indonesian conglomerates, PT Bimantara Citra and PT Rajawali Wira Bhakti Utama, the former being controlled by Bambang Trihatmodjo, a son of former President Soeharto. In August 1990 a ministerial decree was issued allowing RCTI to broadcast unencrypted, to expand its reach outside Jakarta and to increase its broadcasting to up to 24 hours per day [RCTI 1993]. In July 1991 RCTI was permitted by the government to utilise the Palapa B2P satellite. Thus it was effectively able to broadcast to the whole country though its reception would be possible only through satellite dishes (referred to colloquially as "parabolas" in Indonesia), unlike TVRI which was downlinked and re-broadcast terrestrially. In 1996, the Indonesian government prohibited plans by RCTI to float its shares for fear that the station would be controlled by foreign investors, perhaps cognisant of the fact that the latter already owned 30 per cent indirectly [Pardosi 1996b].

Despite the entry of other commercial stations RCTI remained a leader in the ratings stakes since its start. The majority of its programmes had consistently high ratings and by the early 1990s, its top 20 programmes all had ratings in the 30s. In terms of programming categories, the breakdown was as follows (a) 50 per cent sports and entertainment, (b) 20 per cent commercials, (c) 20 per cent education, religion and culture, and (d) 10 per cent government programming and news. In the mid-1990s its ratio of foreign made to locally produced programming was 80:20, but it sought to change that to 60:40 to comply with government policy. Commercial stations were then not allowed to have their own news programmes but they did have current affairs programmes sometimes called "soft news" as a way of circumventing the regulation [Interview Mly 03.07]. Although constrained by government regulations, RCTI achieved market dominance through programming targeted at middle to upper classes while attracting also lower classes, perhaps by appealing to their aspirations (Table 6.2).

Under more liberal governments in the early 2000s, RCTI continued to target the middle to upper classes, with an eye on the mass market, with programming consisting of both local productions and imported programmes. Some of these programmes were available in bilingual form for audiences to choose between. One local programme on RCTI,

Table 6.2
Domestic Television Channel Audience Share in Indonesia, 1995–98

Channel	1995 (%)	1996 (%)	1997 (%)	1998 (%)	Adspend '98 (%)
RCTI	38	36	36	33	27
IVM	13	19	24	21	18
SCTV	20	17	16	18	23
TPI	20	18	15	16	19
Anteve	9	10	9	9	13
TVRI	–	–	–	2	–

Source: AC Nielsen, cited in Initiative Media Indonesia [1999] and Ishadi [1999].

"Si Doel, Anak Sekolahan" made local history in achieving the highest ever rating of 70 in the country. It soon had serious news and current affairs programmes, including and English-language breakfast-time business show called "Indonesia Today". Its market share of prime-time audiences in 1999 ranged between 26 and 30 per cent, trailing IVM but ahead of SCTV [PPPI 2000]. Despite the political and economic upheavals, RCTI continued to be owned by the Bimantara conglomerate, now restructured, but which also had shares in a number of other Indonesia television stations, included newer ones.

SCTV

In 1990 a second commercial station, Surya Citra Televisi (SCTV) was licensed by the Indonesian government for the East Java region [SCTV 1993]. Since 80 per cent of all advertising agencies and advertisers in Indonesia were located in Jakarta, the administrative and marketing offices of SCTV moved there [Interview Mly 04.08] though the main production studios and satellite uplink/downlink facilities remained in the provincial capital of Surabaya. It was founded by a group of Indonesian businesspersons with strong political connections who saw prospects for commercial television centred on Indonesia's second largest city. A major shareholder in the SCTV was believed to be Sudwikatmono, a cousin of then-President Soeharto (Sen 1994a). Other principals of the consortium which owned SCTV were Mohammed Noer who was a former governor of East Java, and Henry Pribadi who was a brother of the Djuhar Sutanto, a business partner of Liem Sioe Liong (Kitley 1994) who in turn was considered a close associate of Soeharto. Though SCTV did not belong to any business conglomerate as such, it had some private shareholders in common with the Bimantara group of companies which owned RCTI [Interview Mly 03.07].

In 1991 the Indonesian government publicly encouraged Jakarta-based RCTI to cooperate with Surabaya-based SCTV in purchasing foreign programming. This might have been in part due to the fact that a major shareholder in SCTV had attempted to gain almost monopolistic control over film import and distribution in the 1980s (Sen 1994b). In any case, in January 1992, RCTI and SCTV commenced joint operations in their four major markets, Jakarta, Bandung, Surabaya and Bali [Interview Mly 04.10]. Thus there was a quasi-network of RCTI and SCTV before both of them went nationwide [Interview Mly 04.09]. Historically RCTI and SCTV were regional stations and so they were able to share programming without conflict [Interview Mly 04.01]. But in August 1993 RCTI and SCTV separated operations, both continuing to use the same transponders on Palapa but different frequencies. The geographical spread of both RCTI and SCTV was nationwide by cooperative agreement through which relay stations were still shared. The competition for market share and advertising revenue caused by the RCTI/SCTV split saw a change in 1994 from zone-structured rate cards to programme performance-based ones [Grafik McCann-Erickson 1994].

SCTV continued to purchase foreign programming and produce "soft news" programming in conjunction with RCTI for the economies of scale. It seemed torn by its obvious succcess with imported tele-novellas such as *Maria Mercedes* which has been imitated by its competitors [Interview Mly 04.08], and the investment cost of local programming production for its longer term success. Alternatively being a relatively new station it simply imitated the formats of popular foreign programmes [Interview Mly 04.03]. Operating in a market in which RCTI and IVM were dominant, SCTV had yet to position itself and establish a clear niche as of the late-1990s. Subsequently SCTV aimed to target women in the morning, and the all-family segment in the evening [Interview Mly 04.08]. Although in the 2000s SCTV's programming was still similar to RCTI in having both local and foreign programmes, it was a leader in providing Latin American tele-novellas. Thus it had a loyal daytime audience among housewives when its market share was 23 to 28 per cent, only slightly below RCTI's and considerably higher than IVM's. It was also popular for its Chinese drama and kungfu films, which cater to younger adults within the middle class market it shares with RCTI [PPPI 2000]. While still owned by Datacom which was controlled by Peter Gontha, there were rumours in the industry of a shareholding in SCTV by the US financier George Soros [Interview Mly 02.18], possibly through an investment firm.

TPI

In 1991, a third commercial broadcaster Televisi Pendidikan Indonesia (TPI) was licensed by the Indonesia government as an educational television service operated nationwide as a private non-profit organisation. The manifest purpose of TPI was to provide educational resources of benefit to Indonesian school students, development agencies, domestic businesses and the wider population in support of national development. Though a private institution, TPI operations were governed by agreements with the Ministry of Information and the Ministry of Education and Culture. Its mandate included the provision of entertainment, information and commercial programmes as a means of generating operating funds. TPI was owned by a holding company whose principal shareholder was Siti Hardijanti Indra Rukmana, the eldest daughter and then political heir apparent of former President Soeharto. Due to this, it enjoyed favours from the government, such as the banning of commercials on TVRI but not on TPI, the use of TVRI studios and equipment and the purchase of television sets for all school in the country [Darusman 1991].

The educational programmes were funded as a joint venture, with production by TPI and free air time from TVRI [Interview Mly 04.10]. These programmes in mathematics, physics, chemistry, biology and language were planned and produced by the Ministry of Education and Culture, who were responsible for content and the utilisation of them [TPI 1993a]. Programmes for Universitas Terbuka, the national open university system, were also transmitted by TPI. Non-formal educational and information programmes on language, agriculture and health catering to children, housewives, unemployed young adults, workers and the general public were the responsibility of TPI which was permitted to fund them from advertising, both in their time slot and in its prime day-time programming [Interview Mly 04.10]. Though programme production was carried out by TPI, the planning of them was done in conjunction with related government and non-government agencies. Since its status as an educational channel required that the majority of its programmes be educational, its own breakdown of total broadcasting hours in 1992 was stated as (a) educational programming 38.7 per cent; (b) information 20.2 per cent; (c) entertainment 25.5; and (d) commercial 15.6 per cent [TPI 1993b]. Independent sources assessed educational programmes to occupy only 33 per cent of its airtime, with 47 per cent non-educational and 20 per cent occupied by commercials alone [Winton 1991]. In 1996 Peter Gontha, the executive director of the Bimantara group of companies which owned RCTI, negotiated to purchase an undisclosed personal share in TPI [Pardosi 1996a], another indication of the interlocking ownership of commercial television broadcasters in Indonesia.

The situation of TPI was unique in comparison to the other pioneering channels RCTI and SCTV because of the transmission support received from TVRI for its greater penetration nationwide. Since TPI used TVRI facilities and high-powered transmitters in the morning, it was able to go national cheaply and lay claim to a sizeable loyal following in rural areas during the day, though not in the evening when it had to rely on its own transmitters. Because 80 per cent of TPI programming was local, it attracted a large audience among lower-income segments of the population [Interview Mly 04.10]. As the in-house production capacity of TPI was limited, up to a third of its programming requirements had to be supplied by domestic production houses resulting in a boom. By the early 2000s TPI abandoned its educational and rural agenda and repositioned itself as a "family" channel. Its programming now featured more variety shows, movies, serials, comedies and music programmes, most of it locally produced. From observation, TPI seems to cater primarily to families with young children in lower socio-economic segment of the Indonesian market.

An Teve

A late-comer to the first batch of domestic-commercial broadcasters, Cakrawala Andalas Televisi was established after the arrival of StarTV. Perhaps it was approved by the government in order to provide its citizens even greater choice in the hope that it would counteract the impact of transnational television. This fourth commercial channel, operating as AnTeve, was inaugurated in 1994 and though national in intent it suffered from poor transmission quality outside of its Sumatran base. It commenced broadcasting in February 1993 and went decoder-less in May the same year. AnTeve was owned by the Bakrie group, a long-standing Indonesian conglomerate not seen as having close ties to the political centre (Sen 1994a). AnTeve was available initially only in Jakarta, Bandung, Surabaya and Medan though it claimed other cities and was soon planning expansion to Semarang, Yogyakarta and Denpasar, Palembang, Ujung Pandang [Lintas Indonesia 1993]. Due to technical difficulties, including the collapse of its transmitter, AnTeve had to hand some of its programmes to TVRI for nationwide broadcast on its behalf while it provided adequate transmission only to viewers around Bandung [Interview Mly 04.08]. The station was relaunched in early 1994 with a commitment to broadcasting 18 hours per day on a national basis [Grafik McCann-Erickson 1994].

AnTeve was positioned in the competitive television market as a "westernised" entertainment station targeting the youth [Interview Mly 03.07], but this strategy was of questionable success with mass audiences and advertisers [Interview Mly 04.01]. AnTeve's market share was high only when it had the broadcasting rights to the Thomas Cup tournament, since badminton was the Indonesian national sport, and other "live" sports [Interview Mly 04.08]. Imported "western" programming comprised 29 per cent of Anteve programming, of which 8 hours per day in the afternoon and late night comprised MTV Asia programmes by arrangement. Having established a reputation for extensive screening of imported game and quiz shows, AnTeve adapted two of them in conjunction with their foreign originators [Television Asia 1995c: 101–04]. In 1996 AnTeve made a formal commitment to being a specialist sports and music channel after claiming increased advertising revenue from re-orientating its programming in that direction [Pardosi 1996c].

While lagging behind the other commercial stations in size, AnTeve has outlived all prognoses of its demise, re-positioning itself as a "youth-and-music" channel by offering MTV programming—albeit with a week's delay—as well as its own Indonesian clones of the same. Sports, variety shows and news programming were other characteristics of the new AnTeve, including quite unique offerings as a business advice show with phone-in facility, a Thai soap opera, a Singapore tele-shopping programme and a Christian sermonette at closing time. In 2001 AnTeve was progressing with plans for a 50:50 joint venture with the US-based ValCom in order to benefit from the latter's expertise in production and consultancy in restructuring the former. Although still perceived as the weakest of Indonesia's domestic channels, AnTeve nonetheless has a reach of 50 million households which makes it the fifth largest television network in the whole of Southeast Asia [Brown 2001j] and indicates the size and importance of the Indonesian market to broadcasters and advertisers.

IVM

The last of the first cohort of licensed commercial broadcasters, Indosiar Visual Mandiri (IVM) offers a contrast in financial size, political connections and broadcast coverage, and therefore was perceived as much greater competition to the existing domestic commercial broadcasters than the transnational broadcasters. Permission was granted by the government in 1994 for an Indonesian conglomerate to form a joint venture channel with TVB of Hong Kong. Known commonly as Indosiar, it was Jakarta-based and part of the Salim Group which is in turn owned by a businessman Liem Sioe Liong with close connections to President Soeharto. It was generally believed in Indonesia, and not just in the media industry, that without that friendship Liem might have found it difficult to obtain a licence, being Chinese and thus a member of a politically-sensitive minority. The concerns were expressed in the industry about the channel's strong financial backing from the Salim conglomerate which would allow it to dominate the market [Interview Mly 04.06], its owner's Chinese ethnicity and catering for that community [Interview Mly 02.06], his political connections in Indonesia and thus exemptions from imported programme limits [Interview Mly 08.08].

Soon after its launch in 1995, Indosiar began to challenge the dominance of RCTI in the Indonesian television market through programming "blockbuster" western movies such as *Terminator2* and *Judgement Day*. Indeed Indosiar's links to TVB had seen the inclusion of *Return of the Condor Heroes*, *Dragon Sabre* and other violent Hong Kong action series. While such violent programmes would not have been allowed on free-to-air television in western countries, in Indonesia they had succeeded in winning top ratings nationwide for Indosiar [Television Asia 1995d]. Indosiar was criticised by the television industry in Indonesia for employing 150 expatriates from Hong Kong in defiance of government policy, but it defended the move by claiming that this reduced dependency on foreign production houses [APT-C 1995: 121]. Opponents claimed TVB-seconded staff were "super producers" capable of high productivity in programme production, in part due to their plan to replicate 800 Hong Kong television drama scenarios in their programme production in Indonesia. Social commentary at the time revealed the fear that the cultural imperialism might then be undetectable, unlike the obvious case of imported foreign programming. But the incident was more accurately a revival of long-standing hostility towards the wealthy Chinese local community in Indonesia, precipitated by the liberalisation of the broadcasting industry (Kitley 1997).

Given the continuing demand for domestic programming, Indosiar commissioned Indonesian directors and actors under loyalty agreements to produce more local comedy for prime time. It had a strong commitment to developing local programmes such as serials, sitcoms and dramas, including the popular "Pondok Pak John" which was a social-educational family drama on child rearing principles. Some adaptation of TVB and other foreign programmes for Indonesia was acknowledged using the principle of "follow the good, avoid the bad and add a new ingredient" [Interview Mly 02.16]. However, observations in 2000 reveal a high proportion of programmes of Chinese origin from TVB. Its target market was the middle class, though IVM also featured programmes for upper and lower socio-economic classes. Although its advertising revenue declined as a result of the political and economic crises of the late 1990s, paradoxically its viewership increased as IVM introduced political talk shows which included the student leaders involved in the protests [Interview Mly 02.16]. In 1999 IVM held a market share of 34–38 per cent of the Indonesian prime time audience in urban metropolises [PPPI 2000].

As a result of the economic and political crisis in the late 1990s and consequent decline in advertising revenue, all the commercial channels cut airtime by between three to six hours to minimise operational costs, and reduced imported programmes from India, China and Latin America while increasing in-house production [Pardosi 1998]. The crisis also saw all the pre-existing commercial stations in Indonesia restructured ownership-wise. Although the former majority shareholders remain, they are largely minority shareholders now and are no longer involved in management and operations. All television stations in Indonesia suffered significant decline in advertising revenue during the economic crisis of the late 1990s, and consequently lacked funds to produce local programmes or even to purchase new imported programmes and viewers had to resign themselves to re-runs. In one way or another, all the original commercial stations came under the control of the Indonesian Bank Restructuring Agency, given the collapse of the banks to which they were indebted.

Newer Commercial Channels

It may seem perplexing that so soon after the economic crisis, the Indonesian government should offer eight further commercial television licences, even if it was a liberalising consequence of the belated broadcasting bill. Some observers suggest that rather than remove licences from existing television stations, the interim Habibie government thus sought to dilute their power through competition, while some critics have alleged that a few of these newer licences might have been granted to businesses possibly sympathetic to that interim government. One explanation for the great interest in Indonesian commercial television licences was believed to be the anticipated possibility of re-selling the same at a premium in better economic times (Table 6.3). Another may lie in the fact that all prime time advertising slots were sold out by mid-2000 on all existing television channels for the rest of the year. Advertisement agencies reveal that marketers are increasing promotion budgets in anticipation of a business boom [Interview Mly 01.12]. During the "crisis", marketers were compelled to re-package, even re-brand products and position them as being more economical. It was their means of convincing consumers not to curtail spending at a time of uncertainty and increasing unemployment. Presently in improving economic times, both those economy brands and the older upmarket brands are being supported by heavy advertising [Interview Mly 01.11]. It may also be noteworthy that one new television licence was sought and won by a major retailing group.

Table 6.3
Indonesian Household Television Data

	1999	2000 est.	2001 est.
TV households (mill.)	28.5	29.5	30.5
Cable homes passed ('000)	190	240	320
Subscriptions ('000)	75	95	135
Penetration (%)	39	40	42

Source: Kagan Media Asia, cited in Loveard [2000].

There were five confirmed takers of licences, two of them soft-launching towards the end of the year 2000. Owned by Surya Paloh, the publisher of the daily newspaper *Media Indonesia*, PT Media TV Baru was granted a licence in 1999 to run a television station known as Metro TV. This channel intended to be CNN-like with an emphasis on news, current affairs and documentaries, perhaps capitalising on the new freedom of information, though some interviewees wondered how viable this business model would be in the long term. It commenced broadcasting in late 2000 and became the first to broadcast a 60-minute Mandarin Chinese news bulletin. Then rather surprisingly in 2001, PT Bimantara Citra, which still controls almost 70 per cent of RCTI, took a 25 per cent stake in Metro TV, which was the first station not associated with the Soeharto family, with an investment of US$3.7 million and loans worth US$11 million [Brown 2001b].

Backed financially by the Para Group and Mega Bank, the other early entrant was Televisi Transformasi, or TransTV for short. On launching in 2001 it was expected to go head-to-head with the major players, RCTI, SCTV and Indosiar, in targeting the middle-to-upper class segment with a broad programming range on offer [Cakram 2000]. In the same year, TV-7 was launched, owned by the Kompas-Gramedia conglomerate, while in 2002 Lativi, owned by the A. Latief corporation, was expected, showing the continued dominance of conglomerates in Indonesia's television industry.

Thus the commercial television stations in Indonesia, especially RCTI and IVM, though fostered to counteract the anticipated influence of transnational television broadcasters, have undermined the long-standing dominance of the TVRI, the domestic public broadcaster. However, the government and TVRI appear to rationalise the commercialisation of broadcasting as a shift in emphasis of national cultural policy in the face of new social and economic realities, rather than a reversal of direction. Although the advent of transnational television broadcasts via satellite was anticipated in Indonesia better than any other country in Southeast Asia, their business strategies could not have been fully predicted. In tackling the consequences of the same transnational competition, neighbouring Malaysia's commercial broadcasters were faced with quite different choices, given their government's greater involvement in the national cultural agenda.

Malaysian Channels

TV3

The first commercial television service and the third channel to operate in Malaysia, hence its name ("TV Tiga" in Malay), was launched in June 1994, and in a short time became the most watched channel in the country. In early 1995 it was allowed by the government to extend its broadcasting hours to 18 from the 11 hours previously stipulated. The government's decision to break its own monopoly on television broadcasting was a major change of policy direction and part of a wider commitment to privatisation. Nonetheless the licence to operate this third channel was granted by the government to a consortium called Sistem Television Malaysia Berhad (STMB) comprised largely of leading Malaysian newspaper publishers, which were controlled financially by the various political parties in the ruling coalition (Karthigesu 1994: 83) which has held power since independence. After numerous takeovers, management buy-outs and reverse-takeovers over the 1990s, TV3 ended up owned primarily by the lead party in the coalition, United Malay National Organisation (UMNO) [Wong 1998]. TV3 concentrated on urban centres, primarily the national capital Kuala Lumpur and then the state capitals in the more populated Peninsula Malaysia. It catered to a market which had been neglected by RTM for political reasons, namely the largely urban Chinese viewers who had previously turned to video rentals for their entertainment.

TV3's policy of importing newer, more expensive programming in both English and Chinese, attracted advertising revenue to the detriment of RTM, which was spurred into competition (Karthigesu 1994: 84–85). By the mid-1990s, 40 per cent of its programming was imported, while 60 per cent was locally produced, *en route* to compliance with the government's stipulation of 80 per cent local programming by 2000. In 1994, TV3 had the dominant share of television advertising revenue of 41.3 per cent, despite government reduction of their advertisement time from 12 to 10 minutes per hour [Baskerville Communications 1996: 166–67]. One of the ways by which TV3 has endeavoured to reduce costs was by utilising "live" programmes involving audience and participation. Still, Badarudin (1997) has argued that such programming encourages materialism and reconstitutes the audience from being a public to being consumers.

Other Private Stations

Metrovision (TV4), a terrestrial service, owned by a local consortium which included a royal family and a newspaper group, was launched in 1995. With imported programming already comprising 60 per cent of content, MetroVision signed an agreement with the regional satellite network StarTV to re-broadcast 12 hours of its music channel, the first for a Malaysian terrestrial channel [Kagan World Media 1996: 165]. Although there is a quota on local programming, the government has granted Metrovision some leeway; consequently the channel was characterised as being of low quality imported programming [Interview Mly 02.15]. Unlike the other terrestrial channels, Metrovision remained a largely urban service in peninsular Malaysia with a consequently small audience of about 1 million and ratings no higher than 10 per cent [Interview Mly 03.10]. It ceased transmission in 1999 but was expected to return under new ownership. Another station, NTV-7, was launched in 1998 and targeted the upper middle class of the urban west coast of peninsular Malaysia [Interview Mly 03.14]. It was perceived as an innovative broadcaster both in terms of programming and advertising options, but it was still a far second to market leader TV3 [Interview Mly 01.14].

SATELLITE/CABLE TELEVISION

Indonesian Direct-broadcast Satellites

Till the mid-1990s all domestic TV stations in Indonesia were transmitted from Jakarta to Jatiluhur and then uplinked to Palapa by Indosat, a government-owned company, and then downlinked to television stations at Solo, Denpasar, Joyga and then transmitted direct to homes [Interview Mly 04.05]. Even with 300 retransmitters of 100 km radius each, only 35 per cent of the Indonesian population would have been covered by terrestrial television because of the dispersion of its islands and its mountainous terrain. These terrestrial stations would have been difficult to maintain, costing an estimated Rp. 150 billion (US$67 million) per year. The government realised that it would need 1,000 terrestrial re-transmitters and because of the high cost it decided to allow satellite dishes [Interview Mly 03.06]. Furthermore, the encroachment of transnational and spillover television was thought to undermine its cultural integration agenda in some more sensitive and often remote regions of the country. Therefore, the government embarked on a US$150 million programme to provide all domestic television and radio services via DBS by 1996 [IndoStar 1993].

Although Indonesia's Palapa-series satellites were managed by Indosat, the newer DBS satellites were owned by MediaCitra IndoStar, a consortium of foreign and local businesses, among them the shareholders of the domestic commercial television stations. The IndoStar system was designed so that viewers throughout Indonesia would have quality reception irrespective of the weather of both analogue and digital channels directly from the DBS satellite using their present televisions, with satellite dishes of less than one metre diameter, compared to the three metre ones required for Palapa. DBS broadcasting required viewers to have new television sets with internal antennae and that was why one of its consortium shareholders was Amcol Graha, the manufacturer of Sony television sets, which made for a good strategic alliance. Perhaps for favourable publicity, the programme also claimed that jobs would be created as the technology for digital television sets was transferred from the US to the Indonesian factories, by the construction of ground facilities and the stimulation of the broadcast entertainment industry [IndoStar 1993].

Over the late 1990s, two business entities were formed to manage Indonesia's other satellites after PT Telekom was privatised and invested in by foreign and domestic corporations, the latter with connections to the Soeharto presidential family. The task of operating the newer Palapa C-generation satellites launched in 1996 was assigned to PT Satelit Indonesia Palapa, or Satelindo as it is more commonly known. The management of the older satellites was given to PT Pasific Nusantara (PSN) in which global telecommunications corporations had shares, namely Hughes Communications and Telesat Canada with 11.53 per cent each, and Deutsche Telecom Mobilfunk with a 25 per cent share. It was generally anticipated that the first satellite would combine domestic public and commercial services, but at the time of research there was still some speculation as to the channel utilisation of the satellite's transponders. Thus satellite technology which had been sold to the Indonesian government in the 1970s and 1980s on the basis of its value in social and economic development was, by the mid-1990s, largely in the hands of the corporate sector, both local and multinational.

Explanations of the low incidence of transnational television viewership seemed to revolve around prohibitive cost of access to the broadcasts for the masses, and the cultural appeal of transnational television programming to only the urban elite (Table 6.4). As dishes were expensive, it was largely expatriates and wealthy Indonesians who could afford personal dishes [Interview Mly 04.01]. In the middle class suburbs of Jakarta and other major cities where teachers, doctors and civil servants live, three out of 10 homes have access to satellite television [Interview Mly 02.07]. So, of the 189 million people of Indonesia only the elite were said to have sought access to satellite television for news, information and education [Interview Mly 02.01]. Satellite television claimed a penetration of 10 per cent of households in the highest socio-economic segment, namely the top 3 to 4 per cent of the Indonesian population. The buying power of this expanding middle income group was great by Indonesian standards and even increasing [Interview Mly 02.06]. But while this top segment of society could appreciate foreign programmes, they still had a preference for local programming as well [Interview Mly 02.05, Mly 03.06]. These views are corroborated in the findings of government research conducted in the early 1990s, which indicated that satellite television was very much a middle-class phenomenon in Indonesia, attracting 77.1 per cent of its audience from that socio-economic strata alone. Only 20 per cent of its audience was drawn from the lower class which constitutes the vast majority of this developing nation [Ishadi 1994].

Table 6.4
Satellite Television Viewership by Indonesian Population, 1998

	Dish Ownership (%)	Ever Watched (%)	Watched in Past Week
Indonesia	7	18	5
Urban	9	25	7
Rural	5	14	3

Source: AC Nielsen research reported in Deal [1998].

Unfortunately there were no statistics on socio-economic classes and income levels for the general population available for comparison.

Research done in East Java in the mid-1990s for Australia Television confirmed the continued dominance of Malaysian television, specifically TV3, in the transnational viewing preferences of Indonesian audiences (Table 6.5). Although access to other regional stations from Singapore, Thailand and Brunei was available, including Malaysia's public broadcaster RTM1 and RTM2, it does seem like TV3 was the most appealing to Indonesian audiences in a similar way to which RCTI dominates domestic viewing. MTV was the runner up to TV3, and so it does appear that music television had the best chance of crossing cultural and language barriers, at least among the youth. The next preferences in transnational channels are the news-oriented channels of CNN, Australia Television (now ABC Asia Pacific) and Canal France International, which accords with news being cited by 91.3 per cent of East Java respondents as being either important or very important among the benefits of having satellite dishes. It is worth noting that 64 per cent of respondents disagreed that transnational television programmes were superior to domestic ones, but 86.5 per cent agreed that they provided better information on international affairs. The research also found that viewing of transnational television programming averaged 2.12 hours daily, which took place mainly between 6 PM and midnight [Cohen 1996: 14–25].

Table 6.5
Transnational Television Preferences of Indonesians in East Java, 1995

Station	Origin	Reception (%)	Watched Last Week (%)	Watched Yesterday (%)	Watched Most Days (%)
TV3	Malaysia	92.7	42.7	22.0	21.0
MTV	Pan-Asian	72.7	40.7	30.0	54.0
CNNI	Global	68.0	20.0	13.3	27.9
AusTV	Australia	78.7	16.7	9.3	12.2
CFI	France	66.7	12.0	7.3	18.8
TV Philippi	Philippines	82.0	8.0	3.3	7.7

Source: Adapted from Cohen [1996].

Data published in 1998 by the market research organisation AC Nielsen confirmed that TV3 of Malaysia still had the highest penetration of all transnational channels; all 3.3 million satellite-capable homes tuned to receive it (Table 6.6). MTV and CNN were a distant second and third at 2.5 million and 2.4 million households respectively, while less than half the satellite-capable households were tuned to watch Brunei Television. By contrast, domestic channels dominated with RCTI having 86 per cent penetration, SCTV 84 per cent, IVM 76 per cent, TPI 72.5 per cent and AnTeve having 61 per cent [Deal 1998]. It is evident that in Indonesia, with the possible exception of a regional channel from within the Malay Archipelago, transnational television via satellite dishes has very low viewership compared with domestic television.

Table 6.6
Transnational Television Penetration in Indonesia, 1998

	No. of Households	% of Satellite Homes	% of Total TV Homes
TV3	3.3 million	100	13
MTV	2.5 million	76	10
CNN	2.4 million	73	9
AustraliaTV	2.1 million	64	8
CFI	2.1 million	64	8
ABN	1.7 million	52	7
Brunei	1.4 million	42	5

Source: Adapted from AC Nielsen research reported in Deal [1998].

Indonesian Pay-TV

Access to transnational television in Indonesia via cable subscription was limited to the major metropolitan cities like Jakarta and Surabaya. Even in the late 1990s, the preference for delivery was via wireless or microwave; besides these two cities, the infrastructure was lacking. Cable television in Indonesia had been a form of informal community access to free-to-air satellite television but the industry was changing to commercial pay-TV services. So potential subscribers had to be persuaded that they were purchasing not just an integrated receiver-decoder system but extensive programming of their own choice [Interview Mly 04.09].

Indovision

The firm of PT Matahari Lintas Cakrawala gained approval from the Indonesian Ministry of Information in late 1993 to sell decoders for transnational television broadcasts. Known as Malicak for short, it was an Indonesian-owned firm with corporate links to other broadcasting and publishing businesses. Among its shareholders were Amcol Holdings, a Singapore corporation; Bambang Trihatmodjo, the son of then-President Soeharto and president-director of Bimantara Citra which then owned RCTI; Anthony Salim, the son of Liem Sioe Liong who was a close associate of Soeharto and owner of Indosiar Mandiri TV; and Peter Gontha, vice-president of Bimantara Citra who was also advisor to SCTV and a close associate of Soeharto's son [*Business Times* 1995]. Furthermore the chairman of Bimantara Citra, which also had a stake in SCTV, was the husband of Soeharto's eldest daughter who owned the "educational" channel TPI, thus illustrating further how the close web of ownership within the Indonesian domestic television industry extended to the pay-TV franchise [Cable and Satellite Asia 1996c].

The pay-TV service marketed as Indovision initially provided access to CNN, HBO, The Discovery Channel, ESPN and TNT/Cartoon Network. Although these transnational channels were transmitted from one of Indonesia's satellites Palapa B2P, the same one that carried the domestic commercial channels (though not TVRI), these were in encrypted form. Indovision was forecasted to have 1 million cable subscribers by year 2004 out of the current 13 million TV households in Indonesia, or 30 to 40 million television audience. Subsequent to the purchase of a decoder at Rp. 1,475,000 (US$670) the subscriber needed to pay US$410 annual or US$120 quarterly subscription fee [Indovision 1994]. A year after it began operations, Indovision had only 5,000 subscribers, much less than its projections, and this was attributed to the high cost of installation and monthly fees. Soon after, Indovision entered into a management and distribution contract with StarTV to offer the latter's four channels in addition to its other foreign and own channels. Under the deal, subscribers received 15 channels in all using a single decoder for a monthly subscription of Rp. 63,250 (US$28), or almost a third less than before [Asian A & M 1996b].

All the Indovision channels would utilise the Digistar digital compression and encryption technologies for which the StarTV parent company, News Corporation, owned the proprietary rights. Naturally these developments which gave StarTV considerable control over Indovision had been viewed by the other transnational broadcasters with some consternation, especially since they were charged up to

US$500,000 each for uplink costs [Cable and Satellite Asia 1996a: 9–10]. In 1995 StarTV withdrew from Indovision and its nine channels withdrawn were replaced by other global channels such as AXN Action Television, Hallmark, Kermit and Animal Planet, as well as a new domestic one called Music Indonesia which showcased local music video clips. Other global channels in the Indovision stable as at the end of 1999 included CNBC, BBC, CNN, Bloomberg, MTV, CMT, MCM, TNT/Cartoon Network, National Geographic, Discovery, HBO and Cinemax. Declining Indonesian currency in the economic crisis made pay-TV a luxury and caused Indovision to adjust its subscription target down from 600,000 to just 50,000 by end 1999. Another consequence of the economic crisis was that Indovision no longer had much cross-ownership by conglomerates and shareholders controlling the domestic broadcasters [Jusuf 1999].

Other Providers

Although Indovision had the only pay-TV licence issued by the Indonesian government as of late 1996, the situation changed, prompted in part by disenchantment over StarTV's control over Indovision (Table 6.7). The overseas telecommunications carrier Indosat teamed up with SCTV and Indovision shareholders to plan a pay-TV service via cable or microwave multipoint delivery service (MMDS), and acquired a film production house to provide programming. Not to be outdone, the domestic telecommunications carrier, Satelindo, had plans to install cable in major cities and has contracted RCTI to provide programming. A privatised Indonesian satellite company, Satelindo planned its own DTH service from Palapa C1 in association with Hughes Corporation of the US. Finally, the Lippo Group, a large Indonesian-Chinese conglomerate purchased equipment for a high-performance cable system, Kabelvision, for initial installation in private housing in suburban Jakarta with plans to go nationwide [Walker 1996: 10–11].

RCTI launched its own cable service with the brand name of Indonusa Television in mid-December 1998 offering 10 to 16 channels including some shared with Indovision. While RCTI owned 20 per cent of the cable service, 45 per cent was held by the state-owned PT Telkom and another 25 per cent by Datakom Asia which was also a parent company for Kabelvision, a rival cable service [Television Asia

Table 6.7
Cable Television Penetration in Indonesia, 1999

Network	Availability	Programme Languages	Household Penetration
Indovision	National	English, Indonesian, Chinese, French, German	3,300,000
TV Kabel	Jakarta only	Indonesian	15,000
Metra TV	Jakarta only	Indonesian	1,000
Indonusa	Jakarta only	Indonesian	200

Source: Initiative Media Indonesia [1999].

1999b]. In 1999 Indonesia's Lippo Group took a 78 per cent share in PT Indovision, already the country's largest cable network [International Cable 1999a]. Although the direct-to-home satellite service Indovision had difficulty rebuilding its subscriber base after the economic meltdown, Kabelvision rolled out broadband cable to the better suburbs of Jakarta in 2000 with intent to claim market dominance in pay-TV. Astro, Malaysia's dominant pay-TV operator offered its channels on Metra TV, another Indonesian cable service which carried StarTV and 15 other transnational channels, in another manifestation of the transborder Malay cultural market [Pardosi 1999]. As at the early 2000s, estimates were that Kabelvision had about 74,000 subscribers, while Indovision and Indonusa had anything between 20,000 to 70,000 homes [Ross 2002], all of them far off earlier projections and confirming cable television as an elite medium in Indonesia.

Prior to the economic downturn, cable and satellite penetration was expected to be around 10 per cent and to generate revenues exceeding US$500 million by 1998 [Book and Krill 1996]. Aided by a growing middle class, choice of more satellite channels and cable providers, and introduction of DTH technology, multichannel households in Indonesia had been optimistically predicted to reach 805,000 by the year 2005 [Flynn 1996: 109]. What channels were to be offered on the newer pay-TV services when established was yet unclear, but they were likely to be a combination of domestic and transnational channels, giving Indovision considerable competition. But given the relatively high cost of pay-TV subscription for this developing nation, transnational satellite television will remain an elite and generally urban medium in Indonesia for the forseeable future (Figure 6.1).

Figure 6.1
Viewership of Transnational Channels in Indonesia, July–August 2001

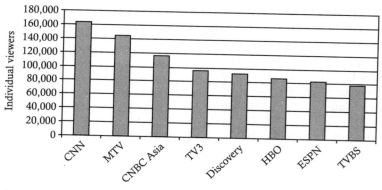

Source: AC Nielsen [2001b].

Malaysian Pay-TV

MegaTV

The government granted its first pay-TV licence to Satellite Network Systems (SNS), a consortium of the public broadcaster RTM and TV3, a commercial station controlled by the ruling coalition, to provide up to eight pay-TV channels [Via Satellite 1995b]. Operating as MegaTV, it began broadcasting in late 1995 as an MMDS to 3,000 subscribers in the Klang Valley, where the capital is situated. It re-broadcast five specialised transnational television channels: CNN, TNT/Cartoon Network, ESPN, Discovery and HBO. However, some news items and documentaries sensitive to the Malaysian government or its ASEAN neighbours were noticeably deleted from its re-broadcasts [Interview Mly 03.11]. Although a pay-TV service, it carried the advertising on the regional channels and had some Malaysian advertising spliced in [Interview Mly 04.10]. As of the late 1990s, MegaTV claimed that it had 95,000 household subscribers and 3,000 hotel rooms [Interview Mly 02.15]. But the advertising industry estimated that it had only 70,000 subscribers after aggressively targeting market segments such as marketing executives and airline staff with discounts and free installations [Interview Mly 03.10].

MegaTV had plans to expand to the rest of Peninsular and then East Malaysia in subsequent years. But its growth was seriously curtailed by the licensing of rival Astro and its consequent growth. This was perceived by MegaTV and TV3 as a breach of understanding by the government which, though already a 30 per cent investor in MegaTV, subsequently became a 15 per cent investor in Astro also. By the early 2000s, however, MegaTV was positioning itself as offering the best in each programming category such as CNN for world news and HBO for movies, against the overwhelming 22-channel offering of Astro [Interview Mly 03.12]. Although it was available free of charge, Australia Television (later renamed ABC Asia-Pacific) did not qualify for carriage on the MegaTV service, perhaps because of diplomatic strains between the countries caused by the then Australian government's perceived lack of cultural and political sensitivity.

Astro

Owned by the Measat Broadcasting Network Systems, Malaysia's first DTH satellite television service provided 22 channels, 24 hours per day, seven days per week and eight radio channels to its subscribers under the brand name of Astro. Measat was a consortium comprising an investment holding company of the Malaysian government, various Bumiputra (ethnic Malay) trusts, and a company owned by family trusts of Ananda Krishnan [All Asia Broadcast Centre 1996], a Malaysian-Indian businessman closely associated with the prime minister. Within a few months of its launch, it was able to achieve 35,000 subscribers but further growth was not expected to be as dramatic [Interview Mly 02.12]. It was also believed that the licensing of Astro was designed by the government to bring an estimated 100,000 owners of private but illegal satellite dishes in East Malaysia into its subscribers fold [Interview Mly 03.11]. In fact Astro acknowledged that enforcement of the law was proceeding apace, now that there was a Malaysian alternative to the direct viewership of transnational television [Interview Mly 02.12]. Since Astro used digital technology throughout, it was able to provide laser disc quality pictures and CD-quality sound, superior to its terrestrial and pay-TV rivals. While Astro offered a wide range of transnational and in-house channels (Table 6.8), the former were downlinked and subjected to government censorship at its ground facilities, the All-Asia Broadcast Centre, and then up-linked for rebroadcast to subscriber homes.

Table 6.8

Transnational and Domestic Television Channels in Malaysia via Astro

Channel	Origin	Primary Programming
Domestic Television:		
Astro Ria	Malaysia	Malay local and regional programmes
Astro Wah Lai Toi	Malaysia	Chinese entertainment and TVB programmes
Astro Vaanavil	Malaysia	Indian entertainment with first-run movies
Astro AEC	Malaysia	Asian Entertainment Channel
Astro Super Sports	Malaysia	Sports programming
RTM1	Malaysia	Malay and English programming
RTM2	Malaysia	Minority language programming
TV3	Malaysia	English, Chinese and Malay programming
Transnational Television		
Star Movies	Regional	English language movies
Star Movies	Regional	Asian language movies
HBO	Global	Current Hollywood movies
MGM Gold	Global	Classic Hollywood movies
Star Sports	Regional	Asian sports
ESPN	Global	International sports
CNN	Global	International news
CNBC Asia	Regional	Asian business and financial news
Discovery	Global	Educational documentaries
National Geographic	Global	Educational documentaries
Channel V	Regional	Asian music videos
MTV	Global	International and Malaysian music videos
Hallmark	Global	Family entertainment
Star World	Regional	Family entertainment
Bloomberg	Global	International business and financial news
TNT/Cartoon Network	Global	Classic movies and cartoons
Disney Channel	Global	Family entertainment
Nickelodeon	Global	Family entertainment
Phoenix	China/HK	General entertainment
TVBS Asia	Taiwan/HK	General entertainment

Source: Astro [2000].

The programming strategy of Astro was that of providing immense choice of channels, at least two of each genre, and up to 480 hours of programming per day, characterised by its own executives as comparable to magazines available at a bookshop. As of early 1997 it claimed to produce 1,000 hours of programming in-house, commission a further 500 hours and purchase 500 hours of imported programming per month [Interview Mly 02.06]. Astro intended to expand its services into the delivery of Near Video-On-Demand (NVOD) access to first-run movies, concerts and major sports events, as well as access to tele-shopping, home banking, internet and other interactive data services. Astro was broadcast via the Measat satellites which had footprints covering not just Malaysia but much of South and East Asia in addition to eastern Australia [Astro 1996]. In the late 1990s both its in-house business news and rebroadcast CNN channel were criticised by the Malaysian government over coverage of domestic political and economic issues, resulting in the termination of the first service by Astro's owner and retractions by the latter [Atkins 2002: 184–94]. In 1999, Astro offered its own channels for carriage on Metra, Indonesia's second cable operator [Pardosi 1999].

The number of Malaysians with access to satellite and cable channels was growing rapidly as evidenced by the 293 per cent growth rate in the late 1990s (Table 6.9). It is noteworthy that the greatest growth came from the Chinese ethnic minority, followed by the Indian minority, whose need for cultural products are less well served by the public broadcaster RTM and even by the commercial terrestrial broadcasters, TV3 and NTV7. Since satellite and cable viewing was not differentiated by the research reported, one has to assume that a major attraction was the dedicated Malaysian or other Asian channels packaged by Astro rather than the global channels such as CNN, MTV and Discovery. Even though access to satellite and cable television was relatively limited, Samsudin and Pawanteh [2001] found that young adults in Malaysia watched it for between seven to 11 hours. In any case, industry projections for the development of television in Malaysia (Table 6.10) are for the number of homes with access to transnational television to more than treble in the early 2000s.

Table 6.9
Malaysians Watching Cable/Satellite Television in the Past Week, 1998–99

Year/Ethnic Group	Malays	Chinese	Indians	Total
1998	91	100,000	47,000	238,000
1999	189	396,000	113,000	698,000
Growth Rate	207%	396%	240%	293%

Source: Adapted from AC Nielsen/CIA Medianetwork as quoted in Selva [2000].

Table 6.10
Television Penetration Projections for Malaysia, 2000–03

	2000	2001	2002	2003
TV households	3,450	3,600	3,700	3,800
Cable homes passed	210,000	350,000	550,000	750,000
Cable basic subscriptions	40,000	70,000	110,000	170,000
MMDS homes passed	1.8 million	2.0 million	2.2 million	2.3 million
MMDS subscriptions	200,000	260,000	310,000	210,000
DTH households	570,000	950,000	1.3 million	1.8 million

Source: Kagan Asia Media Ltd as quoted in Asia Cable and Satellite World [2000b].

PROGRAMME INTERCHANGE

There have been programme import-exports among broadcasters within the Malay Archipelago though this has been minimal. However, by the early 2000s RTM of Malaysia was in a cooperative arrangement with SCTV of Indonesia to exchange programmes and news, perhaps prompted by the Asian economic crisis. RTM which already had a one-hour slot Rancangan Indonesia (or Indonesian programmes) selected four SCTV series and both stations agreed on future co-production [Television Asia 1999d]. In the late 1990s TV3 of Malaysia also signed a programme exchange agreement with RCTI of Indonesia and sought out similar agreements, even joint ventures with media firms in Thailand, Philippines and other ASEAN countries. It was also involved as a partner in Sistem Network Nusantara, a network uniquely targeted Malay-speaking populations in Indonesia, Brunei and Singapore via satellite transmission. TV3 had intended producing only 50 per cent of its programming in Malaysia, with 40 per cent in Indonesia and 10 per cent elsewhere (Badarudin 1998). But the Asian economic crisis of the late 1990s may have stifled these pioneering attempts at Malay language television regionalisation.

Incorporation of the developing countries of Asia into a truly regional market has been envisaged by the Asia Pacific Economic Cooperation (APEC) trade grouping and on a smaller scale in Southeast Asia by the ASEAN Free Trade Area (AFTA). Both of these include the emerging economies of Malaysia and Indonesia, as well as Singapore,

Thailand, Philippines and Brunei which have small Malay-speaking markets. Whether transnational satellite television takes off will then depend largely on continued economic growth in this region, and on whether national governments are enlightened enough to decide like Indonesia on deregulating access by consumers, or like Malaysia on regulating access lightly and variously via DTH satellite dishes, encryption and microwave relay. Transnational television within Greater China represents yet another set of altenative paths to media development and will be examined in the next chapter, before all three Asian regions will be compared together in Chapter 8.

Although Hong Kong was still a British colony in the early to mid-1990s, many decisions about licensing of television broadcasters were being made then with its eventual handover to China in mind, if not actual consultations with the rulers-to-be. In 1997 Hong Kong became a special administrative region (SAR) of China, modelling the concept of "one country, two systems". This concept was designed to maintain global business confidence in Hong Kong, and meant also to allay the fears of Taiwan over the consequences of political re-unification in the future. There are historical reasons, beyond the scope of this book, for the ongoing political rivalry between the nationalists in Taiwan and the communists in mainland China that continues in the form of military and diplomatic posturing. Yet in recent years there have been considerable cultural and economic links between these two countries, sometimes even encouraged by both governments. This extends also into the television industry and contributes to its globalisation as well, as this chapter will demonstrate.

PUBLIC BROADCASTERS

China's CCTV

China commenced broadcasting in 1958 in the capital Beijing and by 1960 there were less than a dozen urban stations which circulated films and tapes among themselves. Television faced a setback during the Cultural Revolution of the 1960s when media policy was confused, and only in the late 1970s did television cover all provinces and become a major part of the lives of the Chinese population. By 1983 it grew to 105 programme-production stations, with 411 mocrowave stations and 7,475 rebroadcasting stations for rural and remote areas (Won 1989: 212–13).

Deng Era

Economic reforms under Deng Xiao Peng during the 1980s triggered unprecedented growth in Chinese television, such that by the early 1990s there was a four-tier network of one national broadcaster, 30 provincial, 295 municipal and 350 prefectural stations reaching 80 per cent of the population. The national or central broadcaster CCTV then had four channels, two of which were nationwide, one local to the capital Beijing and one transnational via satellite and targeted at Taiwan, Hong Kong and Macau. CCTV-1 had an nationwide audience of 300 to 400 million viewers and transmitted the national news through 11 news bulletins per day. Also nationwide, CCTV-2 provided economic information and English language programmes to an estimated 100 million viewers. CCTV-3 is broadcast to 5 million viewers in the Beijing area during the evenings only and its programming comprises repeated feature films, drama and educational programmes. In this post-Mao era, the Ministry of Radio, Film and Television (MRFT) began subscribing to western news agencies and showing about 10 minutes of international news, remarkably, relatively unedited (Won 1989: 221–23). CCTV-4 was transmitted by satellite and so may be seen nationwide as well in much of Asia [Australian Film Commission 1994a: 21–24].

Programmes were increasingly sourced from domestic movie studios and independent production houses, even imported from other Asian countries such as Taiwan and Japan, as well as from the US [Asia, Inc. 1994]. The MRFT set limits on the number of hours of different programming genres that could be imported and broadcasters had considerable freedom of choice within those constraints. Chinese broadcasters seemed to prefer purchasing western programming rather than other Asian productions [Television Asia 1994b]. Chinese television officials justified permitting the broadcast of foreign programming on domestic channels by saying that it helped retain the audiences, perhaps against competitive transnational television, attract multinational advertisers and fill broadcasting hours. By official accounts CCTV was able to produce only one-third of its programming needs in 1990, while provincial and city level stations were able to produce less than two hours of their daily programming. Imported programming was also much cheaper, about 10 per cent the cost of producing similar programming in China. But there was the major constraint of foreign currency exchange and therefore the MRFT ran a quota system, and balanced the programmes imported by genre and country of origin. Foreign currency exchange difficulties were also bypassed by Chinese television stations offering to swap advertising time and part of that revenue for the right to broadcast foreign programmes for free. Thus in practice the quota system was not fixed and Chinese domestic broadcasters were allowed to show as much as they could obtain, with due political clearance (Chan 1994).

Ziang Era

From the mid-1990s many of China's provincial stations began to broadcast nationwide through satellite, much to the displeasure of CCTV. Local provincial and municipal television stations in China achieved higher coverage among them than the national CCTV, with the exception of Beijing [Interview Chn 01.02]. This meant competition for advertising revenue from both domestic business and MNC sources on which all Chinese broadcasters were semi-dependent, though the central government was committed to bailing out CCTV financially if necessary. It was expected that the provincial television stations would eventually broadcast Asiawide to overseas Chinese [Interview Chn 04.03]. In 1995 CCTV contracted with PanAmSat to utilise their Pas-2 and Pas-3 to reach up to 40 million overseas Chinese with its broadcasts. At the same time CCTV was also concentrating its programming sales on overseas Chinese and other Asian markets. It also announced the launch of its own encrypted sports and movie channels within China, allowing CCTV to produce duly censored channel packages for local cable networks [Simons 1995].

Soon CCTV announced that it would launch six digital channels worldwide, through a 10-year distribution agreement with PanAmSat which would take its coverage from Asia alone to North America, Europe and Africa. It also began with extending the reach of CCTV-4, the channel tailored to overseas Chinese, and added a music channel in July and an English language channel in October. In keeping with the expressed aims to promote understanding of China generally and to reach an overseas Chinese audience of 60 million, all of the international channels were to be free-to-air and subsidised by its domestic channels [Masters 1996b: IV]. In 1998, the Chinese government under President Ziang Zemin signalled the restructuring of its media assets, particularly the transformation of CCTV from a government organ into a fully commercial station. Among the possibilities was the establishment of independent corporations for each medium or the dispersion of assets on a provincial or city basis [Television Asia 1999a], though quite the opposite eventuated.

As of the late 1990s, CCTV had eight channels and broadcast 138 hours of programmes daily via satellite, cable networks, microwave and other means. Its flagship channel CCTV-1 reached 84 per cent of the Chinese population of 1.2 billion, while CCTV-2 continued to provide economic, social and educational programmes. CCTV-3 offered operas and music and CCTV-4 catered to overseas audiences though satellite and cable networks abroad. Newer channels introduced in the mid-1990s included CCTV-5 which is a sports channel, CCTV-6 for movies, CCTV-7 providing an eclectic mix of children's, agricultural and military programmes, and CCTV-8 devoted to the arts and entertainment. CCTV also had personnel and programme exchanges with some 250 television stations worldwide [ABU 1998]. But it was evident from audience research that, apart from the capital city, city-based or provincial terrestrial commercial stations dominated the list of top channels by audience share (Table 7.1). In the early 2000s, the Chinese government mandated the merging of national, provincial and city stations, both cable and terrestrial, in order to facilitate programme production but believed to aid closer managerial control. Around the same time it was conducting negotiations with News

Table 7.1
Channel Audience Share in China's Cities, November–December 1998

	Beijing			Shanghai				Guangdong
Rank	Channel	(%)	Rank	Channel	(%)	Rank	Channel	(%)
1.	CCTV5	15	1.	C-Drama	21	1.	GZTJ	25
2.	BTV2	15	2.	STV1	15	2.	GDTJ	21
3.	BTV1	14	3.	OTV20	13	3.	GZAH	15
4.	CCTV6	9	4.	OTV33	12	4.	GDAH	14
5.	CCTV1	8	5.	STV2	9	5.	Others	9

Source: AC Nielsen [1999].

Corporation and AOL Time Warner to have broadcast access to south-ern Chinese cities in exchange for their transmission of CCTV-9 in North America [*The Economic Times* 2001]. Thus as Hong (1998) has documented, the globalisation of China's domestic television pro-gresses with periodic ebbs and flows, due to both national and inter-national factors.

Taiwan's TTV, CTV and CTS

The introduction of television to Taiwan in 1952 was a highly politi-cised decision because the nationalists wanted to demonstrate their commitment to free enterprise in contrast to their communist rivals on the mainland. Hence the then government, the ruling political party and the military banded together with private interests to form an oligopoly in the television industry—a model replicated elsewhere in Asia in recent years of ostensible privatisation. The resultant three com-mercial networks, which dominated the Taiwanese television scene, were TTV (provincial government), CTV (Kuomintang political party) and CTS (military), are discussed in a subsequent section on domestic commercial television. All three networks were partly owned by those entities named in the brackets, and partly by public shares [Interview Chn 04.05], but there were no public television broadcaster as such.

Hong Kong's RTHK

The public broadcasting service, Radio and Television Hong Kong (RTHK) does not broadcast television but produces programmes, such as current affairs, documentaries, drama and civic education, which TVB and ATV are obligated by law to carry on all four channels. RTHK also broadcasts seven English and Chinese radio stations, for a total of 1,148 hours per week, one of the stations being the 24-hour BBC World Service, but no public television channel as such. The only other public broadcaster, Educational Television (ETV) also util-ises the transmission facilities of the commercial stations to provide curriculum-based educational programmes to schools for about eight hours per weekday [Hong Kong Government 1994b]. Reflecting the dominance of the free market in Hong Kong, RTHK has always been an insignificant player, and this has remained unchanged into the early 2000s, regardless of the advent of transnational television in the early 1990s and the handover of the colony to China in 1997.

COMMERCIAL BROADCASTERS

Chinese Domestic Stations

As mentioned earlier in the chapter, all domestic television networks in China were government-owned, though dependent on advertising revenue given declining government subsidy. It was said by some in the broadcasting industry that there has not been any domestic commercial television station in China largely due to a lack of local expertise to match Hong Kong and Taiwan, rather than lack of funding. But it may also be the political risks and dire legal and financial consequences for a domestically-based television station and its managers for offending the communist Chinese government. Perhaps in response to competition by transnational satellite channels there has been some attempt at privatising the television media in China, though in reality the ownership of such so-called non-government stations were still in government or party hands.

Of the major regional stations Beijing Television surpassed CCTV in the capital city region with its three channels, considerable imported programming and an audience of 10 million. One of China's earliest stations, Shanghai Television had two channels and an audience of 70 million, the largest of the regionals. Oriental Television of Shanghai established in 1993 is owned by the city of Shanghai and contributes half of its advertising revenue to the government [Interview Chn 02.11]. Launched in 1993 and catering to the Yangtse Delta, it has ambitions on Taiwan, broadcasting considerable sports programming, some of it obtained from ESPN [Australian Film Commission 1994a: 27–30]. Guangdong Television with two channels catered to southeast China where it competed also with Hong Kong channels available by spill-over. So by the mid-1990s, China had a diversified television market, even if the ownership was either local governments, communist party branches or entrepreneurs with good political patronage.

Taiwanese Domestic Stations

Prior to the 1990s all domestic television networks in Taiwan were owned by the then government and political party, though run commercially. Founded in 1952 as the first station, Taiwan Television Company (TTV) had the Taiwan provincial government as its principal shareholder owning 49 per cent, in conjunction with four Japanese television companies owning 20 per cent between them and the rest held by local businesses. Apparently its monopoly profits were so attractive that other similar players began to enter the television broadcasting industry. Thus in 1969 the China Television Company (CTV) was formed with the Kuomintang (KMT) Party as the majority shareholder at 60 per cent, with some radio stations owning the remaining shares. Though with the KMT voted out of government in 2000 after some 50 years in power, this channel may no longer be considered quasi-government. Then in 1972, a small educational television service was expanded quietly into a thoroughly commercial station called Chinese Television Service, 72 per cent of which was owned by the Ministry of Defence (Lo et al. 1994). All these domestic terrestrial stations remain dominant players in the Taiwan television market, despite the high penetration of transnational television.

Ratings for the three original broadcast networks had been dropping over the 1990s, ever since the transnational channel TVBS entered the market and became very profitable. TVBS achieved popularity through a programming strategy of having political forums and Hong Kong soap operas specifically targeted at the Taiwan domestic market by using Mandarin dubbing. Lacking long-term strategy, other satellite providers were said to lose NT (New Taiwan currency) 5 to 6 million per month and expected to go out of business. However, the advertising income of networks did not decrease significantly since the advertising share grew bigger, even though Taiwan was in the middle of a recession in the mid-1990s [Interview Chn 03.08].

A fourth terrestrial broadcaster, Formosa Television (FTV), commenced in 1997 as the government sought to licence as many as 11 new domestic television stations. These moves were linked to the government's plans to liberalise the media and position Taiwan as a regional centre of Mandarin language television. But industry executives were afraid of further loss of audiences and advertising revenue by CTV, CTS and TTV which had already lost much to the cable networks [Asian A & M 1995b]. Unlike the other stations, the fourth terrestrial broadcaster was owned by former opposition politicians, in conjunction with the US cosmetic firm Estee Lauder which had experience in running its own stations in Europe (Westbrook 1996). Thus with the inauguration of FTV in 1998, Taiwan had for the first time a television station identified with the Democratic Progressive Party (DPP) which had a pro-independence-from-China political platform (Hong 1999). It has joined all the other terrestrial stations in the ratings race in Taiwan, while the cable networks are not represented (Table 7.2). Although then in opposition, the DPP came to power in 2000, and ironically this terrestrial station may now be considered quasi-government while some of the other channels associated with the KMT party considered to be private.

Table 7.2
Top 10 Television Programmes in Taiwan, 1998

Programme	Channel	Rating	Viewers in '000
Super Sunday	CTS	10.38	2,101
Step Mother's Heart	FTV	8.35	1,689
Parents' Heart	FTV	7.83	1,584
Conan	CTS	7.33	1,484
Let Me Guess	CTV	6.58	1,331
CTV Evening News	CTV	6.48	1,312
Variety King	CTS	6.43	1,301
TTV Evening News	TTV	5.64	1,141
Red & White Victory	CTV	5.47	1,107
TTV Weather Report	TTV	5.39	1,091

Source: AC Nielsen, cited in Adweek Asia [1999].

Hong Kong Domestic Stations

Television in Hong Kong began in 1957 as essentially a commercial service when Redifusion was licensed to provide a wired television service comprising two subscription channels. A decade later Television Broadcasters Ltd (TVB) began operating a wireless television service under an exclusive licence. When the government offered two more wireless licences after a broadcast policy review, Redifusion terminated its wired services to take up wireless broadcasting in 1973.

This station subsequently changed owners and was renamed Asia Television (ATV). The other licence was granted to Commercial Television (CTV) which began transmissions in 1975 but ceased operations in 1978 having failed to cope with stiff competition from TVB and ATV. This led to the view that the Hong Kong market could support only two domestic television stations [Hong Kong Government 1994b].

Television Broadcasters Ltd. (TVB)

The commercial station TVB began broadcasting as the first wireless television broadcaster in Hong Kong in November 1967, and was one of the few stations worldwide then to offer all-colour transmission. Commencing with a staff of 200, it broadcast a few local productions along with imported programming. Over the years it increased local production so that by the mid-1990s it was producing an average of 5,000 hours of programmes annually or 85 per cent of the programmes it broadcast and was employing 2,600 people [TVB 1994]. Programmes produced entirely in-house by TVB are news, variety, drama and music for its two Hong Kong channels, the Chinese channel broadcasting 23 hours per day, and the English one for 16 hours per day [Interview Chn 02.04]. In part its production output was due to the lack of alternative sources for Cantonese programming for its Hong Kong and southern China spillover audiences.

As far back as 1991 TVB introduced NICAM, its own hardware innovation, which provides viewers with digital stereo and more significantly multilingual sound tracks which transnational satellite broadcasters have since emulated [TVB 1994]. It has astutely used the technology to provide trilingual programming in Cantonese, English and Mandarin in the post-1997 era under China's rule [Asian A & M 1997a]. More recently a programme distribution deal was signed with the transnational Asian Business News for ABN programming featuring business and financial news, information for which was carried terrestrially by TVB. Likewise, the American CBS Evening News received via satellite was broadcast on TVB each morning. Finally, TVB teamed up with CNN, HBO, ESPN and Australia Television to form a consortium which took up 16 transponders on ApStar1 (Fung and Lee 1994). In 1995 the UK media group Pearsons which has investments in publishing, computer software, multimedia, production houses and television stations, was able to purchase a 10 per cent stake in TVB for US$168 billion from its chairman Sir Run Run Shaw, succeeding where Time Warner had failed earlier [Taylor 1995]. In 2001 TVB became the first "foreign" broadcaster to have two of its channels re-broadcast by China's CCTV. In exchange, TVB would distribute two CCTV channels via satellite in Europe, Australia, North America and Southeast Asia [Brown 2001b], thus illustrating the growing synergies of Hong Kong and Chinese media.

Asia Television Limited (ATV)

This first television service in Hong Kong was previously owned by the Chiu business family which had close links to the Chinese government. Thus they enjoyed the strong support of the Xinhua News Agency, the unofficial Chinese embassy in Hong Kong, in their progressive purchase of ATV in the mid-1980s from Rediffusion UK and an Australian consortium. More shares of ATV were then sold in the mid-1990s to a Hong Kong corporation with major property development interests, the Lai Sun Group (Fung and Lee 1994). Over the 1990s ATV was a weak runner-up to TVB which had an 80 per cent market share, though both had once been head-to-head competitors in the early 1980s (Table 7.3). ATV was said to be traditionally preferred by older audiences, though investments in the early 1990s led to an increase from 10 per cent of prime time audiences to an average of 25 to 30 per cent [Rap 1994]. Ever since the third domestic station CTV closed down within two years of its start, the conventional wisdom has been that the Hong Kong market could at best support two broadcasters [Interview Chn 03.02].

ATV had long been a loss-making operation due to its inferior programming, despite receiving twice the advertising revenue of StarTV, but this began to change in response further competition in the 2000s. Having failed through its earlier attempt to increase market share by imitating TVB programming, ATV adopted a strategy of providing fresh alternatives such as "tabloid" television. By giving Hong Kong audiences controversial stories for the first time, such as interviews with crime victims and anti-China politicians, ATV succeeded in occasional market shares of almost 50 per cent [Interview Chn 02.02]. ATV broadcast about three hours of drama programming every night, producing one hour of it in-house and importing the rest from Taiwan, Japan and increasingly from China. Of the 23 hours daily on ATV

Home (Cantonese), 70 per cent were produced in-house but half of that was repeats. More than 40 per cent of ATV World's (English) programming was imported, mostly from the US though increasingly from Japan and Korea. ATV has marketed its programming overseas, produced special programmes for CCTV and once contracted to supply over 400 hours to StarTV's Chinese channel [APT-C 1995].

Table 7.3
Top Five Rating Programmes on Hong Kong Channels, September 1995

Programme	Genre	Rating	Programme	Genre	Rating
TVB Jade (Cantonese)			**ATV Home (Cantonese)**		
Show by Shobal	Leisure	30	N. Legend of Shaolin	Movie	19
Shobal Challenge	Light Ent.	29	Man of Times	Movie	17
Shrimp	Light Ent.	28	HK Today	Light Ent.	16
Condor Heroes 95	Drama	26	Romance of 3 Kingdoms	Drama	15
Stepping Stone	Drama	26	Fist of Fury	Drama	15
TVB Pearl (English)			**ATV World (English)**		
Thunderball	Movie	6	Mrs Doubtfire	Movie	4
Batman	Movie	5	Racing Night Live	Sports	3
Lethal Weapon 3	Movie	4	Kindergarten Cop	Movie	3
King Kong	Movie	4	Mac & Me	Movie	3
Yesteryou, yesterme	Movie	4	Gotcha	Movie	3

Source: ASIAcom [1995a], citing Nielsen SRG.

In the late 1990s, ATV underwent further ownership change, coming increasingly under mainland China business interests and sharing a major shareholder, Lin Changle, in common with Phoenix Chinese, the affiliate of News Corporation's StarTV. Yet in the early 2000s ATV accused cable operators in Guangdong province of re-broadcasting its terrestrial Hong Kong programmes without paying any fees. By contrast, rival TVB removed encryption on its satellite channel TVB-8 to deliberately target a larger Chinese audience [International Cable 2000a]. The cable operators in southern China argued that their re-broadcasting gave the programmes larger audiences and hence earned Hong Kong channels greater advertising revenues. This suggests that politically correct ownership is no panacea for business conflicts arising from transnational broadcasting even within the Greater China region. From a survey of Guangzhou residents with access to Hong Kong channels, Chan (2000) found that both channels rated highly. With

TVB Jade at 83.7 per cent and ATV at 75.8 per cent, these Hong Kong channels had considerable impact on viewing of domestic Chinese channels, on perceptions of television as primarily an entertainment medium and on social attitudes. Fung and Ma (2002) went on to suggest Hong Kong television as a form of colonialisation, resulting in various modes of consumption by Guangzhou audiences.

SATELLITE/CABLE TELEVISION

Chinese Pay-TV

The development of cable television in China has been characterised by Chinese officials as having undergone four stages: (*a*) community antenna TV, (*b*) closed circuit TV, (*c*) large and medium enterprise cable system, and (*d*) finally administrative region cable network [Jiang 1995]. The stage was thus set for the controlled introduction of subscription cable or pay-TV networks in China. Industrial community television (ICTs), owned or associated with factories and other economic institutions and narrowcast to their housing areas have been a generally unacknowledged part of the Chinese media scene. Originally utilising microwave from domestic television relay stations, it has given way to cable following the growth of the latter and the liberalisation of regulations. While the ICTs' facilities and equipment belonged to the industrial organisation, it came under the direction of CCTV or the local public television station for technology and programme production, the MRFT local bureau for policy implementation, and even the Propaganda Department of the Chinese Communist Party (Shoesmith 1998). All of these relationships have been considerably eroded in recent years, as the ICTs shifted from being primarily informational-educational organs of the government to being leisure-entertainment conduits of domestic and transnational channels in a competitive environment which included multiple cable networks.

The Chinese government seemed to be keen on encouraging subscription cable television networks in order to counter the threat of transnational television, and again the provincial and municipal level broadcasters were designated as major players. Cable networks were city-based under the PRC government's policy maxim of "one city, one system" which oversaw them through the four-tiers of government (To 1998). Utilising MMDS technology, Shanghai Cable TV and Beijing Cable TV were the largest such networks, claiming 3.5 million viewers between them. In early 1996 China was estimated to have 1,200 cable stations with a further 2,000 awaiting approval, each expecting to provide between 10 to 24 channels. For the longer term cable was laid, particularly in the cities, by terrestrial television stations in cooperation with municipal authorities (Table 7.4). To avoid the strains that this proliferation of channels would put on domestic film production and perhaps imports, the central government decided shrewdly that CCTV would be responsible for their programming. By the mid-1990s the 300 largest cable systems with a viewership of 12 million households between them were re-broadcasting CCTV encrypted channels: Channel 5 Sports, Channel 6 Movies, Channel 7 Children's/Farmers, and Channel 8 Variety [Simons 1996].

Table 7.4
Major City Cable Operators in China in the Late 1990s

Cable Operator	City TV Households	Subscribers
Shanghai Cable	3,000,000	2,000,000
Beijing Cable	2,009,000	1,600,000
Tianjin Cable	1,650,000	800,000
Wuhan Cable	1,125,000	600,000
Shenyang Cable	1,200,000	350,000
Chengdu Cable	808,000	500,000
Xian Cable	740,000	280,000
Nanjing Cable	724,000	300,000
Dalian Cable	470,000	280,000
Chansha Cable	400,000	200,000

Source: China—The Media Industry 1998, cited in Schoenfeld [1998].

Although foreign investment in them was prohibited, there were exceptions such as Wuhan Cable Television Enterprise, the joint venture since 1992 between the Foreign Relations Department of Wuhan city and the transnational/regional broadcaster CTN of Hong Kong which provided start-up capital, equipment and technical consultancy [Shoesmith 1994]. Another example was United International Holdings (UIH) of the UK which was in a 49 per cent/51 per cent joint venture with the Broadcast Bureau of Hunan Province in the Hunan

International TV Communications Company, which delivered one channel to cable networks in 14 cities in the province. In this case it was able to circumvent Chinese broadcast laws because the microwave relay used was classified as a communications system and not cable television. It was set to expand its operations and upgrade to digital technology with the assistance of UIH. Finally, Time Warner of the US had a contract to supply Beijing Cable Television with equipment and assistance in expanding an MMDS system, while Singapore Technologies and Singa Infrastructure Investment of Singapore were working with BCTV to build a pilot fibre/coaxial cable system [Flynn 1996: 68]. The latter case may not be seen entirely as a foreign investment because of Singapore's dominant Chinese culture and commitment to cultural and political values compatible with China's. However, as of the early 2000s, Taiwanese satellite channels were still not permitted by the PRC government to be re-broadcast on Chinese cable networks, despite their sizeable investments in production in Hong Kong.

The leading cable market was Shanghai where the city cable network competed with not one but two city-based terrestrial commercial channels by offering specialist channels in sports, music and drama. In less than six years it went from 70,000 to 2.4 million subscribers or 5 per cent of all 50 million cable households in China within a city with a population of 14 million. But it lagged behind the other major cable markets of Beijing and Guangdong in offering cable networks in offering interactive services such as internet, email and stocktrading updates [Chin 1998]. There were also objections from the 210 cable networks about the uneven allocation of investment funds for upgrading by the central government to provincial capitals and other major cities [Schoenfeld 1998]. Foreign media hardware and software firms were keen to tap into China's burgeoning cable market (Table 7.5) but recognised that there were official constraints and regulatory uncertainties, cultural barriers to effective joint ventures and difficulties with collecting revenues from the cable networks. Nonetheless at the start of the 2000s, there were estimated to be 90 million pay-television households, in contrast to just 1.6 million personal computers with access to the Internet [Farmer 2001]. Furthermore, the government's stated policy was to almost double cable television penetration to 150 million by 2005 and then raise it to 200 million by the end of the decade [Leung 2001e].

Table 7.5
China's Cable Television Market and Projections, Late 1990s to Early 2000

	1997	1998	1999	2000	2001
TV households (mill.)	241.89	248.40	254.90	261.34	267.70
Growth %	2.76	2.69	2.62	2.53	2.43
Homes passed (mill.)	61.10	66.80	73.50	81.00	89.00
Growth %	10.52	9.32	10.03	10.20	9.88
Basic subs (mill.)	55.90	57.90	61.00	64.00	67.10
Growth %	10.23	3.72	5.19	4.92	4.84

Source: Kagan Asia Media, cited in Mann [1999], Asia Cable and Satellite World [1999a].

Taiwanese Pay-TV

Democracy Networks

The factors that led to the growth of cable in Taiwan, as in India, were the poor programming previously on the three broadcast channels, and difficulties with their reception due to mountainous terrain and tall buildings. Some 20 years ago local cable operators began a mass antennae system for domestic television, subsequently putting on video channels and later satellite channels. These services provided by small-scale neighbourhood operators came to be known collectively and colloquially by the term "fourth channel". Since the government and Kuomintang party owned or controlled the broadcast channels, members of opposition parties or people sympathetic to their causes started cable channels in the late 1980s, long before the channels were officially made legal in 1991, in order to provide a means of communicating with voters especially at the frequent Taiwanese elections.

These "democracy networks" enjoyed popular support whilst they provided alternative political viewpoints, before a combination of systematic government repression and their own ideological bias which came through in their programmes caused their viewership to stagnate. The (then-opposition) Democratic Progressive Party owned up to 20 cable operations though via different political factions, allowing for some independence of operation [Interview Chn 03.08]. Hence, cable operations were clamped down upon by the then-government of the Kuomintang Party, thus driving them "underground" and allegedly some into the control of criminal elements [Interview Chn 02.09]. Some political parties had also invested in production houses though the programmes they produced tended to be apolitical [Interview Chn 04.04]. At one stage there were an estimated 40 channels island-wide, but the politically-biased views expressed on these so-called "democracy networks" led to some decline in their popularity with audiences [Interview Chn 03.06].

TVBS

In 1993 TVB was an early entrant into the Taiwanese market with its SuperChannel or TVBS, a Mandarin language cable channel delivered by satellite. It did not succeed as well as it was expected to because it used Hong Kong programmes dubbed from Cantonese initially, but subsequently realised that local programmes were needed. So unsuccessful was TVBS with its programming in Taiwan that it achieved only 5 per cent penetration then [Interview Chn 03.01]. Soon TVB began producing Mandarin language programmes in Taiwan, achieving an output of 1,000 hours a year and a penetration of 2.5 million homes representing almost 90 per cent of cable households and 50 per cent of all television households [TVB 1994]. Having become the most popular cable channel in Taiwan, TVBS expanded elsewhere in the region by being available to subscribers in the Philippines via SkyCable, in Singapore via Singapore Cable Vision and in Thailand via Universal Cable TV. It diversified its offerings into TVBS Golden and TVBS Newsnet channels. TVBS Golden featured in-house productions of dramas, made-for-TV movies and music specials broadcasting from 1000–0400 hours. TVBS Newsnet featured international and financial news in the morning and evenings, and lifestyle and entertainment for women and children in the afternoon [TVB 1995b].

Multiservice Operations

In 1995 the Taiwanese government, then KMT, entered the cable industry itself by introducing a VoD service to some 2,000 subscribers which was backed financially by over 13 organisations and companies. These included foreign and local multinationals such as Hewlett Packard, Philips, Acer, Tatung and Chinatrust which contributed US$1.5 million, an amount that was matched by Taiwan's National Science Council [Westbrook 1995]. This coincided with moves by the government to legalise and regulate the cable television industry and permit competition to its oligopoly of the broadcast television industry (Table 7.6). By 1999 only 12 of the approximately 100 cable networks in Taiwan were still under their original ownerships. Through acquisitions and vertical integration, the United Communications Group (UCG) and Eastern Multimedia Group (EMG) controlled about 62 cable networks (60 per cent market share), 2.92 million subscribers (70 per cent market share) and 40 channels available (40 per cent market share). Both these firms were divisions of large Taiwanese business conglomerates, Koos and Rebar respectively, with interests in financial services, manufacturing, real estate, public services and more (Chen 1999).

Table 7.6
Top 10 Taiwan Cable TV Stations by Advertising Revenues, 1998–99

Rank	Channel	January–June 1999	January–June 1998
		NT '000	*NT '000*
1	TVBS	586,411	508,452
2	Sanlih—Variety	564,947	226,323
3	SETN	379,486	80,929
4	TVBS—N	288,904	175,736
5	GTV—Variety	272,533	121,784
6	SuperTV (Sony)	269,800	254,574
7	ET News	253,795	24,219
8	Sanlih—Metro	252,013	159,817
9	FTV—News	226,019	183,969
10	StarTV Chinese	225,803	155,356

Source: Rainmaker Industrial, cited in Davies [1999].

While these newer groups were not directly controlled by a political party, their owners were reputed to be KMT members. One of the first post-1994 Cable Law entrants in the domestic television market, though, was Po-Hsin Entertainment. It began in 1995 as a programme provider, television channel operator and multiple-system operator (MSO) owning nine cable operators around Taiwan. Like CTV, Po-Hsin's PHTV station was KMT-financed. There were also two other media groups active in Taiwan: first, TVBS which was run from Hong Kong and supplied programmes from there, and second, the Taiwan-based but Hong Kong-financed CTN which ran two channels for news and entertainment [Interview Chn 02.10]. Distributed via satellite, CTN channels were targeted at Chinese speaking populations in mainland China, Southeast Asia, the South Pacific and the US as well where it was carried by cable networks [Television Asia 1995c: 33]. A number of Taiwanese firms, including the Po-Hsin group, were interested in a stake in CTN but the latter feared that this would damage its chances of penetrating the Chinese market. A bid from the Pearson's Group of the UK was also unsuccessful [Hughes 1996b]. In 1999, CTV was the first Taiwanese terrestrial broadcaster to go public amidst an erosion of audiences by cable operators, a slowing economy due to the Asian economic crisis and ceilings on foreign ownership (Table 7.7).

Table 7.7
Taiwan Cable Television Market and Projections, Late 1990s to Early 2000s

	1997	1998	1999	2000	2001
Homes passed ('000)	4,750	4,900	5,000	5,150	5,250
Growth %	3.26	3.16	2.04	3.00	1.94
Basic subs (mill.)	4,400	4,500	5,000	5,150	5,250
Growth %	7.32	2.27	2.22	2.17	1.06
Penetration homes passed	92.63	91.84	92.00	91.26	90.48
Penetration of TV hh %	77.19	77.59	77.31	77.69	77.24

Source: Kagan Asia Media, as cited in Davies [1999].

While cable television was a serious competitor to terrestrial television, it was also characterised by unannounced programme changes, failure to broadcast commercials as contracted and blackouts during commercial disputes [Liu 2001]. In the early 2000s Taiwanese cable networks were also increasingly involved in joint ventures with foreign media corporations and seeking new markets, after the Cable Television Broadcasting Law enacted in 1999 allowed up to 80 per cent foreign ownership. GigaMedia formed a joint venture with StarTV/News Corporation, Sega Corporation and Yahoo! to develop broadband interactive platform and content to upgrade its franchised network which passed 2.2 million homes Taiwanwide. ERAnet, another Taiwan player, was selling shares to Pacific Century Cyberworks (PCCW) of Hong Kong and coproducing broadband content with that pro-China company. Pacific Satellite TV of Taiwan won a pay-TV licence in Hong Kong which was a stepping stone to its plans to serve the whole region. Finally, Asia Plus Broadcasting launched the first HDTV channel in Mandarin from Hong Kong, targeted at the whole Greater China region via the satellite AsiaSat3S [Leung 2000c]. Yet it was only in late 2002 that Taiwan lifted its ban on Chinese channels and Phoenix TV, the affiliate of News Corporation's StarTV there, was the first to be re-transmitted on local cable networks.

Hong Kong Pay-TV

Wharf Cable

By 1994 satellite television was offered in Hong Kong by cable as well as by MMDS, but viewership was not growing as well as expected. The cable subscriptions were aimed at those living at government housing estates, seemingly a mass audience to be tapped for satellite television but they seemed quite satisfied with programming on the domestic terrestrial stations. There were also problems with wiring the upper-middle class suburbs of Hong Kong with optic fibre cable, which have led to the process being behind schedule [Davies 1994a]. In actual fact, MMDS access had not been prevalent in Hong Kong except in apartment blocks owned or developed by millionnaire Li Ka-Shing who first owned StarTV. By later acquiring the MMDS subsidiary from his Hutchinson Whampoa group, Wharf Cable gained access to a customer base of 300,000 households and hotel rooms already wired to receive StarTV [Goll 1995]. If it had acquired the rights to distribute three of StarTV's better-known channels, Wharf Cable would have acquired their established audiences as well as an added inducement for would-be subscribers but the negotiations soured. There were 60–80,000 Wharf Cable subscribers by early 1994, while 600,000 to a million homes would be passed by cable eventually. Still by late 1995 the number of end users of satellite television in Hong Kong was not significant [Interview Chn 01.06]. Wharf Cable did not use TVB material since it is considered a competitor for domestic audiences in Hong Kong [Interview Chn 02.04]. But it carried up to 15 transnational channels such as CNN, ESPN, ABN and so on, and while it was not permitted to carry advertising till 1996, the legislation gave it exclusive direct-to-home access.

It is difficult for any government to draft laws for a free market like Hong Kong's, given the rapid technology change, such as the convergence between cable television and telecom networks. This was illustrated by the situation in which Wharf Cable alleged that Hong Kong Telecoms (HKT) was launching an alternative cable service in the guise of a video-on-demand service ahead of the expiry of Wharf's own exclusive licence, and so appealed to the government to intervene [*Business Times* 1994a]. When the Hong Kong government decided in

1996 not to issue any further licences for pay TV until after the next official review scheduled for 1998, Wharf Cable effectively received an extension of its monopoly while being permitted to accept advertising. Wharf Cable utilised this borrowed time to complete its fibre optic cable roll-out by 1998 which would allow it to offer up to 45 channels instead of 20, but it denied any ambitions of expansion into the PRC [Kwang 1996]. Still, in a determined bid to be a regional broadcasting hub, in the mid-1990s the Hong Kong government invited bids for licences to provide pay-TV, VoD, and free-to-air services and even waived its service origination fee to attract investors [AMCB 1996c].

Other Providers

In the early 2000s, the Hong Kong government granted five new licences. The only foreign winner was Elmsdale, owned 90 per cent by UK's Yes TV and 10 per cent by local content provider Shaw Media. Elmsdale would utilise HKT's fibre optics network to deliver Disney movies, BBC news, TIW sports, among other programming fare. Other winners included Pacific Digital Media Corp, which was active in Taiwan and whose 20-channel offering would include HBO, Cinemax, MCM, CNBC, CNN, Bloomberg, Deutsche Welle and Animal Planet. Hong Kong DTV, a subsidiary of StarTV would have its own programming from ESPN and Fox Channels as well as local movies from China Star. Galaxy Satellite Broadcasting, owned by TVB, would have access to its parent's massive programme library. Finally Hong Kong Cable, formerly Wharf Cable, would position itself as being more westernised in programming [International Cable 2000b]. However, StarTV withdrew from the Hong Kong cable market in 2001, alleging keen competition, and was believed to be considering a prospective DTH market in China instead.

Throughout the 1990s Hong Kong was overtly in a race with Singapore to be the regional broadcasting hub but each adopted quite different approaches. While Singapore's push was typically government-driven, Hong Kong adopted a characteristically market-driven approach (Lovelock and Goddard 1999). The jury is still out but Hong Kong seems fairly secure in its traditional role as regional business base for East Asia and especially Greater China, despite competition from Singapore and Shanghai respectively, and this appears to extend to the media industry as well.

PROGRAMME EXPORT

Chinese Output

The television stations in China, especially CCTV based in Beijing, and the provincial and municipal stations of Shanghai, Guangzhou and Sichuan have sold their programming to overseas markets either directly or via China Television United (CTU). Television festivals organised in these metropolitan cities to promote Chinese programmes, have attracted other stations as well which had programmes to sell. However, China's television programmes were not very saleable in the other Greater China markets of Taiwan and Hong Kong. Taiwan restricted the utilisation of China programming though there are loopholes for re-packaging them in Hong Kong or for transmission by illegal cable operators. While Hong Kong had no such restriction, its audiences have found China programmes of poor quality and too ideological, and so the commercial stations tend not to feature them. Instead, Chinese programmes found a more receptive market among the ethnic channels and video shops in North America as well as other regions with sizeable numbers of diasporic Chinese. Although China agreed to swaps of programming of an educational nature as with Discovery Channel, it had not permitted direct broadcast by the latter into its market in return [AMCB 1995]. Another way that China exported its domestic programming was via extending its transnational satellite broadcasts, such as CCTV-4 for Hong Kong and Taiwan, to diasporic Chinese in the US in 1993, in Southeast Asia by 1996 and worldwide by 2000 [Chan 1996].

Although the production of television drama in China was still partly funded through an annual state subsidy of the production houses, this was increasingly supplemented by other sources. These included personal connections in other parts of government and the army which could provide further subsidies, but also enterprises which could enjoy up to 30 per cent return on their investment, as well as marketers wishing to sponsor the production in return for an association of their product with the programme. It was alleged that often the production houses had to modify context to satisfy their benefactors or investors while not offending the censors, thus compromising artistic autonomy and production quality (Keane 1996). The alternative process of raising funds from banks and investment firms and selling the programmes to broadcasters who then raise revenue from advertising has not reduced the compromise of creative integrity in China, as the more recent and popular soap operas and situation comedies indicate. Under the pretext of safeguarding cultural values and perhaps to protect the state-owned television production facilities, the MRFT ruled that imported movies may not exceed 40 minutes on prime time television [AMCB 1996g]. China's entry into the WTO in 2001 has raised hopes of at least partial deregulation, allowing both programme imports and collaboration in programme production. Keane (2000) has suggested that the extensive practice of programme cloning might be an interim measure in anticipation of greater competition from global producers. Meanwhile, StarTV, MTV and other transnational broadcasters have reported greater programme sales to cable operators [Leung 2001b]. In anticipation of further growth, many foreign media organisations have entered into joint ventures with both Chinese and Hong Kong firms in the early 2000s.

Taiwanese Output

Back in 1993, Chinese language television and movie production in Greater China was valued at US$2.8 billion. Of this Taiwan had the highest share at 47 per cent or US$1.3 billion, followed by Hong Kong at 28 per cent or US$0.8 billion and China (PRC) at 25 per cent or US$0.7 billion. Assuming growth of media markets at 5 per cent annually, cable penetration exceeding 60 per cent, and a slight increase in movie and television share of consumer purchasing power, the value of Chinese language programme production in Greater China could be as high as US$14 billion by the late 1990s, not counting subsidiary services [Hu 1995]. The US was the largest source of funding for original Chinese television production through such media firms as Disney and Discovery, while Taiwan firms simply transferred labour-intensive animation contracts for films exported to the US [Weinstock 1996]. By late 1996 China's Ministry of Radio, Film and Television (MRFT) had announced stricter regulations on the use of Chinese personnel in films and co-productions. To combat what it described as the "pernicious social influences of fake domestic films and co-production", the MRFT required that most of the film cast and crew should be native Chinese [Garland 1997]. But such regulatory efforts of the Chinese government might be a case of "too little, too late", and somewhat ineffectual in the highly competitive, global business of convergent media.

The International Media Company, a subsidiary of three Taiwanese commercial networks, TTV, CTV and CTS, has been responsible for selling their programmes to North America. However, because its managing director's position has been rotated regularly through the three networks, each appointee has not remained in the job long enough to build the business. Meanwhile the government-run Broadcasting Development Fund (BDF) promoted its programmes at international television fairs and some BDF programmes were used without charge by an ethnic Chinese satellite channel in North America. Because of its anti-communist agenda, BDF found it difficult to sell its programmes in television markets elsewhere. However, Wharf Cable and the video-on-demand service in Hong Kong sourced programming from BDF for dubbing into Cantonese, while Macau and Singapore broadcasters bought its programmes [Interview Chn 04.05]. In 1995 alone, Taiwan's television stations exported NT$186 million of programming, and over 1994–95 sold 19,535 hours of programming worldwide, including 8,474 hours of television dramas to other Asian markets, over a quarter of it to Malaysia (Hong 1999). Despite an almost 200 per cent increase over six years in the early to mid-1990s, there was understandably a limited market worldwide for Taiwanese productions. Furthermore, China, the largest market for Mandarin language programmes, remained closed to Taiwanese producers, and most overseas Chinese markets were Cantonese language dominant and thus well-serviced by Hong Kong producers.

Hong Kong Output

Hong Kong was one of the key centres of film and television production not only for those of Greater China but overseas Chinese in Southeast Asia as well as worldwide. With an output of 200 full-length features per year it was reputedly the third largest producer of films and the second largest exporter. Firms such as TVB and Golden

Harvest that were prodigious producers have also world-class libraries comprising Chinese drama, kung fu epics, police thrillers, music and comedy programming. Given their unique political, cultural and geographical situation Hong Kong distributors have also served as intermediaries between television stations in China and programme producers overseas, whether western or from other Chinese societies [Australian Film Commission 1994b].

TVBI, the international arm of Television Broadcasters Ltd, was established in 1976 to meet the worldwide demand for Chinese language programming. Each year TVB produced 5,000 hours of programming for its two channels which broadcast in Chinese for 23 hours per day, and in English for 16 hours per day. Programmes produced entirely in-house by TVB were news, variety shows, drama and music [Interview Chn 02.04]. These were then available for export by TVBI's three marketing divisions targeting overseas Chinese communities, national markets in Southeast Asia and western markets. TVBI was the largest single operator in the Chinese video-rental industry with its involvement ranging all the way from production of video programmes to operating video shops.

As far back as the mid-1990s, a TVB affiliate company set up The Chinese Channel, a cable pay-TV channel in Europe, catering to about 800,000 overseas Chinese resident there [Kohli 1994]. TVB was not only exporting programmes but management expertise, such as to Indonesia where it assisted the Indosiar commercial channel, and to India where it was collaborating with a British firm to consult with domestic commercial broadcasters using satellite [Interview Chn 04.03]. The other Hong Kong broadcaster, ATV, has sought to emulate TVB in programme production and export but on a smaller scale. For its Mandarin language channels, StarTV has purchased programming regularly from various Taiwanese producers as well as from ATV which was not a direct competitor in the transnational market, though not from TVB which certainly was.

Given the social and cultural affinities between Hong Kong, Taiwan and China, there has been much synergy in their domestic television industries, despite their ostensible political and economic differences. One unfortunate manifestation is piracy in China (PRC) of Hong Kong and Taiwanese programmes, or at least unlicensed adaptations of programme formats. However, some industry executives do not see piracy as a major problem in China, compared to Thailand, Philippines and India, because of government ownership of the cable networks and the language barriers [International Cable 2000g]. The extent to which the satellite and cable television medium has promoted homogenisation of cultural preferences and markets across Asia and especially within Greater China via programme production and export is worthy of further exploration. Now that they share competition from transnational satellite television and compete among themselves as subregional broadcasters in Northeast Asia, the strategies of TVB, CCTV and various Taiwanese broadcasters are comparable with other regional markets in Asia. In the next chapter, principles are gleaned from the varied responses of regional and subregional broadcasters to the new competitive environment which should be instructive to other developing world markets with regional sociocultural affinities.

That the globalisation of media in Asia has progressed at varying rates, even in distinct ways, is evident in the selected regions, countries and supranational subregions researched. The preceding chapters of this book have contained not just findings of the research but also discussion the impact of transnational television on each of them; it is not possible in case studies to segregate strictly events from causes, problems from solutions, description from analysis. In the study of transnational television there remains a need for an overarching framework for analysing systematically the interacting factors of globalisation. This chapter attempts to provide such an analytical framework to serve as a basis for a critical theoretical stance on the strategic management of transnational television. It needs to be prefaced by a discussion of the various levels of models put forward to understand the media and its development.

STRATIFYING MODELS

In earlier decades some developing countries invested in satellites for public television and telephony as one means of uniting their large territories and integrating the quite diverse cultures within. Today virtually all governments in Asia are concerned about the flows of transnational television in the region, and seek systematic approaches to analysis and policy. On the other hand, corporations need models to understand the implications of environment and the strategies might overcome some their challenges. Coming from an international relations perspective, Mowlana (1986) provided a model for systematic understanding of the international flow of information, one which integrated both sociocultural and economic-technological dimensions. Deducing that much media research concentrates on source and content of messages, he urged more emphasis on distribution and its control, and their political implications all the way from an individual and institutional level to nation-state and global level.

Micro-level Models

To avoid the needless controversy caused by inappropriate levels of analysis in media research, Frederick (1993: 188–93) classifies theories of global communication as being either micro, mid-range or macro theories, a typology which will be adopted in this discussion. Micro-level theories deal with the human mind, its motivations, needs, thoughts, fears and desires. Learning concepts garnered from psychology such as selective perception, frustration-aggression, cognitive dissonance, stereotyping and gaming have their usefulness in explaining the ways in which audiences utilise the widely available media and all the global information it provides access to. Selective perception, for instance, may explain why audiences make quite biased and inaccurate inferences about people in other countries. Gumpert and Cathcart (1984) elaborate an intercultural interaction model of communications which highlights the fact that many individuals and groups have only indirect contact with individuals and groups in other countries through media reporters who may introduce stereotypes and biases. The global media, largely American, has been at least partly responsible for perpetuating such cultural or national stereotypes.

Macro-level Models

Systems theories of global communication, theories of political economy and geopolitical theories deal with such entities as nations, ethnic cultures, regional economic alliances and the capitalist world system. Such theories emphasise the vital importance of the constant flow of information to the maintenance of relations between countries, without which diplomatic, economic or military confrontation might result (Frederick 1993: 202–07). Idealist systems theories believe that the media could be a forum for public opinion which would lead to peace, while realist systems theories believe that the media and public opinion are to be harnessed to serve the ideology of the state. Herman and Chomsky (1988), for instance, sketch a propaganda model of how the political and economic power structure in the US influences the way its mass media selects and frames news of the rest of the world. This phenomenon been demonstrated amply by the transnational television broadcaster CNN to its global audience in recent years.

Mid-level Models

Approaches which deal with social groups, classes, communities, political movements and institutions in relation to global communications may best be characterised as mid-range theories. In adapting the classical Shannon-Weaver model to global communication, Cioffi-Revilla and Merritt (1981–82) add four more actors—observer, organisation, broadcaster and audience—and emphasise the role of gatekeepers and the prevalence of noise at all levels. Frustration-aggression is often cited by governments in the developing world as their underlying concern for seeking to control western programming and advertising which would lead to dissatisfaction with their economic state and thus to political instability. There has been some speculation that television images of the West European capitalist societies may have fuelled the popular revolutions which caused the demise of communism in Eastern Europe. But Lull (1995: 166–68) argues that the effects of media are not one-way from institutions controlled by the dominant political-economic-cultural elite, because messages are often resisted or at least negotiated by audiences, even if unconsciously. Geolinguistic regions form a major focus of research on global television collated by Sinclair et al. (1996) which illustrates for the power of explanation of mid-range models of global communication. Since these models concentrate on the television ecology in each country, comprising institutions in the broadcast industry and their decision makers, such mid-range theories match the objectives of the present research.

ANALYTICAL GRID

Hopes of resolving debate on the impact of global media rest on on-going research and theorisation. Having analysed three regional television markets in South Asia, Southeast Asia and Northeast Asia separately, this chapter will make explicit comparison of their experiences of transnational television through an inductively-derived analytical framework. In analysing the growth of this medium, a "media strategy" approach would seem to avoid the polemics of the earlier mentioned schools, especially of political economy and cultural studies, by taking into consideration the full complexity of its national contexts. Yet in keeping with its political economy and cultural studies roots, such an approach analyses government policies and regulation, the programming appeal to audiences, the role of marketers and advertising, and the like in particular countries and regions. This convergent media strategy approach might then be considered paradigmatic for analysing the impact of transnational television on the broadcasting and advertising industries in Asia.

A conceptual framework was implicit in the research questions that were the focus of data collection in all three regions selected as sites of indepth investigation, namely the Indian subcontinent, Malay Archipelago and Greater China. It is made explicit in the analytical grid (Figure 8.1) which will be partially expounded on below. While not covering all the factors involved in the highly complex impact of transnational satellite television, it highlights the most recurrent ones to surface in the interviews, secondary data and content analysis. In other words, it is inductively derived from the results of field research, as the explanation and application of each of the factors will demonstrate. Each factor may be represented by a continuum that is relevant selectively to the phenomenon of transnational television, especially in the context of developing countries.

In a more traditional model, the business performance of transnational broadcasters might constitute the independent variable, the changes in the media and advertising industries constitute the dependent variables, with the politico-economic and sociocultural factors constituting the intervening variables. However, such a model would be highly deficient given the complexity and multidirectional nature of the relationships between the factors, as indicated by the research data.

Therefore in the following subsections the incidence of or potential for impact of transnational television in the three regional markets in Asia is investigated by utilising this analytical framework and its inventory of significant factors. For comprehensive analysis of borderless media markets, every factor could and should be applied to each of the countries in the region, but for this book different yet comparable countries from each region are used under each category of factors simply for the purpose of illustration.

Figure 8.1
Grid for Analysing the Impact of Transnational Television

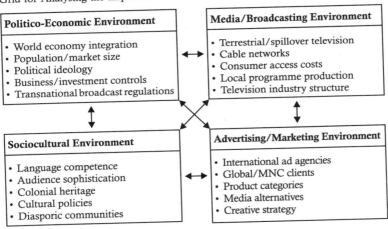

Politico-economic Environment

While recognising that earlier modernisation paradigms had been inadequate, many economists claim that promoting the growth of the information sector via investments in telecommunications would transform developing economies. Although structural-functionalism has its roots in the developed world, its modernisation theory variant is still held to have some relevance to developing countries facing a dilemma over the conflicting values needed for modernisation versus nationalism. So even today there are post-structuralists like Jussawalla (1988) who see the new communications technologies and the dominance of MNCs in cultural industries as being apolitical and value-free, thus deserving to be evaluated solely in economic terms. Though equivocally, this same school which denies any negative consequences of the media, attributes to the new communication technologies all the positive technology-determinist power needed to promote democracy, reduce socio-economic disparity, provide universal education, enhance human work and virtually usher in utopia. The findings of the research for this book suggest that the relationship between media strategy and the politico-economic environment (Figure 8.2) is at least bidirectional, if not multidirectional.

Figure 8.2
The Politico-economic Environment of Transnational Television

Selected Factors	Indonesia	India	China
World economic integration	Free market	Social democratic	Market socialism
Political ideology	Liberal/ democratic	Liberal/ democratic	Paternalistic/ one-party
Business/investment controls	Political patronage	Specific restrictions	Bureaucratic/ restrictive
Transnational broadcast regulations	Liberal access	Controlled access	Latent suppression
Population size	Dense/large	Dense/large	Dense/large

World Economic Integration

Despite their earlier socialist, non-aligned, and somewhat isolationist policies, all three countries have sought greater integration into the capitalist world-system in the last decade or so. Certainly they were not coerced, if by that one meant that they were militarily or diplomatically rail-roaded into joining, but there was simply no viable alternative in a capitalist dominant world especially post-Cold War, unless the consequences for North Korea or Cuba were considered desirable. Whether China will be able to maintain its communist political system while pursuing a market economy, India its socialistic bureaucracy while liberalising, or Indonesia its authoritarian-style government while democratising has yet to be seen. Schiller (2000) for one, continues to doubt that they can resist being drawn via the media into being adjuncts of First World politics, economics and culture. However, one might assume that the erosion of political power evident already in those countries presages greater liberalisation and democratisation in the longer term, be that years or decades from now. Therefore public

broadcasters such as TVRI, DD and CCTV were invariably constrained in their exercise of national hegemony over the television
medium by the incremental integration of their respective nations,
Indonesia, India and China, into a global economic system.

Political Ideology

Quite obviously, it would appear that countries which adopt a free
market approach in their economies are the most integrated into the
capitalist dominant world economy, and by implication would be the
most likely to experience globalisation of its television. However, apart
from the few strictly communist dominated economies which are
necessarily isolated from the international mainstream, a government's
politico-economic complexion has little to do with the country's integration into the capitalist world economy. Most countries have been
compelled to do what Friedman (2000) calls the "golden straight-
jacket" which requires privatising industry, reducing restrictions on
trade and investment, shrinking state bureaucracy, introducing currency convertibility and so on in order to reap the benefits of a global
world economy. Thus regardless of their particular politico-economic
shade, India, Indonesia, China and most other nations in Asia, have
experienced globalisation of their television industries, if not directly
via transnational television, at least indirectly as their domestic
channels faced up to the challenge of global or regional competition.
In this process of globalisation, it is evident that domestic television
in each country often faces a conflict over the control between its more
nationalistic political bureaucratic elite and its more transnationally-
oriented capitalist middle and upper classes.

Business/Investment Controls

Almost all countries have controls on foreign investment to some
degree, and the media industry in particular attracts attention on the
grounds that it is a national cultural resource or even involves issues
of national security. Perhaps more to the point, control of the media
and thus its message content is critical to a particular political power
group or at least a socio-economically elite stratum of society. In
Indonesia, until the economical meltdown in the late 1990s and political reforms in subsequent years, ownership of all businesses had to
be in the hands of locals or be joint ventures, and the licensing of commercial broadcasters reflected the importance of political patronage.

Given its socialist, non-aligned pedigree India still had controls on business and investment, though in over the last decade or so of liberalisation it was increasingly bowing to pressure for foreign investment in all industries, conceding minority equity participation by foreign media corporations. In recent decades China has permitted foreign direct investment in industry, but only in the early 2000s was this extended grudgingly to the media industry. Furthermore the process was said to be highly bureaucratic, and anything more than strategic alliances was frowned upon. However, there seemed to be some concessions made to overseas Chinese entrepreneurs regardless of their citizenship. Thus in one form or another, the three key countries studied maintained strict controls over investment in the media, especially the television industry, though in reality this is being progressively eroded.

Transnational Broadcast Regulations

All countries in Asia exercised some form of regulation of access to transnational satellite television on a range from "active suppression" to "liberal access" though these may shift over time, as explained extensively in Chapter Four. Indonesia granted its citizens access via the liberal licensing of satellite dishes, perhaps counting on their prohibitive cost and the language barrier to limit the audiences. India, on the other hand, finally opted for controlled access after a long period of complacent inaction when it was hamstrung by the legal vacuum created by outdated telecommunications laws. By contrast, China moved from a policy of complacent inaction initially to latent suppression, following some unflattering coverage by StarTV. But it may now be moving towards controlled access in support of multiservice operations owned at least in part by the army, state or communist party. As a general rule, a policy of allowing access or at least of not overtly restricting is favourable to the growth of transnational television in a particular country, though this needs to be qualified by yet other factors. Regulations alone have not been sufficient to deter access, for they often serve to drive the industry "underground" and consequently difficult to regulate.

Population Size

The more large and dense a country, all things being equal, the more likely that it would be targeted by transnational broadcasters because it represents a sizeable market for audiences to be sold in turn to advertisers. All three countries used as comparative case studies on politico-economic environment are populous and that explains in part their interest to broadcasters and advertisers, though the differing levels of interest can be explained by other contributory factors. However transnational television is sometimes a boon to audiences in sparsely populated subnational regions beyond the reach of terrestrial transmission means. Thus in its early years, StarTV attracted sizeable audiences from the western provinces of China (PRC) previously unreached by the national broadcaster. But because they were also the poorer, rural provinces, advertisers were not impressed with the audience size claimed by the transnational broadcaster for the country as a whole. However, in India, a sizeable market of affluent rural landowners has been attributed with causing the growth of satellite commercial channels in subnational ethnic languages. Likewise, the role of population size in the potential impact of transnational television in the case of Indonesia needs to be qualified by the relative level of cultural sophistication and economic affluence of the population of each country or geolinguistic market.

Sociocultural Environment

The cultural impact of transnational television on the general populace is difficult to assess as this has not happened in isolation. For the advent of transnational television in Asia coincided with the end of the Cold War, the rise of democracy movements, the transitions of economies to capitalism, the formation of World Trade Organisation, and so on. With the superceding of public broadcasting the government was left as a referee among the players, one that was sometimes ignored, as it sought to balance national cultural agenda with global economic imperatives. Yet quite evidently transnational television has had a discernible impact on the cultural industries, particularly television, in the various countries as well as vice-versa as seen in the scramble for audiences and advertising. Just how this impact has been mediated by sociocultural factors and why it has varied across Asia and within its subregions is worthy of closer examination (Figure 8.3).

Figure 8.3
The Sociocultural Environment of Transnational Television

Selected Factors	Pakistan	Malaysia	Taiwan
Language competence:	Limited bilingualism	Functionally bilingual	National/subregional monolingualism
Audience sophistication:	Urban/ affluent	Urban/ middle	Urban/ middle
Colonial heritage	Mixed experience	Benign experience	Limited experience
Cultural policies:	Nationalistic/ restrictive	Cosmopolitan/ liberal	Nationalistic/ restrictive
Diasporic communities:	Extensive/ worldwide	Limited/non-migratory	Extensive/ worldwide

Language Competence

On this dimension of facility with a world or major regional language, it is reasonable to compare only urban metropolitan areas across these three markets. In Malaysia, English is utilised largely in the capital city of Kuala Lumpur and the other major commercial centres, usually primarily within MNCs and service industries. Bahasa Malaysia is the lingua franca among the various ethnic groups and is similar to dominant language in Indonesia and Brunei, making them a sizeable market for subregional language programming by spillover or satellite. The situation in Pakistan was somewhat different since there has been a tradition of an English language press in urban areas. However, a considerable proportion of domestic public television is in Urdu, which is similar to Hindi used in northern India. A legacy of colonial rule, English is the language of international business in Pakistan but not of national government. But all of the urban metropolises of Greater China, only in Hong Kong is English spoken to any extent, while even in Beijing, Shanghai, Guangzhou and Taipei it was virtually impossible to operate without a knowledge of Mandarin or the local dialect. Therefore the only transnational channels which have been able to attract viable audiences in Taiwan are those like Star Chinese/ Phoenix, CTN or TVBS which broadcast in Mandarin.

Audience Sophistication

The more affluent and cosmopolitan the urban metropolitan areas of a country, the more likely that it will be a market for transnational satellite television. The prime markets for StarTV would have been those which rank among the NICs of Asia except for the fact that Singapore and Malaysia have government restrictions on access, while in Thailand, Indonesia and to a lesser extent Taiwan there are language barriers to be overcome. But in essence it was the commercial and political capital cities which had driven the demand for transnational television, and so the markets in Asia were largely defined by the greater metropolitan areas of Bombay, Karachi, Taipei, Hong Kong, Shanghai, Jakarta and Kuala Lumpur rather than their respective countries. In general terms, these urban consumers are cosmopolitan in their outlook and consumption habits, given their exposure to western culture. While there might have been affluent audiences in other urban or rural regions of the various countries under the satellite footprint they were better described as being local in outlook by constrast. They often represented a secondary market for transnational television, one better catered to by subregional or subnational language programming. Critical as audiences are to the performance of transnational broadcasters, advertisers are less interested in their size *per se* as with their buying power and cultural sophistication.

Colonial Heritage

Especially with its sale to Murdoch's News Corporation, there had been concern among nations in the Asia region over cultural imperialism via StarTV, though this attitude was often at odds with their determination to achieve economic development. Despite the mixed colonial experience and traumatic transition to political independence, an affluent segment of the Pakistani population proved receptive to the western-geared programming initially predominant on transnational television. Wider audiences followed with the development of Hindi-language television from India, cultural affinities overcoming political allegiances. While Malaysia chose to adopt Malay as its national language, given its relatively benign colonial experience under the British, western culture in general and English-language programming in particular remained desireable to a significant segment of the population. Taiwan was only briefly colonised by the Portuguese, Dutch and Japanese, the last of which explains the popularity of Japanese cultural products including television programming in the country. In a sense the Mandarin language might be thought of as part of a colonial culture brought by the majority Han Chinese migrants and enabling sharing of television programmes with mainland China. Like many developing countries worldwide, Pakistan, Malaysia and Taiwan had utilised public television as a means of promoting national integration, social development and economic modernisation. Similarly, concern about past colonialism or neo-colonialism has been responsible for restrictions, often in vain, on access to transnational television by their citizens who, by virtue of a post-colonial legacy in education and culture, appreciate such broadcasts.

National Cultural Policies

The more stringent the cultural policies of a nation in its commitment to national integration, the more likely it is to control domestic television broadcasting. Ironically, the more restricted the domestic programming fare, the more motivated are consumers to gain access to transnational television regardless of governmental controls on access. Public broadcast television in Asia in the past has been paternalistic in reflecting primarily the tastes of the political-bureaucratic elite whose ranks were often dominated by members of a particular ethnic-geographical subnational group. While accusing transnational satellite broadcasters of cultural imperialism, government leaders often remained blinkered to the same phenomenon within the nation-state by one dominant ethnic group over its minorities, such as the ethnic Malays in Malaysia, Urdu speakers in Pakistan and Mandarin-speaking mainlanders in Taiwan. Unfortunately, as national public television broadcasters worldwide compromise their public service ideal of nationwide appeal in order to survive in a commercialised broadcasting market, ethnic minorities often have even less hope of gaining a cultural voice within their nation-state. Yet where it may not be economically viable as a domestic market basis, there might be a market for such an ethnic channel on a subregional-ethnic or global-diasporic basis as India's commercial satellite channels in Bengali, Gujarati and Tamil, and Hong Kong's similar channels in Cantonese seem to demonstrate.

Diasporic Communities

There is a tendency to think of population in terms of national size, although for transnational satellite television, the relevant population size is all those conversant in a particular language of broadcast or of similar culture under its footprints. This is the case with Pakistan which shares ethnic groups with Pakistan, Afghanistan and India. Then there are South Asian expatriates such as in the Middle East, or historic immigrants in Southeast Asia, Fiji, East Africa, the Caribbean and more recently in North America and Europe. A parallel situation exists in Greater China and among overseas Chinese, predominantly in East Asia such as in the urban areas of Thailand, Philippines, Malaysia and Indonesia, and also practically worldwide. Malaysia has a national language similar to Indonesia's and Brunei's, namely Malay, which is spoken only in a limited fashion also in Singapore, southern Thailand and southern Philippines. In contrast to South Asia and Northeast Asia, there are few Malay speaking migrants outside the Southeast Asia region, largely confined to the Netherlands and its former colonies of Suriname and South Africa, where the language is in relative disuse. Thus while pan-Asian English language television did not work well, regional South Asian language and Chinese language channels have proven very successful. Through the pay-TV services the programming on these channels, if not the channels *in toto*, have been made available to smaller markets for these ethnic groups outside the continent. There is therefore considerable correlation between the existence of migrant and expatriate markets, and the growth of transnational television using one of the major languages of Asia.

Other Environments

Due to the length needed to do justice to them, the media-broadcasting and advertising-marketing environments alluded to in the analytical grid will be discussed in a sequel anticipated to be published within a year of this book. But briefly, as to media-broadcasting environment, the more diversified and liberal the domestic television industry and/ or greater the access to spillover terrestrial television in a country or subregion, the less of a market for transnational television it is. Similarly for the advertising-marketing environment, the stronger the presence of international advertisement agencies in a country the more likely that a transnational medium such as StarTV would be utilised for advertising in that national market as well as for the region, subregion or diaspora of which that market was a part.

ASIAN RENAISSANCE

The media seems to have perpetuated, even exacerbated, the economic disparity between developed and developing worlds. In an empirical test of world-systems theory, Peacock et al. (1988) demonstrated that over time there has been increasing divergence in economic development and wealth distribution between the core, semi-periphery and periphery countries, and that there was convergence only among core countries. Failure to achieve economic development compelled developing or peripheral countries to assert their desire for economic independence or interdependence in a new international economic order (NIEO), rather than continued dependence on developed or core countries (Amin 1984). Regardless of their analytic preferences most thinkers acknowledge that some form of global economic system has persisted over the last few centuries. Thereby they vindicate Wallerstein (1979) who pioneered analysis of social change on a global rather than solely national basis, even if he erred in the direction of ignoring the diversity and dynamism of Third World countries. Thus there is a growing basis for arguing that Third World media cannot follow the pattern of media growth in the First World because of their quite different politico-economic place within the global context.

In an adaptation for Asia of his populist analysis of megatrends Naisbitt (1995: 14–32) makes much of the trend from nation-states to networks. Most pertinent for this book, he highlights the ethnic Chinese globally as the third largest economy in the world and yet relatively invisible. Another business consultant, Ohmae (1990) points to the rise of what he terms instead the "interlinked economy" of the triad of the US, Europe and Japan joined by Taiwan, Hong Kong and Singapore. Though he does not direct it at the media industry, his treatise called for the minimalist intervention from national governments, new IGOs emphasising interdependence rather than competition, and businesses maximising the benefits of operating in a borderless world. Writing also for the business community, the academic Thurow (1993) sees the same triad of nations leading the global economy though in dire competition. Thus many thinkers anticipate the NICs in Asia, such as those researched for this book, being part of an Asia-wide trading bloc. This augurs well for their culturally interlinked media industries expansion within an Asiawide market and participation in the global marketplace.

The inductively derived analytical grid sketched in the chapter seeks to elucidate the major factors in the development of transnational television in Asia, largely as seen by key decision makers in the region's cultural industries. At this stage of the diffusion of transnational television in Asia, the descriptions of the selected factors are perhaps more accurate concerning the urban-metropolitan areas of each country than as generalisations about each country as a whole. The wide choice of television channels now in much of Asia's urban areas does mean that television has changed from being a window into the rest of the nation-state, into being a wallpaper representation of the world, variously alienating and alluring. What is insidious about the change is that it seems to be shifting people from being citizens sharing a national ideology and identity, however flawed in its design, to being consumers vital to capitalist production and marketing systems, if not global, at least regional or subregional. The following chapter will revisit the research issues first raised in Chapter One in the course of summing up the findings of this study. Through answers to these questions the key issues surrounding the environments of transnational television will be expanded upon, and generalised with caveats to other developing countries in Asia and beyond.

POLICY DIALECTICS

The global market for goods and services has grown exponentially since the 1970s, due in part to new technologies in transportation, communications, information and production. It is now both quicker and cheaper to move goods, services, information, capital and people between countries, increasing their accessibility to and from markets. This was accompanied in the late 1980s by the demise of the communist economic system of planned production and trade, deregulation in capitalist-oriented economies and a decline of ideologically-driven national development among developing countries. All of these changes have contributed to the growth of the global economy which forms the macro-environment for the development of transnational television and advertising in Asia. Thus the dialectics of each politico-economic and sociocultural issue raised by the experience in Asia need to be addressed in endeavouring to arrive at general principles governing the choices facing developing countries there and in other parts of the world.

REGULATION/LIBERALISATION

As evidenced in earlier chapters, most governments in Asia felt challenged by the advent of transnational television and sought various means to moderate their citizens' access to it. The countries most concerned were those that had the strongest ideological commitments to national cultural and political integration, and/or centralist social and economic planning. Realising that their various media regulations had failed to achieve sufficient control, some governments went on to make concessions to or collude with the transnational broadcasters, while others simply conceded defeat or were overwhelmed by events. Deregulation of the media, by which governments abdicate control and allow private enterprise to operate with minimal restraint, is one of the key symptoms of economic and political globalisation, and this has been increasingly in evidence in Asia over the 1990s.

Patrolling the Borders

Governments are by their very definition nationalistic and fear the intrusion of transnational television, over which they have little control over, into their political environment. Based on the perceived threat to its national culture, each developing country on the continent has sought to adapt in differing ways to the advent of satellite television. The controls exercised, ranging from "active suppression" to "liberal access", have been elaborated upon in Chapter Four and the shifts in policy made by countries over time reiterated there and more specifically in the case studies. The prime response of Asian governments has been some deregulation of their terrestrial-domestic television industries as in Indonesia, India and Thailand, either in anticipation of transnational television or in forced response to overwhelming competition. In the more politically conservative countries, the preferred option is expansion and diversification of the government-owned or controlled media, as in China, Malaysia and Singapore. While the more liberal countries such as the Philippines, Nepal and Thailand seem content to let market forces prevail, others like Korea and Pakistan appear to adopt a wait-and-see attitude, though clearly biased towards a more conservative alternative of regulation.

In any case control over access grows increasingly difficult with technological advances, such as greater power of DBS satellites making dishes for reception smaller and less detectable, and the liberalisation of world trade which means pressure on countries to open their markets to foreign media. Contrary to misinformation at the time, the audio-visual sector like other service industries was not left out of the GATT Uruguay Round and so forms part of the purview of its successor WTO. But French and Richards (1996: 343–58) counterbalance this with the reminder that despite its rhetoric, GATT is difficult to enforce especially in the arena of audio-visual services such as television where even free marketers recognise a case for some cultural autonomy. Of the 13 countries which made commitments to offer access to audio-visual services, most were from Asia, though a number of them like India, Hong Kong and Malaysia offered qualified access. Other countries such as Indonesia, Australia and the European Union made no such commitment and are under no obligation to liberalise their present practices because, as Kakabadse (1995) points out, the GATT agreement recognises the autonomy of countries to regulate their media industries as they deem fit. But this does not preclude liberalisation of the audio-visual sectors of those recalcitrant countries in successive rounds of negotiations when they could be placed under considerable pressure. Gershon (1997: 116–29) went so far as to argue that as part of an interdependent global economy, host nations are duty bound to protect the rights of global media corporations. Yet he considers corporate influence in the pursuit of business opportunities to be unintentional, and that governments have the right to regulate such cultural trespass. So it is not a question of whether but when countries will yield and make their national cultural policies subservient to world trade imperatives for the liberalisation of their cultural industries.

Power Partnerships

While strict regulation of broadcasting may not be acceptable to MNCs, considerable deregulation may be unacceptable to developing countries, and so a tension exists between transnational television broadcasters in Asia and the countries under their satellite footprints. Still, commercial television and Asian governments have not been at odds as it might have seemed on the surface. For instance, in an Indian election in the mid-1990s, ZeeTV offered to broadcast political rallies for the party in government when the latter was in a dilemma over not being able to use the public broadcaster DD for political campaigning purposes. In an attempt to win friends in the government, StarTV broadcast "live" the traditional prime minister's speech on independence day, previously carried solely by DD. In 1999 and 2001, StarTV took a very partisan stand on the Indo-Pakistani conflicts, seeking to identify with its major subregional market of India at the risk of alienating a lesser market. For a time CNN was broadcasting from a Indian government satellite, while assisting DD to improve its news service. News Corporation made amends with the Chinese government over Murdoch's speech in 1994 about satellite television threatening totalitarian states by dropping BBC World from its stable. Later it published the memoirs of China's "paramount leader" Deng Xiao Peng worldwide through its subsidiary Harper Collins, whilst cancelling its contract for the memoir of the last British Governor of Hong Kong, Chris Patten, which was not complimentary of the Chinese government. StarTV has more recently formed joint ventures for programme production, channel provision and cable networks in China, India and Indonesia, with domestic businesses which have the right political and business connections to facilitate greater penetration of its services.

The need to differentiate between the "hard" power of economic clout and "soft" power of cultural cooption by the developed world which developing countries face, especially in their determination to be globally competitive and yet culturally autonomous, was spelt out by Ferguson (1993). While agreeing that economic aspects such as the migration of capital, goods, services, data, technology and labour are primary in globalisation, she also highlighted functional ideologies, for instance that "big is better" which justifies corporate expansion on a global scale, or the myth that "more is better" which rationalises increased consumer choice as a public good. Mulhearn (1996) has demonstrated the globalisation of the world economy through such indications as the increasing integration of world markets, the emergence of global economic institutions such as IMF and GATT, and the growth of internationally-oriented businesses in the industrial and financial sectors, as well as a protectionist backlash by regional economic groupings. The prevalence of transnational television and other media may be yet another indicator of globalisation of the country's economy and culture. Global integration may be expedient but not as inevitable as it is made out to be by vested interests of countries, regions and corporations which benefit from the inequity of the globalisation process. More subtle is the risk of economic decline for many developing countries as a consequence of integration into a global economic system, with the possible exception of newly industrialising countries (NICs), as a result of these globalising processes.

Concessionary Conduits

One compromise made by countries such as Malaysia and Singapore, which restrict the reception of free-to-air satellite television, has been to provide a cable television service on which is available programming similar to transnational satellite broadcasters or downlinked selectively from them. Similar to the case for terrestrial television, their authorities are able to apply pressure, if not outright control, over programming and advertising either legally or morally on cable providers in a way not possible with transnational broadcasters. Oftentimes, such pressure is somewhat superfluous since the domestic cable services are run either by a corporation owned by the government, by a political party in government, or by the family, friends and business partners of political leaders. Some governments such as China and India have even entered the transnational television business themselves, while others are contemplating doing so, at least on an Asiawide basis as an extension of their use of satellites for domestic television which results in considerable spillover anyway. The underlying rationale of such concessions must be that the wider the choice of domestic broadcasts and the more readily available terrestrially or via regulated cable, the less likely their citizens are to be influenced by watching transnational television directly.

To a considerable extent all these strategies to control transnational television seem to have succeeded because in many Asian countries local dramas and news on domestic television continue to be the programmes with highest audience ratings. The growth in transnational television viewership, even in those countries which do permit access to it, does not seem to be at the expense of domestic terrestrial television watching. Neither did advertising revenue for domestic broadcasters decline, possibly due to the high economic growth among many Southeast, Northeast and South Asian nations in the early 1990s spurring expansion of marketers' budgets. As Hutchinson (1999: 35–47) pointed out, governments are seriously constrained by the role of media in society, economic policy, technology and increasing globalisation in formulating media policy effectively. Thus regulation is a poor predictor of the impact of transnational television because there are other factors to be considered in the equation, in recognition of which some governments in Asia have since deregulated their television industries. Turner and Hulme (1997) argued that, since the end of the Cold War, developed countries have stipulated fundamental changes in economic management and governance in developing countries as a precondition for development aid. So while some governments in Asia hold fast to their regulations or make pronouncements on further control, most of them fail to implement them. A few try to, erratically, but like all governments are constrained by their own aspirations for greater integration of their nation-states into the capitalist world economy.

OWNERSHIP/CITIZENSHIP

Transnational television in Asia was an initiative of regional or global businesses to provide a pan-Asian advertising medium, and not of governments or IGOs to provide a public service to countries or subregions. So from the start, MNCs of either regional or First World origin have dominated the transnational television industry in Asia, as has been the case elsewhere in the world, whether it involved the hardware of satellite and cable technology or the software of programming or advertising. With the increasing incidence of collaboration between transnational broadcasters and domestic cultural industries, and the trends in domestic television towards privatisation and deregulation, the role of media conglomerates and marketing multinationals seems to be expanding in tandem with commercial and political interests in the emergent economies of Asia.

Technology Dependence

Even before the era of transnational television, communications satellites for development were recommended to the governments of Third World countries such as India and Indonesia by First World governments or their surrogate IGOs, usually at the lobbying of their MNCs, as seen in the case studies. But the purported benefits of national integration, administrative effectiveness, provision of educational services and of news/information, and their deliverability, may be questioned. For it is doubtful whether the medium of domestic satellite television can realistically overcome the need for local autonomy, bureaucratic centralism and inefficiencies inherited from colonial powers, and general deficiencies of finances, trained personnel and support equipment which are often characteristic of developing countries. Extensive research funded by the governments and their donors/sponsors did reveal some positive social and economic change with the use of satellites. But the reality is that this somewhat minuscule change might have been achieved more cost-effectively by alternative communications media, including traditional forms. So even the public broadcasters of Asia were in a dependency relationship with the First World and its MNCs for technology, well prior to the arrival of commercial transnational television via satellite.

Some theorists seek to mitigate allegations of foreign technology impact by emphasising their role in mediating cultural experience rather than determining it. Like a number of others, Tomlinson (1991: 34–67) saw media at the core of the cultural imperialism debate, comprising as it does the cluster of programming, advertising and news whose economics of production and dissemination is dominated by MNCs of the capitalist world market. But cultural imperialism is more than media imperialism, as he argued strongly, since the media are not the totality of cultural experience but are merely the "mediation" of capitalist modernity which is a form of global capitalist imperialism. Defining national culture could be near impossible in globalised societies and cultural imperialism may be an irrelevant argument where the colonised seeks out the imperialist culture. If this be true, interdependence between governments and corporations in the media industry and in cultural production may serve to cynically exploit the economic opportunities afforded by globalisation. In acknowledging the role of electronic technologies in uneven globalisation, Wittkopf and Kegley (1998) suggested that some would focus on the benefits and others on the marginalisation caused. Therefore cultural imperialism is a far more complex and possibly too vague a phenomenon to be measured by research on media alone. It is better characterised as an ongoing discourse largely in the academia of the West than within the television industry of Asia.

Orbits and Trajectories

Although ideally under space treaties the benefits of outer space should be shared by all countries, in reality they have accrued largely to developed countries rather than the developing countries. This is because the former's commercial satellite businesses often apply pressure via their governments on the International Telecommunications Union (ITU), as regulator of global telecommunications, for satellite orbital slots (Westerway 1990: 61–66). Besides it is difficult for ITU to allocate slots equitably because there are multiple users of each commercial satellite, each of different corporate citizenship, and also because some territories such as Hong Kong are not signatories to the space agreement. Countries like Indonesia, India and China that have used their own satellites in their assigned orbital slots to enhance their social and economic development are well within their rights. But many other countries, such as the Pacific island nations, are in no position to utilise effectively any slots they are entitled to and are often persuaded by commercial interests in the First World to lobby for slots and then sublease these to them for television and telecommunications purposes. So the role of broadcast satellites operating over Asia probably warrants some judicial attention under the international treaties relating to the commercial utilisation of outer space.

From classifying the major satellite platforms in Asia in the 1990s for this book, it is quite evident that the field is dominated by MNCs. Even where the satellites are owned by national governments or corporations owned by them, as for instance Indonesia's Palapa satellites, or IGOs such as Intelsat, most of the television channels they carry are commercial and owned by domestic and transnational broadcasters, a trend that continues unabated. Other satellites are owned or part-owned by regional or domestic conglomerates, such as AsiaSat, Apstar, Thaicom and Measat satellites, although most of such firms have connections with or participation by government, political parties, armed forces or other important domestic power bases. With few exceptions such as the cases of India and China, the satellites are constructed by First World MNCs to the specifications of their Asian owners and their potential broadcaster clients, and launched at facilities owned by First World governments or consortia of them. The search for markets by developed countries has overtaken the struggle for territory in the post-Cold War era, claimed Samarajiva and Shields (1993), while the economic priorities of developing countries have been sidelined. Some satellite owners and even manufacturers are diversifying into the business of programming and channel establishment, in other words forward integrating from hardware into software. Although on the surface broadcasters from within the Asia region appear to be holding their own against the transnationals, even occasionally beating them at their own game, the reality is of continued domination of the industry's hardware markets and gradual encroachment on their software markets by MNCs from the First World.

Satellite–Cable Symbiosis

Transnational satellite channels might be said to have a symbiotic relationship with domestic cable networks, despite their sometimes conflicting business agendas and unwillingness to acknowledge dependence on one another. Re-distribution of television signals to cable networks was the first major use of satellites to be made by the television industry in the US and continues to be a prime factor in the utilisation of satellites in Asia. Extensive pirating of signals by individuals and illegal cable operators using satellite dishes in countries such as Taiwan and India, has necessitated the scrambling of signals by transnational satellite broadcasters in Asia, and again involves utilising technologies patented and thus controlled by First World conglomerates, including News Corporation. Although technology for direct broadcast satellites (DBS) has been in existence for decades and in Asia for half a decade now, it has not gained widespread acceptance in the marketplace due to the higher cost of reception via satellite dishes for consumers. Some Asian countries such as Japan, Indonesia and Taiwan have adapted it for pay-TV purposes in their attempts to regulate access to transnational broadcasts as discussed above.

In Asia, as earlier in the US, the slow growth of cable television in some countries could be attributed to failure to recognise its unique quality of narrowcasting. Glazer and Batra (1989) argued that it mistakenly tends to mimic the programming of broadcast television in order to compete with it, rather than competing with specialty print media and direct mail. Instead of seeking to attain large audiences in order to attract advertisers, they advocate that the cable industry promotes the ability of the medium to tailor advertising to editorial content, and even eliminate the boundary between them, by producing highly targeted and localised programming. On the other hand, Tracey (1988) reasoned that the restructuring of television audiences in Europe, brought about by the new media systems such as cable and satellite television, would spur growth in advertising revenue, if governments, suppliers and unions did not get in the way which must be the dream of most capitalists. But in Asia, government attempts in the 1990s to regulate the multitude of small domestic cable networks have usually opened the door to foreign MNCs from the First World which then formed multiservice operations (MSOs) in joint ventures or strategic alliances with domestic or regional corporations, medium or large.

Coveting Ownership

This book has demonstrated also how domestic television in key markets of Asia was in the hands of a domestic political and economic elite in the 1990s. In Indonesia, for the most part the public broadcaster TVRI was in the hands of a politicised government bureaucracy while the early domestic commercial broadcasters such as RCTI, TPI and IVM, narrowcasters such as the pay-TV monopoly Indovision, and satellite owners such as IndoSat were all controlled by conglomerates with close links to the then political elite. Likewise in India, despite legislated reforms, the domestic broadcaster remains in the hands of a quasi-government agency based in Delhi in the Hindi-speaking north and subject to considerable political influence. The domestic commercial broadcasters in India have been largely a marriage of NRIs, local business elite as well as political parties and state governments particularly in the non-Hindi-speaking south, who together have increasingly taken on the role of multiservice providers. In China, national, provincial and city-based television networks as well as cable networks are largely owned by the state, military or communist party subsidiaries. Hong Kong itself is exceptional in not having a public television station, and its commercial stations and cable networks are owned by leading business families and local corporations sympathetic to China and highly regulated by the local government. The present reality in Asia then is admittedly one of growing domination of media industries by commercial interests, whether multinational, regional or even subregional, rather than by public and civil society interests which tend to be largely national in focus.

There is no doubt that global media corporations are not driven by nationalistic cultural agendas but by market imperatives that often transcend borders. But even domestic broadcasters, commercial or public, have been compelled to emulate the programming practices of transnational broadcasters in order to compete for audiences and advertisers, as with programme cloning or global format adaptation. Due to consumer demand for culturally contextualised programming, transnational broadcasters in Asia have become dependent on domestic production houses for some of their programming. Pragmatically they prefer to outsource such production, for greater flexibility, creativity and lower costs as well as reduced risk. At the same time, production operations for both domestic and transnational consumption tend to be geographically clustered, as in the case of Bombay and Hong Kong, to enjoy business synergies and economies. These industries are then protected by their national governments, less as developers of subregional or geolinguistic cultural identities, but more as contributors to the domestic economies through jobs, technology, industry expertise and export income. Tomlinson (1991) questions whether Third World citizens themselves might not think some sort of cultural imperialism well worth the social development which accompanies it, such as clean water and good roads. Perhaps cultural imperialism ought to be studied in terms of the wider socio-economic changes in developing countries in which the media play a crucial role by mediating the complexity of the new culture of development to its citizens. Certainly the increasing commercialisation of television in Asia has resulted in considerable convergence of interests between transnational and domestic television broadcasters, and between public and commercial sectors in related media industries.

NATIONALITY/ETHNICITY

The distinct experience of the early transnational television broadcasters in Asia has been that they are unable to attract any significant audiences despite having more than half the world's population under their satellite footprints. StarTV was rather modest in claiming to appeal to only the socio-economic elite of the major countries where its signal reached, but even this failed to attract advertising income despite competitive rates. This could be due to scepticism of marketers over their audience research which provided large potential penetration figures, often bolstered with evidence of higher-than-average household income levels but little actual viewership figures or ratings. Whatever independent research was conducted previously, even if somewhat unsystematically, seemed to indicate almost insignificant audience ratings for transnational television programmes in most markets. There are various reasons put forward by those executives interviewed for this research and writers of articles for industry media as to why transnational television has not lived up to its original vision in Asia, and has had to metamorphise into regional, subregional and quasi-national television.

Culture and Class

Transnational broadcasts in world languages, such as what StarTV provided initially in English, were able to attract only minuscule audiences across Asia, largely expatriate executives or an urban cosmopolitan elite who are able to relate to the content and be comfortable with the language. As seen in the secondary data provided in this book, domestic television channels, whether public or commercial, tend to attract far larger audiences in any single Asian country than any pan-Asian ones such as those via satellite and cable, with very few exceptions. This is because any country's cultural milieu affects the role that television plays in it and its appeal to particular segments or the broader population. Instead of dealing with the cultural hegemony of certain social classes within any society via the media, Martín-Barbero (1993) theorised rather about "mediations" or, in other words, how the masses use the media and incorporate them in their everyday lives. Hailing from the context of Latin America, he dissented from the view of "western" homogenisation as the only form of modernity and cites the diversity of cultures globally out of which the masses formulate their own culture. Likewise, Smith (1992) argued that global culture today may be an artificial construct mediated into our consciousness by the media, especially television. Still, ethnic and national cultures seem to remain the strongest filters of the transnational images we receive via television. Writing likewise of contemporary communications in the Third World context, Reeves (1993) agreed that interpretation by audiences might reflect class and subcultural affiliations and challenge the "preferred readings" of the text.

However, he reminded that "the whole, continuous development of the media, and their conventions, institutional arrangements, values of practice, and role in the construction and reproduction of ideology and culture was always constrained by their capitalist nature" (ibid.: 151). A critical theory approach to understanding media does well to be counterbalanced with a political economy one. Hence in its analysis of transnational television this book has adopted the middle path of a "media strategy" approach which highlights the role of various players including governments, media corporations, marketing MNCs, advertising agencies, programme producers as well as audiences.

What the pioneer StarTV took a few years to concede, other transnational broadcasters such as CNBC, HBO and Discovery realised quite soon after their entry into the Asian market: that in order to command significant audiences in each country and thus attact advertisers, they had to thoroughly localise or at least culturally contextualise their programming somewhat. Domestic broadcasters then discovered that in order to beat the transnationals or at least not suffer significant erosion of their audiences, they had to upgrade the quality of their locally produced and imported programming. Another strategy was to provide or emphasise subregional ethnic programming which the transnationals would not have expertise in doing. Public domestic broadcasters had been previously averse to doing this, as in the case of DD in India, CCTV in China or TVRI in Indonesia, because of their political mandate as public broadcasters to promote national cultural integration. On the other hand, domestic and transnational commercial broadcasters saw every need to do so in their pursuit of audience segments within the mass market. In much the same way that Jeffrey (2000: 217) argued has happened with Indian newspapers, regional commercial television seems to be re-making the masses into ethnic Tamils, Cantonese and so on and thus undermining the notion of culturally integrated nation-states.

Urban-middle, Rural-rich

Transnational television first took off in the urban metropolitan areas of India and Taiwan because it was compatible with existing practices of watching cable television. It could also be tried at a low cost in contrast to the situation in Indonesia and Hong Kong for instance, where expensive satellite dishes or pay-TV had to be installed. Furthermore, transnational programming represented a quantum leap in quality over the existing programming fare on domestic television in the former countries, and so represented a relative advantage to potential adopters who could observe this for themselves in advance through their social networks. To extend the application of Roger's (1962) classic model of diffusion, "innovators" in the adoption of transnational television in all of these countries were culturally "cosmopolitans" rather than "locals", and generally financially better off. Thus its diffusion in the metropolitan areas of these countries represented acceptance by the early majority of adopters, only later spreading to the rural towns of Indonesia, India and China where the "late majority" are largely represented by small entrepreneurs and landowners, a process aided also by the increasing cultural contextualisation of the programming and breadth of channels.

While early cultural studies research looked at the relationship between media interpretation and class structures within national society, later cultural studies exponents extended it to gender (Ang 1985) and ethnic groups (Lull 1990) globally. Given the design of the present research it was not possible to assess in detail the impact of transnational television on specific audiences. In any case the notion of impact is difficult, if not impossible, to measure because the medium might well be consumed differently in various cultural and economic contexts. How transnational television fits into viewers' lives in Indonesia, India or China, or for that matter any subnational group there may differ greatly. Unless extensive ethnographic studies are conducted, it is only possible to speculate or generalise. If indeed cultural texts are polysemic, then how the urban elite in any Asian country views the programmes and advertising of StarTV could be very different from how the rural poor of the same country or urban elite in any other might. Perhaps the popularity of RCTI, ZeeTV, TVB and other regional commercial channels represents largely middle class and subcultural resistance to the cultural hegemony of the political elite via the domestic public broadcasters in their respective nations. While the trend towards expansion of media choice holds promise for the development of a multiethnic public sphere within nations, Husband (2000) cautioned this might not be commercially viable and require public subsidy. In the case of South, Southeast and Northeast Asia, satellite and cable television seems still largely a phenomenon of the largely urban middle and upper classes, and it is arguable whether by regionalised or localised programming and advertising they are invariably being incorporated into the expanding global market for goods and services.

Production and Reproduction

The highest rating programmes on domestic television in most Asian countries are often either local productions or clones of foreign programming, or at least foreign produced and locally dubbed. All of these are especially popular with heavy viewing domestic audiences, usually of the lower middle socio-economic classes. Thus they are probably more effective at cultivating values and attitudes desirable to advertisers among a developing country's citizens than any transnational television programmes in a foreign language. Furthermore, programming directions on domestic television channels sometimes reflect the cultural hegemony of the country's urban politico-economic elite who can be from a dominant ethnic or minority subcultural group within that country. In other words, there is often as much cultural hegemony exercised within a country than from without. As transnational television channels increasingly target domestic markets with quasi-localised programming, domestic broadcasters are using direct broadcast satellites and expanded channels to increase penetration, a trend which is already discernable in Japan, Malaysia and Taiwan. But the risk for domestic broadcasters is still that of centralising programming for the whole of their countries, rather than decentralising it to states or subregional cities and therefore relinquishing some measure of control. Otherwise they would afford little access for non-capital city cultural sources, and it may simply mean perpetuating the intranational cultural imperialism that has already been the case for years via domestic terrestrial television.

The MacBride Commission report (1980) had begun with a review of the current state of communications but said little about satellite and cable systems. At that time Intelsat and Intersputnik were the only transnational satellites and other systems were either domestic, marine/aeronautical and military, while cable television was then strictly a North American and West European phenomenon. Instead the Commission commented on language diversity, literacy, traditional media, mass media technology, cooperative news dissemination and

the growth of entertainment and leisure. It dealt with more controversial issues such as dominance of communications by transnational
corporations, state subsidies and monopolies in the media, regional
disparities in consumption of communication products. Outdated as
it might seem now, one of the Commission's enduring recommend-
ations relevant to this book was that developing countries develop
their own broadcast systems. This included training and production
facilities, adding that national production of broadcast materials was
crucial to reducing dependency on external sources. But it betrays a
"social communications" viewpoint that Schlesinger (2000) has argued
assumes a strictly defined national communicative space, which no
longer holds true in a globalised world, economically and culturally.

Global-diasporic, Subnational-ethnic

StarTV and its followers into the Asian market may not have succeeded
in their original aim of being pan-Asian media, but somewhat belatedly
they stumbled on the reality of diasporic ethnic/language groups across
national borders, as well as minorities within many of the countries
under their footprints. In fact it would be reasonable to suggest that it
was advertisers who first used the medium in innovative ways such as
Indian advertisers using StarTV to reach NRIs in West Asia, or consumers who responded unpredictably, such as the high viewership of
StarTV among Taiwanese (when it had been originally targeting
China) which raised the attention of the transnational broadcasters
to this untapped market. Although StarTV and other transnationals
have expanded their channel offerings subsequently, in actual fact it
was not the pan-Asian but ethnic channels such as TVBS, CTN and
ZeeTV which blazed the trail. Other latecomer channels such as
SunTV and Asianet had no major transnational ambitions but were
using the satellite medium to circumvent national regulations. Instead,
they heightened industry awareness about subregional ethnic groups
whose cultures and languages were not catered to by the dominant
domestic television media. Even in this case, it led to the discovery of
major markets among expatriates in West Asia and migrants in
Southeast Asia, reachable only via a transnational medium.

If globalisation does not necessarily imply sociocultural homogenisation, then the question arises whether the concept of post-
modern society prevalent in the First World has as much currency in

the countries of the Third World. Knox (1995) delineates the role of world cities such as London, New York and Tokyo as centres of economic and cultural importance in the world system, even though they are palpably different from each other on either of those dimensions. He also hints that with the growth of the global information economy these cities may be superseded by cities currently further down the hierarchy but more technologically adept. So on the one hand, postmodernism might well be irrelevant in the Third World which could be said to be still largely pre-modern, let alone modern. Yet on the other hand, King (1991) quite rightly asks whether Singapore and Calcutta early in the twentieth century might have presaged the cultural diversity and social polarisation said to be symptomatic of all postmodern societies presently. The multicultural characteristics of those cities of the colonial world then have been seen only more recently in cities of the First World as a result of post-colonial migration and the renaissance of subnational ethnicities. Perhaps the world cities of the early twenty-first century may be those which are less unencumbered by the infrastructures of long historical development and which, like Kuala Lumpur, Taipei and Bangalore, have made concerted efforts to become information technopolises through rapid implementation of new communications infrastructures.

RE-IMAGINING NATIONS

Transnational television has certainly blurred the arbitrary boundaries between nation-states and undermined the artificial notions of national cultures, resurrecting older cultural contours in place of "imagined-nations". The notion of globalisation as westernised homogenisation may have come from ardent nationalists under threat, alleging of their political rivals what they have been doing themselves to homogenise culture, unwittingly or otherwise. Perhaps in time cultural and social entities might be defined by overlapping satellite footprints, cable networks and web-spaces, rather than inaccurately and questionably defined by fixed geo-political boundaries as at the present. If domestic media can been seen as assisting in the formation of national cultures out of various ethnic cultures within the country, then these so-called subcultures might be said to be finding their expression both in smaller, community media as well as in global-regional mass media. The narrowcasting and interactivity made feasible through newer communications technologies might in future represent a key means of accessing such alternative media favoured by ethnic groups within a country or across borders. This book has proffered evidence that transnational television in Asia has been instrumental in the renaissance of ethnic cultures often geographically dispersed or the fusion of local ethnic sub-cultures with foreign neo-colonial cultures.

While domestic television gave expression to national cultures, however artificial, transnational television seems to further the development of globalised cultures. Like other new electronic media technologies, transnational television makes accessible geographically-distant cultures and thus socialisation from afar, or at the very least globalisation of consumption behaviour. By giving their people a choice of imported cultural products and allowing them freedom to make their own selection, governments might be complicit through deregulation in turning them into postmodern consumers for a global market rather than remaining citizens loyal to a nation-state or even a cultural-economic region. The convergence of urban elite lifestyles and consumption patterns worldwide is undoubtedly precipitated by the ubiquity of television made possible by satellite and cable. Hence transnational television might be detrimental in commercialising and commodifying culture, even if of value to societies in undermining repressive nationalism. The ways in which marketing and advertising have been contributors to and beneficiaries of such nascent cultural change within this region, will take another book to explore.

Just as the process of modernisation has not been uniform across developing countries given their heterogeneity politically, economically, socially and culturally, likewise globalisation of the media in our postmodern world takes place at differential pace and scale from country to country, and even in ethno-geographical subregions or socioeconomic levels within or across borders. The regional case studies within this book of South, Southeast and Northeast Asia have illustrated amply this diversity between developing countries as well as within each, both prior to and since the advent of transnational television. Still, an inference from this book must be that the very same growth of transnational television that has rewritten national cultural policies around Asia, may also be facilitating the formation of newer socio-cultural identities, on a subnational, regional, even global basis.

Through the involvement of civil society, non-government organisations, professional associations, nation-states, inter-goverment agencies and other participants in democratic political processes, globalisation via newer media, even if driven by commercial imperatives, need not spell escalating homogenisation but synergistic hybridity of cultures. Towards that end we ought all to hope and work.

ABU News [1998]. "CCTV turns 40", *Asia-Pacific Broadcasting Union News,* 17 (4).

AC Nielsen [1999]. *AC Nielsen China Peoplemeter Service.* Hong Kong: AC Nielsen (China) Ltd.

———— [2001a]. *CabSat Asia Brochure.* Hong Kong: AC Nielsen.

———— [2001b]. *Indonesia CabSat and Netwatch Report.* Hong Kong: AC Nielsen.

Adweek Asia [1998]. "TVBI Launches of Service". *Adweek Asia,* 25 September.

———— [1999]. "Adweek Asia Top 10 Adspend Summary", *Adweek Asia,* 23 April.

All Asia Broadcast Centre [1996]. *Astro: Fact Files.* Kuala Lumpur: All Asia Broadcast Centre.

Ambez Media and Market Research [1999]. "Satellite Reckoner". *Indiantelevision.com.*

AMCB [1995]. "Discover and CCTV in Programme Swap", *Asian Mass Communications Bulletin,* 25 (6), November–December.

———— [1996a]. "Bangladesh to Get Second Channel", *Asian Mass Communications Bulletin,* 26 (1), January–February.

———— [1996b]. "Korea Gets More TV Channels", *Asian Mass Communications Bulletin,* 26 (2), March–April.

———— [1996c]. "Hong Kong to Liberalise TV Market", *Asian Mass Communications Bulletin,* 26 (3), May–June.

———— [1996d]. "Discovery Asia to Move HQ out of Hong Kong", *Asian Mass Communications Bulletin,* 26 (5), September–October.

———— [1996e]. "Anteve Targets US2.4 billion Revenue in Channel Revamp", *Asian Mass Communications Bulletin,* 26 (5), September–October.

———— [1996f]. "Indian Regional Channels Enjoying Best of Broadcast Boom", *Asian Mass Communications Bulletin,* 26 (5), September–October.

———— [1996g]. "China Clamps Down on Broadcasting of Acquired Productions in Prime Time", *Asian Mass Communications Bulletin,* 26 (5), September–October.

———— [1997a]. "First Private Nepali Channel Goes on Air", *Asian Mass Communications Bulletin,* 27 (1), January–February.

AMCB [1997b]. "Indonesia and Vietnam Restrict Access", *Asian Mass Communications Bulletin*, 27 (2), March–April.

APT Satellite [1996]. "APT Advertisement", *Via Satellite*, May.

APT Yearbook [1998]. "Asia: Regional Satellite Systems", *Asia-Pacific Television Yearbook*, March, published at www.icompub.co.uk and accesssed February 1999.

APT-C [1995]. *Asia Pacific Television: Channels*. Thousand Oaks, CA: Baskerville Communications Corporation.

APT-C&S [1995]. *Asia Pacific Television: Cable and Satellite*. Thousand Oaks, CA: Baskerville Communications Corporation.

Asia Cable and Satellite World [1999a]. "National CATV Company A New Telco Force in China", *Asia Cable and Satellite World*, May.

———— [1999b]. "India: Never the Same Audience", *Asia Cable and Satellite World*, October.

———— [2000a]. "Satellite Transponder Guide—Asia", *Asia Cable and Satellite World*, March.

———— [2000b]. "Malaysia Moves towards Convergence", *Asia Cable and Satellite World*, February.

———— [2000c]. "Satellite Transponder Guide-Asia". *Asia Cable and Satellite World*, March.

Asia-Pacific Broadcasting [1992]. "New Star Shines in Asian Skies", *Asia-Pacific Broadcasting*, June.

———— [1998a]. "Potential and Risks: China Focus" and "Satellite Launches", *Asia-Pacific Satellite*, April.

———— [1998b]. "Telkom 1 Set to Launch in 1999", *Asia-Pacific Satellite*, June.

———— [1998c]. "Binariang in Multimedia Super Corridor Bid", *Asia-Pacific Satellite*, June.

———— [1998d]. "Pas-8 is Fourth Asian Satellite for PanAmSat", *Asia-Pacific Satellite*, December.

———— [1998e]. "Changes in the Air: Thailand Report", *Asia-Pacific Satellite*, December, pp. 34–35.

———— [2001]. "A New Identity for Times to Come", *Asia Pacific Satellite*, October.

Asia, Inc. [1994]. "The Billion-Dollar Battle for China's Airwaves", *Asia Inc.*, March.

Asia Magazine [1990]. "A Bird's Eye View of the Future", *Asia Magazine*, 6–8 July.

ASIAcom [1995a]. "Facts and Stats: Hong Kong TV Viewing", *ASIAcom*, 24 October.

———— [1995b]. "Taiwan Terrestrials Lose Ad Support as Cable Snowhalls", *ASIAcom*, 1 (5), 24 October.

Asian A & M [1995a]. "Star Blacked Out to Protest Switch", *Asian Advertising and Marketing*, November 17.

Asian A & M [1995b]. "Fifth Terrestrial for Taiwan?", *Asian Advertising and Marketing*, 1 December.
——— [1996a]. "TVB Talks in Tongues", *Asian Advertising and Marketing*, 11 July.
——— [1996b]. "Looking Ahead with Indovision" and "Research: Profile of Indonesia", *Asian Advertising and Marketing*, 1 November. Hong Kong: Zindra Ltd.
——— [1997a]. "A and M Hong Kong Profile", *Asian Advertising and Marketing*, 24 January.
——— [1997b]. "Foreign Satellite Relays Banned", *Asian Advertising and Marketing*, 27 June.
——— [1997j]. "NBC in Two Million Indian Homes". *Asian Advertising and Marketing*, 21 February.
Asian Business News [1994]. *ABN Media Pack*. Singapore: Asian Business News.
Asian Communications [1993]. "Regional Focus: Thailand's Local Markets", *Asian Communications*, November.
Astro [1996]. *Welcome to the Future—the World of Astro*. Kuala Lumpur: Astro.
——— [2000]. *A Gift so Perfect*. Kuala Lumpur: Astro.
Australia Television [1996a]. "Australia Television Rebroadcasting Agreements" and "Regional Audience Research". *ATVI Media Pack*. Sydney: Australia Television.
——— [1996b]. *Australia Television: Working in Partnership with Australian Business* (brochure). Sydney: Australia Television.
Australian Film Commission [1994a]. *People's Republic of China* (South East Asian Television Study, Volume 1). Sydney: Australian Film Commission.
——— [1994b]. *Multi-Region* (South East Asian Television Study, Volume 7). Sydney: Australian Film Commission.
AWSJ [1993a]. "Broadcasters Join to Lease Transponders on Apstar2", *The Asian Wall Street Journal*, 2 December.
——— [1993b]. "India may Limit Satellite TV Broadcasts", *The Asian Wall Street Journal*, 4 August.
——— [1994]. "China Issues Satellite-TV Curbs", *The Asian Wall Street Journal*, 1 March.
Badarudin, Noor Bathi [1998]. "The Changing Malaysian TVscape: Road to Regionalisation and globalisation", *Media Asia*, 24 (3).
Bailes, Andrew and Neil Hollister [1996]. *Asian Cable and Satellite: Unrivalled Growth Opportunities*. London: Financial Times Telecoms & Media Publishing.
Bamzai, Sandeep [2000]. "Will this Early Bird get the Worm?", *Business India*, 27 November–10 December.
Baskerville Communications [1996]. *Asia Pacific Television: Channels*. Thousand Oaks, CA: Baskerville Communications Corp.
BBC World [1999]. www.bbcworld.com/content.

Boeke, Cynthia [1997]. "The Asia-Pacific Satellite Scene", *Via Satellite*, January.

Book, Sam and Eileen Krill [1996]. "Late Entrants Post Strong Growth", *Cable and Satellite Asia*, May–June.

Broadcast Asia [1994]. "Cable TV: Impact on the Philippines", *Broadcast Asia*, March.

——— [1998]. "China's Cable TV Promising", *Broadcast Asia*, May.

Brown, Gerald [2000a]. "Stations and Networks: Pakistan", *e-broadcastnewsasia*, 3 (4), 23 October.

——— [2000b]. "Stations/Networks", *e-broadcastnewsasia*, 3 (5), 22 November.

——— [2001a]. "Stations/Networks: ESPN Star Sports", *e-broadcastnewsasia*, 4 (1), 14 March.

——— [2001b]. "Stations/Networks: Indonesia", *e-broadcastnewsasia*, 5 (4), 24 April.

——— [2001c]. "Stations and Networks", *e-broadcastnewsasia*, 7 (1), 27 June.

——— [2001d]. "Regulatory Matters: Anteve Network", *e-broadcastnewsasia*, 7 (2), 3 July.

——— [2001e]. "Satellite", *e-broadcastnewsasia*, 7 (6), 21 October.

——— [2001f]. "Stations/Networks", *e-broadcastnewsasia*, 7 (8), 1 December.

Business Times [1994a]. "Wharf in Bid to Stop HK Telecom's Video-on-Demand", *Business Times*, 16 August.

——— [1994b]. "Hindujas to Launch Cable TV Network", *Business Times*, 5 September.

——— [1995]. "StarTV and Indovision Make Deal for Broadcast of 15 Channels", *Business Times*, 15 March.

Cable & Satellite Asia [1996a]. "Pointing Five Ways", *Cable and Satellite Asia*, May–June.

——— [1996b]. "Asian Channel Guide" and "Cover Story", *Cable and Satellite Asia*, November/December.

——— [1996c]. "All Shook Up", *Cable and Satellite Asia*, March–April.

——— [1996d]. "China Rising", *Cable and Satellite Asia*, September–October.

——— [2001p]. "Stations/Networks: Singapore". *e-broadcastnewsasia*, 7 (2), 3 July.

——— [2001h]. "Regulatory Matters". *e-broadcastnewsasia*, 7 (4), 29 August.

——— [1998]. "News Digest", *Cable and Satellite Asia*, May–June.

——— [2000]. "Channel Guide", *Cable and Satellite Asia*, January–February.

Cable and Satellite Europe [1994a]. "Getting Down to Business", *Cable and Satellite Europe*, July.

——— [1994b]. "A Filip for Expansion", *Cable and Satellite Europe*, July.

Cable Quest [1994a]. "Jain's Proposal for Cable Operators: Will it Unite Them?", *Cable Quest*, July.

——— [1994b]. "ZeeTV Finds a Way to Bengali Heart", *Cable Quest*, August–September.

Cable Quest [2000a]. "National News", *Cable Quest,* 7 (4), July.

——— [2000b]. "RTV (UK) Grows to 8 Channels", *Cable Quest,* 7 (7), October.

Cakram [2000]. "Peta Baru Pertelevisian Nasional". *Cakram,* August.

Chan, Joseph Man [1996]. "Television in Greater China: Structure, Exports and Market Formation", in John Sinclair, Elizabeth Jacka and Stuart Cunning Ham, (eds). *New Patterns in Global Television: Peripheral Vision.* Oxford: Oxford University Press.

Channel 9 Gold [2000]. "Television Penetraion in India". Bombay: Channel 9 Gold.

Chin, Edward [1998]. "Shanghai Cable: Big Shots." *Cable and Satellite Asia,* July/August.

Ciotti, Paul [1994]. "Why Satellites Will Prevail Over Censorship", *Asia, Inc.,* March.

Clifford, Mark [1993]. "Getting wired", *Far East Economic Review,* 8 July.

CNN [1994]. *Media/PR Pack.* Hong Kong: CNN International.

——— [1999]. Asia Pacific website, www.turner-asia.com/cnni.cnni _worldofcnn.

Cohen, Hart [1996]. *Satellite Television in Medan, North Sumatra* (Research Reports Part 1). Sydney: University of Western Sydney.

Conlon, C.J. [2000]. "Bhutan", in Shelton A. Gunaratne (ed.), *Handbook of the Media in Asia.* New Delhi, Thousand Oaks and London: Sage Publications.

Cooperman, William [1995]. "Communications Satellites for the Asia-Pacific Region: 1995 Status Report". Pacific Telecommunications Council 17th Annual Conference Proceedings, Honolulu.

Darusman, Taufik [1991]. "Station Abandons Lofty Objective", *Asia-Pacific Broadcasting,* September.

Davies, Simon Twiston [1994a]. "Wharf Wires Up Territory", *Asian Advertising and Marketing,* 11 March.

——— [1999]. "Taiwan on the Verge", Asia Cable and Satellite World, June.

DD-ARU [1999]. *Annual Report.* New Delhi: Doordarshan Audience Research Unit.

DECORE [1991]. "Communications and Media Patterns in Nepal" (Report submitted to Unicef-Nepal). Kathmandu: Development Communication and Research Consultancy Group.

de Sousa, Vatsala [1994]. *Synergy: The Newsletter of UTV.* Bombay: Source Communications.

Deal, Helen [1998]. "Who's Watching", *Television Asia,* July–August.

Department of Information [2000]. *Indonesia 2000: An Official Handbook.* Jakarta: Department of Information/National Communication and In- formation Board.

DPI [1993, 1990]. *Directives on TV Broadcasting.* Jakarta: Departemen Penerangan Indonesia (Indonesian Department of Information).

Discovery On-Line [2004]. "Discovery Networks Asia—Corporate Profile". (http//:asia.Discovery.Com/jsui/copyright/company. Html)

Dubey, Suman [1993a]. "India's State TV Draws Static as it Takes on Foreign Rivals", *The Asian Wall Street Journal*, 16 August.

—— [1993b]. "Zee TV Expects Broadcast Deal to Spur Growth", *The Asian Wall Street Journal*, 27 December.

Dziadul, Chris [1994]. "Agents of Change", *Cable and Satellite Europe*, July.

e-broadcastnewsasia [2001]. "India", *e-broadcastnewsasia*, 7 (5), 29 September.

Economic Times [2001]. "China Mulls giving News Corp and AOL Time Warner Access to TV Audience", *The Economic Times*, 6 September.

ESPN [1994]. "Fact Sheet". Hong Kong: Entertainment and Sports Program Network.

Euroconsult [1995]. "Asia-Pacific Communications and Broadcasting Market Opportunities: Prospects to 2005". Paris: Euroconsult.

Farmer, Jim [2001]. "Observing China's Cable TV Market". *Communications Technology International*, March.

Flournoy, Don [2001]. "Coverage, Competition and Credibility: The CNN International Standard", in Tony Silvia (ed.), *Global News: Perspectives on the Information Age*. Ames: Iowa State University Press.

Flynn, Robin (ed.) [1996]. *Kagan's Asia Pacific Cable/Pay TV*. Carmel, CA: Kagan World Media, Inc.

Forrester, Chris [1999]. "Global Ambitions", *Television Asia*, March.

Garland, John [1997]. "New Regulations on Personnel for Chinese Films and Co-Productions", *Television Asia*, January.

Goll, S.D. [1995]. "Wharf Cable Agrees to Buy Hutchison"s Satellite Unit", *Asian Wall Street Journal*, 8 June.

Grafik McCann-Erickson [1994]. *Media Monitor*, March. Jakarta: Grafik McCann-Erickson

Green, Andrew [1994]. "Asian Television: Massive Growth but Uncertain Opportunity", *Screen Digest*, April.

Hamid, Farida [1991]. "Pay TV Heats up in Thailand", *Asian Advertising and Marketing*, October.

Hingorani, R.T. [2000]. "Regulating Pay Channels—a Priority", *Cable Quest*, 7 (5), August.

Hong Kong Government [1994a]. *Hong Kong 1994*. Hong Kong: Government Information Services.

—— [1994b]. "Television Broadcasting in Hong Kong". Hong Kong Information Note, Chief Secretary's Office, March.

HTA [1993a]. *The Changing Media Environment*. Hindustan Thompson Advertising, Bombay office.

—— [1993b]. "The Sun TV Count" *Media Update*, December Bombay: Hindustan Thompson Advertising.

—— [1994]. *Media Update*, August–September. Hindustan Thompson Advertising, Bombay office.

Hu, Jason [1995]. "An Asia-Pacific Media Center for the Age of Transnational Broadcasting" (pamphlet). Taipei: Government Information Office:

Huang Yu [1994]. "Peaceful Evolution: The Case of Television Reform in Post-Mao China", *Media, Culture and Society*, 16.

Hughes, Owen [1996a]. "Robert Chua Enlists Investors for CETV", *Television Asia*, January.

—— [1996b]. "Stake in CTN Still on the Market", *Television Asia*, April.

—— [1997]. "Homing in on Japan's TV Market", *Asian Advertising and Marketing*, 21 February.

Hughes, Owen and Constance Soh [1999]. "SES Closes Satellite Deal with AsiaSat", *Television Asia*, January/February.

Hughes, Owen and Nick Masters [1996]. "Measat Launches as Astro", *Television Asia*, Satellite and Cable supplement 1996.

Hukill, Mark [1993]. "Impact of satellites on Singapore", presented at the *Seminar on the Social and Cultural Impact of Satellite Broadcasting in Asia*. Singapore: Asian Mass Communication Research and Information Centre.

IMRB [1998]. "Television Ratings Points". Bombay: Indian Market Research Bureau (www.imrbint.com/trp/top25c.html)

Indiantelevision.com [2001]. "Satellite Reckoner". *Indiantelevision.com*

—— [2002]. "C&S and All-TV Homes". *Indiantelevision. com* (www. indiantelevision.com/tvr accessed 7 September 2002).

Indostar [1993]. "Indonesia Signs Direct Broadcast Satellite Contract Launching ASEAN Information Age" [press release, 8 December]. Jakarta: MediaCitra Indostar & International Technologies Inc.

Indovision [1994]. *Publicity Package for Potential Consumers*. Jakarta: PT Matahari Lintas Cakrawala.

Initiative Media Indonesia [1999]. *MediaFact Indonesia 1999*. Jakarta: Initiative Media Indonesia/Lowe Lintas.

International Cable [1995]. "Networks Compete for Chinese Audience", *International Cable*, December.

—— [1996]. "Cable TV Spices up the Indian Palate", *International Cable*, February.

—— [1999a]. "Asian Subs to Quadruple", *International Cable*, 10 (3), March.

—— [1999b]. "Asia: Taiwan Opens Market", *International Cable*, 10 (4), April.

—— [1999c]. "India Cable & Satellite Forecast", *International Cable*, 10 (6).

—— [2000a]. "Asia's Cable Piracy Issues", *International Cable*, 11 (7), July.

—— [2000b]. "Hong Kong Waits for Big Investments", *International Cable*, 11 (9), September.

—— [2000g]. "Asia's Cable Piracy Issues". *International Cable*, 11 (7), July.

Ishadi, S.K. (ed.) [1994]. *The Reception of News and Information Programmes from Foreign Television Stations through Parabolic Antenna*. Jakarta: The

Centre of Research and Development of Information Media and Japan International Cooperation Agency.

Ishadi, S.K. [1999]. "TV Content in Asia: More Waste or Substance—The Indonesian Experience". Paper presented at the AMIC 8th Annual Conference, Chennai, India, 1–3 July.

Jacob, Paul [1994]. "TV Stations Reminded to Reduce Foreign Content", *Straits Times*, 26 August.

Jiang Chen [1995]. "CATV and Satellite Development in China", *ABU Technical Review*, 158, May–June.

Jusuf, Antariksawan [1999]. "Still Standing", *Television Asia*, April.

Kagan World Media [1996]. "Malaysia", *Asia Pacific Cable/Pay TV 1996*. Carmel, CA: Kagan World Media, Inc.

Karnik, Kiran [1993]. "Satellite and Cable TV Invasion: Its Socio-economic Impact", in *Mass Media in India 1993*. Delhi: Publications Division, Ministry of Information & Broadcasting, Government of India.

Karp, Jonathan [1994]. "Spin Doctor: Medical Man Uses Video for Politics, Profit" and "TV Times", *Far East Economic Review*, 15 December.

King, Thomas [1996]. "A Golden Era for Pakistan TV", *Asia-Pacific Broadcasting*, October.

Kohli, Sheel [1994]. "Shaws Start TV Channel for Chinese in Europe", *South China Morning Post International Weekly*, 19–20 February.

Kwang, Mary [1995]. "Pacific Rim Watch", *International Cable*, November.

——— [1996]. "Wharf Cable: Waiting for Tomorrow", *International Cable*, November.

Lahiri, Indrajit [1995a]. "Hindujas" IN Network Unties the Tangle of Cable", *Television Asia*, September.

——— [1995b]. "Viewing Researchers Fail to Come to a Consensus", *Television Asia*, December.

——— [1996a]. "School's Out in Calcutta", *Television Asia*, April.

——— [1996b]. "Speaking your Language", *Television Asia*, November.

——— [1999]. "Intersputnik to Launch Satellite over Indian Ocean", *Television Asia*, January–February.

——— [2001]. "Home is Where the Heart is", *Television Asia*, July–August.

Leung, W. H. [2000a]. "Newbytes: Satellite", *International Cable*, October.

——— [2000b]. "Newsbytes: Cable", *Communications Technology International*, November.

——— [2000c]. "Taiwan's Cable TV Expands", *Communications Technology International*, December.

——— [2000d]. "Rough Seas for Stand-Alone Cable Models", *Communications Technology International*, November.

Leung, W. H. [2001a]. "Newsbytes: Milestones", *Communications Technology International*, January.

——— [2001b]. "China's Liberalizing Cable Markets", *Communications Technology International*, February.

APPENDIX 227

Leung, W. H. [2001c]. "India's Long Road", *Communications Technology International*, April.
———— [2001d]. "China's Ambitious Plan", *Communications Technology International*, May.
———— [2001e]. "Rough Seas for Stand-alone Cable Models", *Communications Technology Internatioal*, November.
Lintas Indonesia [1993]. *Media Guide 1993*. Jakarta: Lintas Indonesia.
Liu, Jeanne [2001]. "Advertising in Taiwan", in Ingomar Kloss (ed.), *Advertising Worldwide: Advertising Conditions in Selected Countries*. Berlin and Heidelberg: Springer.
Loveard, Keith [2000]. "Indonesia Media Plays Catch Up as Lippo Carves Out New Territory", *Asia Cable and Satellite World*, March.
Malhotra, S. [1994]. "Coming up to Speed", *Cable and Satellite Europe*, July.
Mann, Collin [1999]. "Convergence Reaches China", *Asia Cable and Satellite World*, 2 (23), May.
Masters, Nick [1996a]. "Territories: India". *Guide to Satellite and Cable 1996*. Singapore: Partners in Media Ltd.
———— [1996b]. "CCTV goes Global with PanAmSat", *Television Asia*, Show Edition, May.
Mitra, Ananda [1993a]. *Television and Popular Culture in India: A Study of the Mahabharat*. New Delhi: Sage Publications.
———— [1993b]. "Cable Operators against ZeeTV", *The Hindustan Times*, 15 December.
Mullick, A. [1994a]. "Popular Serials to go off Zee", *Business Times*, 6 September.
———— [1994b]. "ABN to Beam on DD's Channel 3", *The Times of India*, 17 September.
Narang, Rakesh [1996]. "India Watch", *International Cable*, December.
Nielsen SRG [1995]. "Satellite Guide to Asia" (poster). Hong Kong: Nielsen SRG.
Nimbus [1994]. "Laughter. Tears. Passion. Frenzy. Who said Marketing TV Programmes Only Involved Negotiating Rates?" (appointment advertisement). *The Times of India*, 30 July.
Noble, Grant [1989]. "Some Comments on Video in India", *Australian Journal of Communication*, 16 December.
Noordin, Mazlan [1992]. "All this Big Fuss has to do with Values", *New Straits Times*, 18 September.
Panday, Narendra [1993]. "Satellite Television in Nepal". Paper presented to the AMIC Seminar on the Social and Cultural Impact of Satellite Television in Asia, Singapore, 1–3 February.
Parapak, Jonathan [1990]. "The Progress of Satellite Technology and its Role in the Development of the Asia Pacific region—the Case of Indonesia". Paper presented at the Seminar on Socio-Economic Impact of Broadcast Satellites in the Asia-Pacific region, Jakarta, 25–27 July.

Pardosi, Karidun [1996a]. "Gontha to purchase a stake in TPI", *Television Asia*, January.

Pardosi, Karidun [1996b]. "Government Forbids RCTI to Float Shares", *Television Asia*, January.

———— [1996c]. "Anteve Targets Revenues of US$2.4 Billion in Revamp", *Television Asia*, July–August.

———— [1998]. "Cost-cutting by Indonesian Stations", *Television Asia*, March.

———— [1999]. "StarTV to Offer Programmes to Metra", *Television Asia*, January–February.

Pathania, Geetika [1996]. "Ambivalence in a STAR-ry Eyed Land: Doordarshan and the Satellite TV Challenge". Paper presented at the 20th Conference of the International Association for Mass Communication Research, Sydney, September.

Pendakur, Manjunath [1991]. "A Political Economy of Television: State, Class and Corporate Confluence in India". In Gerald Sussman and John A. Lent, eds., *Transnational Communications: Wiring the Third World*. Newbury Park, CA., London and New Delhi: Sage Publications.

PPPI [2000]. *Media Scene 1999–2000*. Jakarta: Indonesian Association of Advertising Agencies.

Rahim, Abdur [1994]. "Impact of Cable TV on Television and Video Viewing in Hyderabad: A Survey". *Media Asia*, 21 (1).

Rai, U. [1994]. "Modalities for DD-CNN Tie-up on News Coverage Finalised", *Indian Express*, 7 March.

Rap [1994]. "Chinese Language Markets Beckon Tough Competition", *Rap magazine*, June.

RCTI [1993]. *Corporate Brochure*. Jakarta: Rajawali Citra Televisi Indonesia.

Reminiscent TV Network [2002]. "Company information" and "Advertise". *Reminiscent Television Network* [www.rtvnetwork.com accessed September 2002].

Ross, James [2002]. "Foreword", *Pay TV in the Year 2002: Time For a Reality Check*. Report Commissioned by Bloomberg Television and produced by Howorth Communications, December.

Rout, Kamila [2000]. "Caught between Zee and Zia", *Himal South Asia*, June 2000 (www.south-asia.com/himal/June/zia.htm].

Samsudin A. Rahim and Latiffah Pawanteh [2001]. "The Emerging Generation: Media Penetration and the Construction of Identity Among Young Adults in Malaysia" [unpublished paper]. Bangi: University Kebangsaan Malaysia.

Schoenfeld, Susan [1998]. "China Research: Many Happy Returns", *Cable and Satellite Asia*, July/August.

Selva, James (ed.), [2000]. *Media Guide 2000*. Kuala Lumpur: Whiteknight Communications.

Severin, Werner J. [1994]. "The New Cultural Revolution: The Spread of Satellite Dishes in China", *International Journal of Public Opinion Research*, 6 (1).

SCTV [1993]. *Corporate Brochure and Programme Schedule*, December. Surabaya: Surya Citra TeleVisi.

Setiawan, B. [1994]. "Satelit Palapa di tengan Persaingan Satelit Komunidasi di kawasan Asia (Seminar paper in Indonesian). Singapore: Asian Mass Media Information and Research Centre.

Sekhar, K. [1999]. "Emergence of Religious and Regional Language Programming in Indian TV", *Media Asia*, 26 (1).

Shimizu, Shinichi [1993]. "The Implications of Transborder Television for National Cultures and National Broadcasting: A Japanese Perspective". Paper prepared for the Symposium on the "New Television", University of Colorado, 17–19 September.

Sidhu, B.K. [1996]. "ZeeTV Seeking Tie-ups to Broadcast in M'sia", *The Star*, 2 January.

Simons, Rowan [1995]. "CCTV to Launch Global Chinese Language Service", *Television Asia*, March.

———— [1996]. "Chinese Cable TV", *Television Asia*, Cable and Satellite supplement, March

Siriyuvasak, Ubonrat [1993]. "The Social and Cultural Impact of Satellite Broadcasting in Thailand", Paper presented at the *Seminar on the Social and Cultural Impact of Satellite Broadcasting in Asia*, Singapore: Asian Mass Communication Research and Information Centre.

StarTV [1992]. "Star Chinese" [publicity brochure]. Hong Kong: StarTV.

Stein, Janine [2001]. "China", *Television Asia*, July–August.

Straits Times [1993]. "Satellite TV Plans Not for the Faint-hearted". *Straits Times*, 19 December.

———— [1994]. "How Li ran StarTV", *The Straits Times*, 21 January.

Stuart, Theresa H. [1993]. "Satellite Broadcasting in the Philippines: Policies and Potentials". Paper presented at the *Seminar on the Social and Cultural Impact of Satellite Broadcasting in Asia*. Singapore: Asian Mass Communication Research and Information Centre.

Suparto, Ina Ratna Muriani [1993]. "The Social and Cultural Impact of Satellite Broadcasting in Indonesia". Paper presented at the *Seminar on the Social and Cultural Impact of Satellite Broadcasting in Asia*. Singapore: Asian Mass Communication Research and Information Centre.

Taylor, Michael [1995]. "Very Important Pearson". *Television Asia*, March.

Tele-Satellite [2002]. "SatcoDX2", *Tele-Satellite International*, June–July.

Television Asia [1994a]. "Broadcasters Shooting for Star", *Television Asia*, September.

———— [1994b]. "Overview: People's Republic of China", *Television Asia Supplement*, December.

———— [1995a]. "Shorts", *Television Asia*, March.

Television Asia [1995b]. "CCTV to Launch Global Chinese Language Service", *Television Asia*, March.

——— [1995c]. "Going Against the Grain", *Television Asia*, December.

——— [1995d]. "Surf's Up: Indonesian Television's Second Wave", *Television Asia*, October.

——— [1995e]. "The Heart Belongs to Dadi", *Television Asia*, March.

——— [1996a]. "India Prepares for the Next Wave with Insat2C" and "Preparing for the second round", *TelevisionAsia*, January

——— [1996b]. "New Radio and Television Stations for Sri Lanka", *Television Asia*, March.

——— [1996c]. "Satellite Operators", *Guide to Satellite and Cable 1996*.

——— [1997]. "CNBC Claims Penetration in Four Million Homes", *Television Asia*, January.

——— [1998a]. "And the Two Shall Become One: ABN/CNBC Merger", *Television Asia*, January.

——— [1998b]. "RPG Launches Local Cable Channel". *Television Asia*, January.

——— [1998c]. "National Geographic Channel Asia Launches". *Television Asia*, July–August.

——— [1999a]. "China's TV Industry to Change Forever", *Television Asia*, January–February.

——— [1999b]. "RCTI Launches Cable Service Indonusa", *Television Asia*, January–February.

——— [1999c]. "MTV Programming Passes 100 Millionth mark", *Television Asia*, March.

——— [1999d]. "SCTV and RTM Exhange Programmes and News", *Television Asia*, April.

——— [1999e]. "CTN Lays off Staff to Cut Costs", *Television Asia*, April.

——— [1999f]. "In brief" and "Government Claims Media Programme Benefits TV Industry", *Television Asia*, April.

——— [2001]. "Gen-X cops", *Television Asia*, March.

The Hindu [1994]. "Satellite TV: A Boom for Entertainment Industry", *The Hindu*, 14 June.

TPI [1993a]. *Company Profile*. Jakarta: Televisi Pendidikan Indonesia.

——— [1993b]. *Marketing Presentation*. Jakarta: Televisi Pendidikan Indonesia.

TVB [1994]. *Television Broadcasters Limited* (corporate brochure). Hong Kong: TVB Ltd.

——— [1995a]. "TVB International Invests in Chinese Satellite Channel for Europe" (press release, August). Hong Kong: Television Broadcasters International.

——— [1995b]. "TVBS ... the Super Channel" (press release, October). Hong Kong: Television Broadcasters Ltd.

UTV [1994]. *Synergy*. Bombay: United Television.

UTV [1996]. *UTV International* (brochure). Singapore: United Television International.

———— [2000]. *Shareholder Communication*. Mumbai: UTV Software Communications Ltd.

Verlini, Giovanni [1999]. "Regional Satellite Systems", *APT Forum 2000*, September.

Via Satellite [1994a]. "1995: The Banner Year Ahead", *Via Satellite*, January.

———— [1994b]. "Footprints over Asia: Hot Birds in the Making" and "Arabsat: Serving the Middle East", *Via Satellite*, February.

———— [1995a]. "Satellite TV in the Middle East", *Via Satellite*, March.

———— [1995b]. "Malaysia's Fast-Growing Economy: Setting the Stage for Satellite Communications", *Via Satellite*, June.

———— [1996]. "AsiaSat, KoreaSat and ChinaStar", Communications Solutions Supplement, *Via Satellite*, August.

Videoland.com [2003] "Agency Presentation", [www.videoland.com.tw/5ab/5abvl_e008.asp].

Vilanilam, John [1996]. "The Socio-Cultural Dynamics of Indian Television: From SITE to Insight to Privatisation", in David French and Michael Richards (eds), *Contemporary Television: Eastern Perspectives*. New Delhi: Sage Publications.

Vista TV [1993–94]. *TV Guide*, 24 December–2 January issue. Jakarta: Vista TV.

Vora, Swapana [1997]. "India Watch", *International Cable*, June.

Walker, Sarah [1996]. "All Shook Up", *Cable and Satellite Asia*, March–April.

Wanvari, Anil [1996a]. "A Paying Proposition", *Asian Advertising and Marketing*, 22 March.

———— [1996b]. "Southward Bound", *Cable and Satellite Asia*, May–June.

———— [1997]. "The Jewel of the East", *Asian Advertising and Marketing*, 7 March.

Weerackody, Irvin [1993]. "The Social and Cultural Impact of Satellite Broadcasting in Sri Lanka", Paper presented at the AMIC seminar, 1–3 February, Singapore.

Weinstock, Neal [1996]. "Preparing for a Chinese Century", *Asia-Pacific Broadcasting*, April.

Westbrook, John [1995]. "Taiwanese Government Pilots VOD", *Television Asia*, March.

———— [1996]. "Estee Lauder wants Stake in New Taiwan Station", *Television Asia*, March.

White, D. [1994]. "Policy and Strategy of ABC TV Broadcasting to Indonesia". Paper presented at AMIC Seminar on "The Penetration Intensity of Foreign Television Programs Through Parabolic Antenna", Jakarta.

Williams, John W. [2000]. "Mass Media in Post-Revolution Mongolia" (http://userpage.fu.berlin.de/~corff/im/Landeskunde/john.html).

Winton, Karen [1991]. "Commercial TV Shakes up Media Scene", *Asian Advertising and Marketing*, August.

Won, Woo-Hyun [1993]. "The Social and Cultural Impact of Satellite Broadcasting in Korea". Paper presented at the AMIC seminar, 1–3 February, Singapore.

Wong Lay Kim [1998]. "Malaysia: Ownership as Control", *Development Dialogue*, 2.

World Broadcast News [1993]. "Asia, Part 1", *World Broadcast News*, November.

———— [1993–94]. "International News" and "Israel: Franchise Battles". *World Broadcast News*, December–January.

———— [1994]. "Vietnam TV Switches to Thaicom2", *World Broadcast News*, June.

———— [1995]. "Singapore: Telcom Plans Test on Video-on-Demand", *World Broadcast News*, February.

ZeeTV [2000]. "Zee & Asianet: Yet another Market, Another Value Chain". Zee Network Online. [www. zeetelevision. com/zee/]

Zuberi, Nisar Ahmad [1993]. "Social and Cultural Impact of Satellite Broadcasting in Pakistan". Paper presented at the AMIC Seminar, 1–3 February, Singapore.

APPENDIX B INTERVIEW SOURCES/PRIMARY DATA

A s they were keenly aware of the issues surrounding transnational television, key decision makers in the media sector of each Asian region were interviewed as sources of primary data for this book. Most of the advertising industry representatives were drawn from among chief executives or media managers of international agencies or large domestic agencies with international affiliations. For the broadcasting industry, interviews were obtained with executives of leading domestic and transnational television broadcasters in each country and they tended to be either public relations, research or operations managers. The researchers were sought from market research firms, social research institutes and universities, while the policy makers/regulators approached were either government officials or members of broadcasting advisory bodies.

Table B.1
Distribution of Expert Interviewees

	Indian Subcontinent	Malay Archipelago	Greater China	Totals
Advertising Agencies/Marketers:				
Account	6	6	4	16
Media	9	7	5	21
Creative	2	1	–	3
Sub-total	17	14	9	40
Media Owners/Programme Producers:				
Domestic	16	17	7	40
Transnational	5	6	5	16
Sub-total	21	23	12	56
Market/Media Researchers:				
Market/Media	9	8	6	23
Academic/Social	6	8	5	19
Sub-total	15	16	11	42
Policy Makers/Opinion Ldrs:				
Government officials	4	6	5	15
Community leaders	4	5	1	10
Sub-total	8	11	6	25
Total:	**61**	**64**	**38**	**163**

INDIAN SUBCONTINENT

Advertising Agencies/Marketers [Ind 01.01–Ind 01.17]

Everest Advertising, Mumbai (Saatchi & Saatchi affiliate)
Chaitra Leo Burnett, Mumbai (Leo Burnett affiliate)
J Walter Thompson, Chennai
Hindustan Thompson Advertising, Mumbai (J. Walter Thompson affiliate)
Mudra Communications, Mumbai
Ammirati Puris Lintas, Bangalore
Lowe Lintas, Mumbai
Sobhagya Advertising, Mumbai
Euro-RSCG, Mumbai
Radeus Advertising, Mumbai
ImageAds & Communications, Mumbai
Anugrah Madison DMB&B, Chennai
TBWA/Anthem, Delhi
Ogilvy & Mather, Mumbai
Advertising Agencies Association of India, Mumbai
Hindustan Lever, Mumbai
FCB-Ulka Advertising, Bangalore

Media-Owners/Programme Producers [Ind 02.01–Ind 02.21]

Doordarshan (DD), Delhi
ZeeTV, Mumbai
Sun TV, Chennai
United Television, Mumbai
Tara Channel, Mumbai
Nimbus Communications, Delhi
Siticable, Delhi
StarTV, Mumbai
Eenadu Television
JainTV, Delhi
Discovery Channel, Delhi
Final Take Films, Mumbai
Channel 9 Gold, Mumbai
Cable Operators Federation of India, Delhi
CNN, Delhi
NDTV, Bangalore

Market/Social Researchers [Ind 03.01–Ind 03.15]

Indian Institute of Mass Communication, Delhi
Indian Institute of Management, Bangalore

Centre for Media Studies, Delhi
University of Poona, Dept. of Communication and Journalism, Pune
Tata Institute of Social Research, Delhi
Times of India Response, Mumbai
TAM Media Research, Mumbai
A and M (Advertising and Marketing) magazine, Delhi
Resource Centre for Media Education and Research, Pune
Indian Market Research Bureau (IMRB), Mumbai
IMRB, Chennai
ORG-MARG (Marketing and Research Group), Mumbai
Indian Newspaper Society, Delhi

Policy Makers/Opinion Leaders [Ind 04.01–Ind 04.08]

Indian Reserve Bank, Mumbai
Indian Space Research Agency, Ahmedabad
Frederich Egbert Stiftung (FES), Delhi
Consortium for Education Television, Delhi
Board of Censors, Delhi
Ministry of Information and Broadcasting, Delhi
DD Audience Research Unit, Delhi

MALAY ARCHIPELAGO

Advertising Agencies/Marketers [Mly 01.01–Mly 01.14]

Grafik McCann, Jakarta (McCann-Erickson affiliate)
Cabe Rawit Advertising, Jakarta
Leo Burnett, Kuala Lumpur
Perwanal Advertising, Jakarta (D'Arcy affiliate)
Matari Advertising, Jakarta (BBDO affiliate)
Ogilvy & Mather, Jakarta
Citra Lintas Indonesia, Jakarta (Lintas affiliate)
Lowe Lintas, Jakarta
Inter-Admark, Jakarta (Dentsu affiliate)
B&B Advertising, Jakarta
Sil-Ad, Jakarta
Saatchi & Saatchi, Singapore
JWT Advertising, Kuala Lumpur

Media Owners/Programme Producers [Mly 02.01–Mly 02.23]

Astro/Measat, Kuala Lumpur
RCTI, Jakarta
Anteve, Jakarta
SCTV, Jakarta

TV3, Kuala Lumpur
Indosiar Visual Mandiri, Jakarta
NTV-7, Shah Alam/Kuala Lumpur
TPI, Jakarta
Malicak/Indovision, Jakarta
Cableview/MegaTV, Kuala Lumpur
Indosat, Jakarta
Kabelvision, Jakarta
Multivisions Plus, Jakarta
Indostar, Jakarta
Prambors Radio, Jakarta
Asian Business News, Singapore
TransTV, Jakarta
StarTV Southeast Asia office, Singapore
Dunia Visitama Produksi, Jakarta (Pearsons affiliate)

Market/Social Researchers [Mly 03.01–Mly 03.16]

Survey Research Indonesia, Jakarta (AC Nielsen affiliate)
Survey Research Group, Singapore
AC Nielsen, Kuala Lumpur
Inmar Infos Sarana, Jakarta (media research firm)
Institut Technologi Mara, Kuala Lumpur
Dept of Mass Communication, University of Gajah Mada, Jogjakarta
Faculty of Communication Science, University of Padjajaran, Bandung
University of Indonesia, Depok
University of Malaya, Kuala Lumpur
Open University, Ciputat
MASTEL (Telecomunications Society)
Institute of Mass Communication Research and Development, Jakarta
Media Information Centre, Department of Information, Jakarta

Policy Makers/Opinion Leaders [Mly 04.01–Mly 04.11]

Dept of Posts, Telecoms and Tourism, Jakarta
Bureau of Information and Communication, Jakarta
Bappenas, Jakarta
Radio-Television Malaysia
Dept of Information, Jakarta
Universitas Terbuka (Open University), Ciputat
Asia-Pacific Broadcasting Union (ABU), Kuala Lumpur

GREATER CHINA

Advertising Agencies/Marketers [Chn 01.01–Chn 01.09]

Ogilvy Media Asia, Hong Kong
McCann-Erickson, Hong Kong
J. Walter Thompson, China
D'Arcy Masius Benton & Bowles, HK
DDB Needham Worldwide, Hong Kong
Leo Burnett, Hong Kong
Grey Advertising, Hong Kong
United Advertising, Taipei

Media Owners/Programme Producers [Chn 02.01–Chn 02.12]

TVB International head office, Hong Kong
Po-Hsin Multimedia, Taipei
Turner International/CNNI Far East regional office, Hong Kong
ATV head office, Hong Kong
TTV, Taipei
StarTV head office, Hong Kong
Wharf Cable head office, Hong Kong
Oriental TV, Shanghai, PRC

Market/Social Researchers [Chn 03.01–Chn 03.11]

Survey Research Group, Hong Kong
AC Nielsen, Hong Kong
Chinese University of Hong Kong
Research Asia, Hong Kong
Frank Small and Associates, Hong Kong
Survey Research Taiwan, Taipei (Nielson SRG affiliate)
World College of Journalism and Communication, Taipei
Rainmaker Industrial, Taipei (media research firm)
National Chengchih University, Taipei

Policy Makers/Opinion Leaders [Chn 04.01–Chn 04.06]

Television and Entertainment Licensing Authority, Hong Kong
Hong Kong Broadcasting Authority
Government Information Office, Taipei
Broadcast Development Fund, Taipei

The goal of this research was a comprehensive understanding of the development of transnational television on the domestic broadcasting and advertising industries in Asia. Hence the research design involved an examination of both the politico-economic and sociocultural environments of the region, with a particular focus on three regions. It aimed to observe the processes of change and identify the specific factors that mitigated or enhanced the impact of the new medium as measured largely by viewership and advertising expenditure. By design, the research sought to determine if there was consensus or diversity of opinion on the impact of the medium from the vantage points of different key players in each of the major markets targeted by transnational television. In the pursuit of these objectives, a number of data collection techniques were employed, and the reasons for their selection are explained here along with their limitations. But first, some working definitions are called for.

CLARIFYING CONCEPTS

The research for this book was concerned largely with programming and advertising on transnational television or the software of the medium, and less with the communications technology or hardware. Nonetheless there is much technical language in the field of satellite and communications, and so this section will seek to provide some basic definitions of terminology as utilised in this book. Other definitions are provided in the course of the analysis within the book's chapters and in the glossary.

Transnational versus Domestic

Transnational television is defined in this book as any broadcast service by television stations aimed deliberately at attracting an audience across national borders within a region or broadcast footprint. It is usually transmitted via satellite and sometimes re-transmitted by domestic cable, and by this definition it does not include terrestrial signals which spill over borders unintended. Generally the transnational broadcaster is not subject to regulatory controls in all the countries where its broadcast signals may be picked up, though there may be controls on its reception by viewers in those countries. The country from which the broadcast signals are uplinked to the satellite invariably attempts to regulate the channels uplinked from its territory, though the extent of control tends to vary considerably from country to country. Transnational television channels are usually owned by private commercial interests, such multinational conglomerates and media corporations, though they may also be owned by governments—often through state-owned or dominant political party-owned businesses with some foreign policy or economic agenda. Domestic television refers to any broadcast by channels owned either by governments or local corporations subject to government regulation, usually transmitted terrestrially, though sometimes via satellite in order to reach remote parts of the country. Unlike transnational television, it is aimed solely at audiences within the country, even though there is often spillover of the broadcast signal into border regions of neighbouring countries.

Satellite versus Terrestrial

It is necessary that a clear distinction be made in this book between terrestrial and satellite broadcasting. Terrestrial television is transmitted by microwave from broadcast antennae mounted on high geographical terrain or man-made structures to a local area within its line-of-sight, that is, between the antenna and the horizon. Satellite transmission is able to overcome the physical limitations of terrestrial microwave transmission because every satellite in geosynchronous orbit has line-of-sight access up to a fixed third of the world's surface that constitutes its footprint. Thus a communications satellite can receive and/or transmit signals from and to an unlimited number of earth stations anywhere within the satellite footprint, with the costs being irrespective of distance. With the advent of direct-broadcast satellites (DBS), it is now possible for such satellites to broadcast direct-to-home (DTH), without needing retransmission terrestrially via microwave or cable; only a satellite dish of small aperture is required for each home.

While geostationary satellites can and are used for telephony, meteorology, navigation, land surveying and a host of other uses, commercial television broadcasting are their major use today—whether for domestic or transnational consumption. It is a fallacy to equate transnational television with satellite transmission, and domestic television with terrestrial transmission because each broadcast medium can use either form of transmission technology. In other words, domestic television channels may use satellite transmission exclusively or in conjunction with terrestrial transmission, as those in Indonesia, India and China have chosen to do in order to reach their citizens over a wider geographical area. On the other hand, transnational television channels may use terrestrial re-transmission in order to reach audiences in other countries across borders whose governments may not permit direct access to satellite signals. It is then intentionality of transborder reach across a region or continent which is the defining characteristic of transnational television which this book primarily investigates.

While cognisant of the innumerable permutations of television channels and media technology in these developing countries within Asia, the focus of this book is on transnational television broadcasting. StarTV and the other transnational television channels investigated in this research are transmitted primarily via satellite, though increasingly they are being made available in conjunction with domestic broadcasters in Asia and beyond, either via microwave transmission, direct-to-home technology or local cable networks. But it is the transnational reach of these channels across the Asia region that primarily concerned this book.

Cable and Pay-TV

Although cable television may be an alternative and thus competitor to satellite television, they are often interdependent. Cable television can be delivered by various distribution systems such as coaxial cable, fibre optic cable, satellite master antennae television systems and multichannel multipoint delivery systems. In other words, some cable television is not delivered by cable at all! The major advantage of cable television is the high channel capacity of coaxial cable and especially of the newer fibre optic cables. Fibre optic cables also have the capacity of delivering telephone, computer as well as video transmissions, contributing to convergence of communications technologies. A major disadvantage of cable is that it is a capital intensive technology and one that is not suitable for highly dispersed populated regions, unlike satellite television which is more cost effective in that circumstance.

Wireless cable, or multichannel multipoint delivery system (MMDS) as it is commonly known, is an alternative to traditional cable which is expensive in urbanised areas that require underground installation of cables. Using microwave signals it transmits from a tower or tall building to a limited local area, and it can be adversely affected by terrain, tall buildings and the weather. Cable television is often used to relay programming downlinked by an earth station or large satellite television receive-only (TVRO) dish. However, it might be undermined by direct broadcast satellites (DBS) which are high-powered satellites capable of delivering signals to TVRO dishes the size of a pizza pan. Both cable and satellite television can be encoded to grant access only to those who pay for the service, and in those cases is known also as pay-TV or subscription television.

Asia and its Regions

For the purposes of this book, Asia is described as encompassing the countries traditionally grouped under South Asia, Northeast Asia, and Southeast Asia, from which countries for the three regional case studies are drawn. Excluded are the countries of Central Asia which were previously part of the former USSR, and as such conventionally if erroneously grouped with Europe. More recently this subregion has come under the political, economic and cultural influence of Iran and Turkey, both seeking to win the hearts and minds of its people, via satellite television no less. Turkey which forms the western most border of Asia has in recent years sought incorporation into the European Union. Only cursorily treated is West Asia, traditionally referred to as the Middle East and often associated with a culturally similar Arabic region which extends across North Africa. Another subregion neglected is Australasia and Oceania, and as such satellites and television services from Australia and New Zealand which dominate the region, for instance, are classified as foreign to the Asian continent. The many culturally diverse and small island nations in Oceania are considered too obscure a market to most major transnational broadcasters.

When used in this book the term "continent" therefore generally refers to Asia as defined above, while the term "region" refers to countries traditionally grouped by geographic proximity or cultural similarity such as Southeast Asia, South Asia or Northeast Asia. "Subregion" refers to entities within countries which are usually referred to either geographically such as southern Indian states, by the state or province such as Guangzhou and its Cantonese speaking siblings of Hong Kong and Macau, or by their ethno-linguistic identity such as Javanese, some of which may cross provincial or national borders. Diasporic ethnic communities, which exist across countries, regions and continents, are usually defined in this book as in most statistics by their original nationality and in the terms most commonly used namely non-resident Indians (NRIs), overseas Chinese or Indonesian migrants.

The countries primarily researched for this book, India, Pakistan, Indonesia, Malaysia, Taiwan and China are classified as developing countries, though sometimes designated under the subcategory of newly industrialising countries (NICs) or big emerging markets (BEMs), given their spurts of rapid economic growth. Definitions of development, and therefore of developing or Third World versus developed, First World or western countries have been implicit in the literature review of globalisation of the polity and economy in Chapter Two. Further definitions of terminology used in this research are to be found in the glossary.

International and Global

Though terms such as international, multinational, transnational and global are not strictly synonymous, they are often used interchangeably of strategies and organisations in the literature referred to, and by respondents interviewed for this research. This book will endeavour to use the terms in the way they are most commonly used. The terms "international" is used for the general all-inclusive business concept and of advertising agencies which operate around the world. The term "multinational" is used of corporations which operate in a number of countries and which usually utilise somewhat modified business strategies in each, leading to it being called a "multidomestic" strategy. The term "global" is used of corporations which straddle the whole world using strategies which are virtually uniform worldwide, as is sometimes the case of global broadcasters. Finally the term "transnational" is generally used in this book in lieu of the term 'transborder' of broadcasting which crosses borders. The former term is often used in academic literature also of corporations which utilise or adapt successful strategies from one international market in which it operates to another where it is suitable. Such practices are certainly true of the crossborder broadcasters that the research in question investigates. The preferred meanings of these terms are made clearer through their extensive and consistent utilisation within this book.

MULTIMETHOD APPROACH

The choice of a qualitative approach was determined largely by the fact that this research on transnational television was exploratory, the variables unknown and a theory lacking (Creswell 1994: 21). This study adopted a quasi-ethnographic methodology since it involved the author visiting the country, interviewing knowledgeable persons at their workplaces, observing locally available television, collecting documents and audio-visual samples and so on. According to Kellehear (1993: 21), the ethnographic-inductive research design is "less a method than an approach to analysing and portraying a social system from an "insider's point of view". Thus in such research designs the literature review is usually not followed by a theoretical framework but ethnographic description as the researcher endeavours to enter with empathy the social world being researched. This research attempts to test the degree to which there an on-site consensus of informed opinion on the impact of transnational television in each country studied, rather than imposing an "outsider" perspective.

As an exploratory study this research needed to be multimethod, without being over ambitious, allowing the strengths and weaknesses of each method to compensate for those of others. As Brewer and Hunter (1989) advise, some combination of ethnographic fieldwork, audience surveys, experimental studies and non-reactive research gives greater credibility and validity to the results through triangulated comparisons. Since the objective of this research was to obtain a multifaceted perspective on the impact of transnational satellite television on domestic broadcasting industries, a number of data sources and collection techniques were employed. Qualitative case studies are typically heuristic, helping to construct theories inductively in a pioneering area of application where theory is lacking rather than testing established theories deductively (Merriam 1988: 57–59). The end result of this research has been three regional and comparative case studies on the development of transnational television in Asia which incorporate primary data from interviews and content analysis, secondary data from government and industry, as well as media research done by others in the countries.

As is consistent with the dominant inductive paradigm that qualitative research adopts, models are somewhat disdained as potentially constraining factors, particularly early in the process. Although there was some flexibility of design at the pilot study stage, given the time and financial constraints for the fieldwork in three regions and the need for comparability across them, a working model based on the research questions above was adopted prior to the actual fieldwork. Miles and Huberman (1994) recommended making thoughtful trade offs between tight, pre-structured and loose, inductive research designs, depending on the nature of the problem being investigated, constraints of time, comparability of cases, the issue of data overload, and so on. This research on transnational television leans towards being structured, in being confined to impact of the new medium on domestic broadcasting and advertising industries in specific national markets in Asia. All the same it was intended that this research arrive at an inductively-derived analytical framework for understanding the corresponding process of globalisation elsewhere in the developing world.

The research design described in this section makes judicious use of methodologies endorsed by various theoretical schools in media research in arriving at an integrated multimethod approach suitable for investigating the development of transnational television in Asia. Such research plans need to be tempered by the realities of fieldwork especially carried out in developing countries overseas that have had implications for subsequent processes of analysis, all of which took about five years. Thus the following section chronicles the actual experience of data collection in the field and data analysis back at the home base, then in Australia, along with explanations of the challenges encountered and the rationale for the solutions chosen.

FIELDWORK AND ANALYSIS

This study focuses on the advent of transnational television and developments in its first five years. While some data was collected before and after the fieldwork, the research was based primarily "snap shots" of the situation in 1994–95 and then five years later in 1999–2000, with updates from secondary data sources for the periods in between and since. Given the multimethod approach adopted to facilitate a comprehensive coverage of the research topic, the multisite and comparative and historical nature of the research, the process of data collection, preparation and analysis was spread over the 1990s. The preliminary fieldwork was conducted in late 1992, with a second phase of fieldwork between early 1994 and late 1995, when StarTV was the pioneering broadcaster of transnational television and unchallenged market leader, allowing sufficient time to evaluate its impact prior to the arrival of other major satellite broadcasters. More recent fieldwork was conducted in 1999–2001 approximately eight years after the inauguration of transnational television in Asia.

The book was finally written during a sabbatical in 2002–2003 incorporating additional secondary data collected in those years on continuing developments in the Asian broadcasting industry. The countries researched represent, to some extent, major sociocultural and politico-economic regions under the footprint of StarTV, namely Southeast Asia, Northeast Asia and South Asia. Indonesia was selected as it had a history of using satellite television domestically and had also maintained an open sky policy to foreign broadcasts, while Malaysia was chosen for having taken a diametrically different approach initially. Hong Kong was selected because it was the headquarters of StarTV, the point from which the broadcasts are uplinked, and where regional advertising decisions are made for much of East Asia. Along with Taiwan it was used to as a base to gather data on Greater China since it would have been difficult, if not almost impossible, to conduct this research within the Peoples' Republic of China (PRC) for cultural and political reasons. Finally, India was selected as a country in which satellite television was officially restricted and yet widely watched, while Pakistan was chosen for being the country in the region which officially embraced the new medium but whose own broadcasts did not gain a following regionally. Of all the

South Asian countries, India was the most accessible politically as well as culturally to the researcher. More importantly, all these countries were selected because they represented key markets targeted by most transnational television broadcasters operating in Asia.

DECISION MAKER INTERVIEWS

As appropriate and almost indispensable in exploratory research, interviews were conducted with key personnel involved in the cultural industries of three countries in Asia under the footprint of StarTV, primarily Indonesia and Malaysia (from Southeast Asia), India (from South Asia) and Hong Kong, and Taiwan (from Northeast Asia). A sample of executives stratified by advertising agencies, broadcast media, research organisations and regulatory bodies was necessary in each country because this would provide adequate representation by these homogeneous subsets to enhance accuracy of perception of the variables under investigation (Babbie 1992: 215–218). Potential interviewees in each of these subsets were identified through professional contacts as well as through bibliographic sources, and in most cases were approached in advance regarding participation. Within each strata or organisational subset, the sampling was purposive as each interviewee was selected on the judgement that he or she would be a key informant, able to provide specialist or professional insight into the impact of transnational television via satellite on the national market in general, and its media industries in particular (Kinnear and Taylor 1996: 398).

As the research was exploratory, the interviews were semi-structured in form. Issues raised by the researcher were based on the research questions listed in Chapter One, beginning with those most relevant to the expertise of the interviewee in question. The interviews were also an iterative process in that responses of previous interviewees were raised anonymously with subsequent interviewees for their comment. In this manner, both flexibility and consistency across the interviews of decision makers from different organisations and with diverse roles in related industries could be attained (Patton 1990). The interviews were not audiotaped as the author believed that this would significantly affect the responses as some of the issues discussed were either politically or commercially sensitive or both, in most of the countries researched. With the permission of the interviewees, brief notes were taken of their comments using a secretarial notepad, explaining that it was to assist in recalling their opinions and reassuring that they would not be identified individually but that their views would be aggregated qualitatively. The interviews were a combination of objective information giving and subjective opinion, perception and speculation, and the line between these was not always clear. Even where there had to be some speculation, given the dearth of hard data, these opinions or estimates were the basis on which these executives, officials and researchers carried out their professional responsibilities, and were thus of no less import (Kinnear and Taylor 1996: 399).

The interview data was analysed utilising the NUD•IST software package which allows the development of a framework for qualitative analysis incorporating these main functions (Richards and Richards 1993). The interviewee sources are not identified in this book except by an alpha-numeric code for reasons of confidentiality. Their region of origin is identified by the initials "Ind" for Indian subcontinent, "Mly" for Malay Archipelago and "Chn" for Greater China, and their professional status by the initial digits of "01" for advertising agency staff, "02" for broadcasters, "03" for researchers and "04" for policy makers. More specific data on their organisational affiliations and job designations are provided in Appendix B, in a way that does not allow identification of the respondents. Where an opinion was expressed repeatedly, only one or two interviewees were accredited with it, usually the ones who expressed it best. Consensus has yet to be achieved on how to analyse and present semi-structured interview data so as to reveal its richness, while being succinct and without undue interpreter influence (Fontana and Frey 1994).

GOVERNMENT/INDUSTRY DATA

In order to increase the validity and generalisability of the interview data, a wide range of secondary data was collected. The interviewees were asked for secondary sources of data that they may have access to, such as audience research, demographic data, annual reports, corporate brochures, clippings files. Additional documents were collected from a variety of sources within the country. Extensive bibliographic searches in the region were conducted at the Asian Media, Information and Communication Centre (AMIC), Chinese University of Hong Kong, and Indian Institute of Mass Communication (IIMC) libraries, among others. This effort uncovered books and reports published in each country, sometimes in native languages, which were often not known or available outside the country or region, and relevant sections were photocopied at libraries or the books purchased through local bookshops and publishers. To some extent this procedure of utilising as multiple sources of information and publication overcomes the problem of bias towards literature and data more easily accessible to the researchers at their home base which Cooper (1984) cautions against.

These secondary data were collected both through published or archival sources as well as through the in-house resources of advertising and broadcasting executives, research organisations and government officials. Some research on transnational television had been done at Asian universities or research institutes, usually in the form of consultancy reports for the government in conjunction with overseas aid agencies. Wherever possible, access to or purchase of these documents was sought. Surveys of audiences done by public service organisations often use national government staff accompanied by local officials which could lead to response bias, but often there is no other way to conduct field research in many countries in Asia, given their political climate. Wherever possible, research conducted by nationals of the countries investigated were evaluated for partial incorporation in this book, thus overcoming any criticism of foreigner bias even though this researcher is originally from Asia. In any case, it was not feasible logistically for this single researcher to mount extensive audience research in countries and markets researched.

Some research on transnational television has also been done by commercial entities but this tends to be proprietary information, only limited parts of which were revealed to this researcher. Due to commercial sensitivities these were not always made available or those released were reasonably out-of-date though occasionally, as in the case of India, some such data was published in a national newspaper. Some data was obtained only after the researcher was able to assure respondents that the process of academic research meant publication of the book some years in the future, thus rendering the proprietary data provided quite valueless commercially. By stating in writing ahead of the interview that the research was for academic research purposes and not for any funded consultancy, this researcher found most respondents cooperative in providing secondary data, referrals, and other forms of practical assistance. Audience ratings reports were sought through the negotiated cooperation of media owners and/or media research organisations as a measure of the viewership for each medium and of advertiser interest. Whenever a television broadcaster was not prepared to make ratings data available to researchers and advertising agencies alike, an inference that could be drawn quite reasonably was that the data was not favourable towards their own channel.

Since such articles and reports were extensively utilised as secondary data for this research, they were not incorporated into the bibliography but referenced separately as secondary data in Appendix A, as were the details of the interview sources in Appendix B. To assist in locating their full references, both secondary data sources as well as primary data such as the interviews, are referred in the text of this book, exclusively in the case study chapters, using square brackets to indicate that their references are to be found in the appropriate appendices rather than in the bibliography. In a few cases where journal articles and book chapters are alluded to also in the literature review, methodology and chapters or vice versa, there are references in both locations. By weaving data from intermedia, secondary sources and interviews to build comprehensive country case histories within the three regions, a serious attempt was made to reflect on-site perceptions in Asia of the advent and development of transnational television.

Satellite Platforms

Apstar/Galaxy:	www.apstar.com/
AsiaSat:	www.asiasat.com.hk
Astra:	www.astra.lu
Inmarsat:	www.inmarsat.org
Intelsat:	www.intelsat.int
Measat/Binariang:	www.measat.com.my
Optus Communications:	www.optus.net
PanAmSat:	www.panamsat.com
SingTel:	www.singtel.com
Shinawatra/Thaicom:	www.thaicom.net

Footprint Maps

Geo-Orbit:	www.geo-orbit.org/easthemipgs/ fcrackp.html
Measat2:	www.measat.com.my/footprint2.html
SatcoDX:	www.satcodx-op.com/
SeaTel:	www.seatel.com/footprints/
ISatAsia:	www.isatasia.com/cmeng.html

Transnational Broadcasters

ABC Asia Pacific:	www.abcasiapacific.com
BBC World Asia:	www.webhk.com/bbc
China Entertainment TV:	www.cetv.com
CNBC Asia:	www.cnbcasia.com.sg
CNN International:	www.turner-asia.com
Channel News Asia:	www.channelnewsasia.com
Channel V:	www.channelv.com
Chinese Television Network:	www.ctn.net
Deutsche Welle:	www.dwelle.de
Discovery Channel Asia:	www.discovery.com
ESPN Star Sports:	www.espnstar.com
MTV Network Asia:	www.mtvasia.com

NHK International: www.nhk.org.jp
Phoenix Satellite Channel: www.phoenixtv.com
STAR TV: www.startv.com
Sony Entertainment TV: www.setindia.com
ZeeTV Network: www.zeetelevision.com

Domestic Broadcasters

Asia Television (ATV):   www.atv.com.hk
China Central TV (CCTV):   www.cctv.com
Doordarshan India (DD):   www.ddindia.net
Formosa TV (Taiwan):   www.ftv.com.tw
Indosiar (Indonesia):   www.indosiar.com
Media Corp of Singapore: www.mediacorp.com.sg
MetroTV (Indonesia):   www.metrotvnews.com
Munhwa Brdcst Corpn (Korea):   www.mbc.co.kr
Oriental TV (China):   www.orientaltv.com
Radio TV Hong Kong: www.rthk.org.hk
Radio Television Malaysia: www.asiaconnect.com.my/rtm.net
RCTI (Indonesia):   www.rcti.co.id
SCTV (Indonesia):   www.sctv.co.id
Shanghai TV (China):   www.stv.sh.cn
TPI (Indonesia):   www.tpi.co.id
Taiwan TV Enterprise: www.ttv.com.tw
TV3 (Malaysia):   www.tv3.com.my
TV Corporation of Singapore: www.tcs.com.sg
TVB (Hong Kong):   www.tvb.com.hk
TV New Zealand: www.tvnz.co.nz

Cable/Pay-TV Networks

ABS-CBN (Philippines):   www.abs-cbn.com
Asian Television (Canada):   www.aci.on.ca/AsianTvnet
Astro (Malaysia):   www.astro.com.my
Chinese TV Service (Taiwan):   www.cts.com.tw
Hong Kong Cable/Wharf: www.cabletv.com.hk
Indovision (Indonesia):   www.indovision.co.id
ITV (Thailand):   www.itv.co.th
JET TV (Japan):   www.jettv.com
Kabelvision (Indonesia):   www.onklik.com/ontv
MegaTV (Malaysia):   www.megatv.com.my
Optus Vision (Australia)   www.optus.net.au
Philippines Cable: www.geocities.com/televisioncity/
                                           studio/2608
Singapore Cablevision: www.scv.com.sg

Advertising Agencies

Euro RSCG Advertising:	www.eurorscg.com
J Walter Thomson:	www.jwtworld.com
Leo Burnett:	www.leoburnett.com
Lowe Lintas Indonesia:	www.lowelintas.co.id/
McCann Erickson:	www.mccann.com
Mudra Advertising:	www.mudra.com
Ogilvy & Mather:	www.ogilvy.com
Saatchi & Saatchi:	www.saatchi-saatchi.com

Regulatory/Policy Bodies

Government Information Office (Taiwan):	www.gio.gov.tw
Ministry of Information and Broadcasting (India):	http://mib.nic.in/
State Administration of Radio, Film and Television (China):	www.chinaembassy.org.in/eng/nt/jyjs/t61109.htm
Television and Entertainment Licencing Authority (Hong Kong):	www.info.gov.hk/tela

Industry Resources

ACNielsen:	asiapacific.acnielsen.com.au/home.asp
Broadcast & Broadband Asia:	http://web.singnet.com.sg/~meson/aboutus.html
Cable Quest:	www.cable-quest.com/
China Marketers' Guide:	www.shanghai-ed.com/j-market.htm
Communications Technology:	www.cabletoday.com
The Economic Times, India:	http://economictimes.indiatimes.com/
Indiantelevision.com:	www.indiantelevision.com
Television Asia:	www.tvasia.com.sg/homepage.html
Transnational Broadcasting Studies:	www.tbsjournal.com
Via Satellite:	www.omeda.com/vs/

Academic Resources

Asian Media Information and Communications Centre:	www.amic.org.sg
Asian Journal of Communications:	www.amic.org.sg/ajcv11n2.html
Centre for Media Studies:	www.cmsindia.org

Continuum:	www.cowan.edu.au/pa/continuum/
Journal of International Communications:	www.mucic.mq.edu.au/JIC/
Media, Culture and Society:	www.sagepub.co.uk/journals/details/ j0088.html
Media Development:	www.wacc.org.uk/publications/md/ directory.html
Institute for Media and Communications Management:	www.mcm.unisg.ch

ABN:	Asian Business News, the first Asiawide satellite business news service, owned by a consortium of foreign and regional news corporations; merged with CNBC.
AC Nielsen:	Global market research company which monitors television ratings and advertising expenditure, formerly known as Survey Research Group in Asia.
Adspend:	Expenditure by marketers on various advertising media, which is a major consituent of agency "billings" which include creative development and production charges.
Ad agency:	Advertising agency, a firm specialising in advertising services such as creative production of television and print advertisements, selecting and buying media time and space, which works on behalf of a number of marketing organisations.
AMIC:	Asian Media, Information and Communications Centre, a non-governmental research and consultancy organisation based in Singapore.
AMCB:	Monthly media industry news bulletin produced by AMIC for its members.
APTC and APTC&S:	Asia Pacific Television: Channels and Asia Pacific Television: Cable and Satellite, annual reference guides to the media industry in the region.
ASEAN:	Association of South East Asian Nations comprising initially the non-communist countries of Malaysia, Indonesia, Thailand, Singapore, Philippines and Brunei, and later expanding to include the countries of IndoChina such as Vietnam, Myanmar (Burma), Cambodia and Laos; proposing in future to act as a free trade area, Asean FTA or AFTA.
Asian A&M:	Asian Advertising and Marketing, leading regional bi-monthly magazine for practitioners, which later became *Adweek Asia*.

Asianet:	A commercial television service via satellite in Malayalam serving the dominant ethnic group of the southern Indian state of Kerala as well as expatriates from there in West Asia.
ATV:	Asia Television, a Hong Kong-based commercial television station.
ATVI:	Australia Television International, the original name of the satellite television channel of the ABC broadcasting to Southeast Asia, which now prefers to be known simply as Australia Television to differentiate it from the Hong Kong broadcaster immediately above. Now known as ABC Asia Pacific.
AWSJ:	Asian Wall Street Journal, regional edition of the finance/business newspaper.
Beam:	Signals from a satellite aimed at a particular area on the earth; broad beams covering almost a third of the earth's surface and spot beams focussing on a small area. See also "footprint".
BEMs:	Big emerging markets, a term used to characterise countries such as India, Brazil, China, Poland, etc., which have belatedly adopted free market policies and are anticipated to be significant engines of economic growth in their regions.
Bollywood:	Colloquailism for the prodigious Indian movie industry based in Bombay, hence the term is a condensation of "Bombay-Hollywood".
BPS:	Acronym in Bahasa Indonesia for the Central Bureau of Statistics (Biro Pusat Statistik), which conducts census.
Broadband cable:	Usually in the form of fiber optics technology which can carry multiple communications and high speed, including television, telephony, video-on-demand, e-commerce and the Internet, and thus enabling bi-directionality and interactivity between service provider and consumer.
Cable television:	A system of delivering television channels from a number of terrestrial or satellite sources via underground or overhead cable to subscriber homes.
Canto-pop:	Popular or rock music composed in or translated into Cantonese from English, though often used generically of pop music in other Chinese dialects.

C-band:	A frequency band, around 4–6 Ghz, allocated for the transmission of satellite signals, but prone to interference from other terrestrial services using microwave transmission.
CATV:	Traditionally standing for "community access television" but currently used to refer to any cable-delivered television.
CCTV:	China Central Television, the central government-owned network in PRChina which broadcasts nationwide and increasingly regionally.
CEO:	Chief Executive Officer of an organisation or corporation, though in Asia variously called managing director, president-director, general manager or president.
CETV:	China Entertainment Television, a commercial satellite broadcaster based in Hong Kong noted for its "no sex, no violence, no news" programming policy to gain acceptance with authorities in the Peoples' Republic of China.
CTN:	An all-Chinese all-news satellite service headquartered in Hong Kong, owned by interests there and in Taiwan, and serving the whole Greater China region.
CTS:	China Television Service, a Taiwanese terrestrial broadcaster, owned by the Taiwan ROC army.
CTV:	China Television Company, a Taiwanese terrestrial broadcaster, owned by the ruling KMT party.
CNN:	Cable News Network, a global news network established by the US-based Turner Broadcasting Network which has since merged with the AOL (America On-Line) Time Warner media conglomerate.
Channel providers:	Often cable systems which compile channels for their subscribers out of other terrestrial and satellite channels, domestic or transnational, and from programme providers.
Critical theory:	Political economy perspective exemplified by the thinkers of the pre-Second World War "Frankfurt School".
Crore:	Ten million (or one hundred lakhs), often used in India, usually to quantify money in rupees without having to string together numerous zeros.

Cultural imperialism:	Often subtle imposition of a culture by a dominant economic and political power on other nations in support of its interests.
DBS, DTH or DTU:	Direct broadcast satellites, direct-to-home or direct-to-you satellite transmissions for which homes need use only a small satellite dish to receive the television signal and not have to go through a cable/MMDS service.
DD:	Doordarshan, the Indian public television broadcaster which accepts advertising.
DD-ARU:	Audience Research Unit of Doordarshan, which monitors broadcasting and advertising in India.
Developed countries/ economies:	See First World
Developing countries/ economies:	See Third World
Digital cable:	Often an optional service by broadcasters that encodes transmission to produce better reception of sound and pictures, arguably of "CD quality" or "cinema quality".
Digital compression:	Technology using binary numbers to convey information; in satellite television it enables transmission of multiple channels from a single transponder with improved sound and picture quality and interactive services.
Downlink:	Process of obtaining television signals transmitted from a satellite transponder via its beam.
DPI:	Acronym in Bahasa Indonesia for the Ministry of Information (Departemen Penerangan Indonesia), which regulates broadcasting.
E-commerce:	The marketing and sales of products and services via the worldwide web or Internet either as a supplementary channel to a "bricks-and-mortar" business or solely as a "clicks-and-views" one.
Encryption:	Scrambling of television signals to allow reception only by paying subscribers using a decoder.
EL-TV:	An Indian pay-TV channel available via satellite, a joint-venture of ZeeTV and its affiliate StarTV.
ESPN:	Entertainment and Sports Program Network, a US-based satellite channel now in strategic alliance with StarTV in Asia.
EU:	European Union, a regional economic and political union comprising countries of Western

Europe and increasingly some of the transitional economies of Eastern Europe; previously known as the European Community (EC) and European Common Market (ECM).

FEER: *Far East Economic Review*, a leading political and business newsmagazine in East Asia, comparable to *The Economist*.

First World: Refers to the industrialised economies or developed countries of North America, Western Europe, Australasia and often Japan; sometimes collectively, if inaccurately, referred to as the "North" or "West".

Footprint: The area on the earth's surface covered by signals from one or more beams from the satellite's transponder.

Fibre optic cable: A fine glass fiber through which digitally-encoded laser light is passed, capable for carrying about 10 times the capacity of the older coaxial cable.

GATT: General Agreement on Tariffs and Trade, which governed international trade through rounds of negotiation; superceded by the World Trade Organisation (WTO).

Geostationary orbit: A satellite placed at 35,800 km about the equator, known as the Clarke Belt, would have an orbital speed equal to that of the world's rotation. Hence it is also known as geosynchronous orbit, though satellites need occasional assistance from rocket propulsion to remain perfectly stationary.

GIO: Government Information Office in Taiwan/ROC which regulates broadcasting.

HBO: Home Box Office, a US-owned channel offering largely Hollywood movies on satellite/cable television via subscription.

HDTV: High-definition television using digital technology to provide better resolution and picture clarity.

Head-end: A central facility where television signals from diverse sources are received, processed, often encrypted and even converted into new channels for re-transmission by local cable networks.

HK: Common acronym for Hong Kong, the British colony returned to China's sovereignty in 1997 and now a Special Administrative Region (SAR) of the PRC under the "one country, two systems" political-economic policy.

HK$:   The Hong Kong dollar; pegged at about HK$8 to the US$, and hence relatively stable.

Homes passed: All the homes in the community that are passed by the cable network and could conceivably connect to it on subscription.

HTA: Hindustan Thompson Advertising, the Indian affiliate of the international advertisement agency J Walter Thompson (JWT). In the early 2000s, after five decades, it reverted to using the latter name.

Hybridity: Characteristic of new composite cultures formed out of the fusion of two different cultures, often one "Western/Occidental" and the other "Eastern/Oriental".

IGOs: Intergovernmental organisations, which include Intelsat, the UN and its agencies, WTO, NATO, ASEAN and so on.

IMF: International Monetary Fund, closely affiliated to the World Bank, and both funded largely by the US and to a lesser extent other Western governments.

IMRB: Indian Media Research Bureau, which compiles television ratings in India, now affiliated with the global media/market research firm AC Neilsen.

Intelsat: International Telecommunication Satellite Organisation, a consortium of governments to share satellite technology, which makes transponders on its own satellites available to developing countries on concessionary terms.

Interactive services: Enables subscribers to use the television to shop, bank, make travel arrangements, play games, etc., independently or in conjunction with television programmes.

Internet: Is another definition really necessary for something so prevalent that every reader of this book would be personally acquainted and conversant with?!

ITU: International Telecommunications Union, regulatory body for transborder telecommunications, whether terrestrial or satellite, which seeks to allocate orbital slots on a national basis equitably, without regard to each nation's ability to utilise the slots immediately.

JWT:	A major US-based international advertising agency operating in Asia, now part of the British-owned mega-agency group WPP (originally standing for Wire and Paper Products!).
Ku-band:	A frequency band, around 11–15 Ghz, allocated for the transmission of satellite signals potentially direct-to-home, and free of interference from microwave transmissions but reception is affected by weather such as rain.
Lakhs:	One hundred thousand, often used in India to quantify currency in rupees.
LDCs:	Less/Least Developed Countries, sometimes used as a synonym for developing or Third World countries in general, but usually to refer to a subset of them which have been even slower at achieving social and economic development.
MIB:	Ministry of Information and Broadcasting, India which regulates telecommunications and broadcasting, including cable and satellite television.
Microwave transmission:	High-capacity signals utilised for terrestrial re-transmission of television broadcasts.
MMDS:	Multichannel Multipoint Distribution System, a cable or microwave system transmitting TV channels to households within a limited area.
MNCs:	Multinational corporations or businesses whose operations span a number of countries; sometimes referred to by the UN as transnational corporations (TNCs) or by others as global corporations though these terms are not strictly synonymous.
MRFT:	Ministry of Radio Film and Television in China (PRC), which regulates broadcasting, subsequently renamed SARFT.
MSO:	Multiple System Operator, a company owning more than one cable system and providing hardware, channels, programme production, internet services, VOD, etc.
NAM:	Non-Aligned Movement, a group of Third World nations which sought to be independent of the parties in the Cold War, particularly the US and USSR; not to be confused with American colloquial abbreviation of Vietnam.
News Corporation:	One of the leading global media conglomerates, controlled by the family of Rupert Murdoch;

	of Australian-origin but involved in media industry on most continents.
NGOs:	Non-governmental organisations, which include worldwide bodies such as Greenpeace, International Red Cross, Amnesty International, Medecins Sans Frontieres, Intermediate Technology Group, World Wildlife Fund and the like.
NICs:	Newly Industrialising Countries or a subset of developing/Third World countries that have been successful at achieving rapid economic development. Those in East Asia also referred to as "Tiger Economies".
NICAM:	Near Instantaneously Compounded Audio Multiplex, an innovation allowing television viewers choice of multilingual sound tracks in digital stereo.
NIEO:	New International Economic Order, proposed by Third World countries under the auspices of UNCTAD and the United Nations, and largely ignored by the First World in favour of GATT and the WTO.
NT:	New Taiwan dollar; at the time of the research fieldwork in the 1990s worth about NT27 to the US$.
NTSC:	The US colour transmission standard used in a number of countries, disparaging called "Never The Same Colour" by those who prefer the technically superior European PAL standard.
NWICO:	New World Information and Communication Order, proposed by Third World countries under the auspices of UNESCO and the UN in the 1970s and 1980s.
O&M:	Ogilvy and Mather, a leading MNC advertising agency with offices throughout Asia, now part of the mega-agency group WPP.
Orbits:	Equatorial, polar or inclined paths around the earth in which satellites are placed and which could be either circular or elliptical.
Orbital slot:	Point in the Clarke Belt above the equator where geostationary satellites are "parked" and designated by geographical coordinates relative to the earth.

PAL:	A superior color transmission system developed in Germany and the standard for television in most of Western Europe, Latin America and Asia.
Pay-TV:	Cable or satellite channels offered to households or businesses for a subscription fee; usually providing superior programming to that available free-to-air and without interruptions by advertisement breaks.
Political economy:	Theoretical stance that is a critique of the ownership and organisation of the economy, including the media-communications industry, drawing on its Marxist roots.
Post-modernity:	The fluid, fragmented social condition currently in the developed world characterised by lack of objective standards and overarching structures, affecting all forms of culture from art, literature, music, architecture and media.
Programme providers:	Often film/video production houses and sometimes media brokers who trade programming to television channels in return for advertising time.
PRC:	Peoples' Republic of China, communist-led nation of mainland China.
PPPI:	Acronym in Bahasa Indonesia for the Indonesian Association of Advertising Agencies, which produces comprehensive data on advertising and media.
Region:	Used in this book to refer to parts of the continent of Asia, such as South Asia, Greater China, West Asia and Malay Archipelago.
Rmb:	Renminbi, the PRC currency; at the time of research fieldwork in the 1990s worth about Rmb 8 to the US$.
RCTI:	Rajawali Citra Televisi Indonesia, a dominant Indonesian commercial domestic broadcaster.
ROC:	Republic of China, the pre-1947 anti-communist government of China; in exile, based in Taiwan, though claiming sovereignty over mainland China as well till the 1980s.
Rp:	Rupiah, the Indonesia currency; at the time of the research fieldwork in the mid-1990s worth about Rp 2,200 to the US$, but by the early 2000s, worth about Rp 8,000 and fluctuating.

Rs: Rupees, the Indian currency; at the time of the research fieldwork in the 1990s worth about Rs 35–40 to the US$.

RTM: The Malaysian public broadcaster of radio and television, which accepts advertising.

SARFT: State Administration of Radio, Film and Television in China (PRC), which regulates broadcasting, formerly MRFT.

Satellite: An artificial object placed in space and moving in orbit around a planet relaying telecommunications and television signals.

Satellite dishes: Dish-shaped antennae which can receive television signals from satellites but not transmit them; known variously as satellite dishes, TVRO (TV receive-only) antennae, parabolic antennae, and simply parabolas (in Indonesia).

Satellite television: Transmission of television programming via the use of satellites which may be directed either primarily at a domestic market or a transnational one.

SCMP: *South China Morning Post*, a respected English language newspaper published in Hong Kong.

SCTV: Surya Citra TeleVisi, the second Indonesian commercial television domestic broadcaster to be established.

SECAM: French improvement on the NTSC colour broadcasting system, used largely in Eastern Europe, Francophone Africa and the CIS (ex-USSR).

Second World: Usually refers to the former planned economies of the USSR and Eastern Europe and often included their satellites such as Cuba, Angola and Vietnam. Previously collectively referred to as the "Eastern Bloc" or "East" in contrast to the "West". See also Transitional Economies.

SMATV: Satellite master antennae television systems, where one TVRO dish feeds a number of television sets inside an apartment block, office building or hotel.

Smart card: A key that allows only authorised subscribers to unscramble encrypted pay-TV television signals.

SonyET: Sony Entertainment Television, a joint venture between Sony Corporation and Indian interests to provide satellite television, mainly for South Asia though also for diasporic and expatriate

	Indians abroad.
SRG:	Survey Research Group, a leading research company in Asia subsequently taken over by ACNielsen, which specialised in media and marketing research, known then in each country as SRI (Indonesia), SRH (Hong Kong) and SRT (Taiwan).
StarTV:	Strictly an acronym for Satellite Television Asia Region but used as a brand name for the pioneering transnational satellite television broadcaster in Asia.
Subregion:	Used in this book to refer to parts of a country such as Southern India, the Cantonese-speaking areas of China, and Peninsular Malaysia, that is subnational regions.
SunTV:	A commercial television service via satellite in Tamil serving the dominant ethnic group of the southern Indian state of Tamil Nadu as well as migrants from there in Southeast Asia.
TELA:	Television and Entertainment Licensing Authority, which regulates domestic and transnational broadcasts originating in the territory of Hong Kong.
Third World:	Usually refers to developing countries/economies which were former colonies of European powers in Asia, Africa and Latin America; sometimes collectively, if inaccurately (geographically) referred to as the "South".
TPI:	Television Pendidikan Indonesia, or Indonesian Educational Television, a quasi-commercial station.
Transnational or trans-border television:	Television signals which deliberately cross national boundaries, usually through the use of satellite technology.
Transitional countries/ economies:	Formerly communist/socialist planned economies, mostly in Eastern Europe, now seeking full membership in the capitalist world economy and regional organisations like the EU through marketisation/privatisation. See also Second World.
Transponder:	Equipment on a satellite which receives and transmits a television or other telecommunication signal (made up from the words "transmitter" and "responder").

TTV:

Taiwan Television, a terrestrial broadcaster owned by the Taiwan provincial government.

TV3:

The dominant commercial television broadcaster in Malaysia, known locally in the Malay-Indonesian language as "TV Tiga".

TVB:

Television Broadcasters Ltd, a major Hong Kong-based television broadcaster and programme producer, operating internationally as TVBI.

TVBS:

TVB's Superchannel, a transnational satellite television service in Mandarin to Greater China and more recently to diasporic communities of ethnic Chinese elsewhere.

TVRI:

The Indonesian public broadcaster, which does not accept advertising but "taxes" advertising income of the commercial broadcasters.

TVRs:

Television Rating Points, sometimes referred to by the acronym TRPs.

TVRO:

TV Receive-Only, describing satellite dishes which can receive television signals but not transmit them; a.k.a. parabolic antennae.

TVNZ:

Television New Zealand, previously a public broadcaster, now privatised and active in Pacific Islands television markets.

UNESCO:

United Nations Educational, Scientific and Cultural Organisation, an intergovernment body responsible for issues of culture and media, among other social, scientific and educational matters. It has a general mandate to enhance global communication flows among nations, and funds 'communications development' projects to increase the communications capacity of developing countries.

Uplink:

Process of transmitting television signals from earth to a satellite, usually through large uplink centres though increasingly possible from small mobile equipment.

UTV:

An Indian programme production house, subsequently part-owned by News Corporation and since then expanding operations to other Asian countries.

VoD:

Video-on-Demand, a cable television system which allows subscribers to select programming to watch at their own time on a pay-per-view basis; also known as interactive cable.

WTO:
World Trade Organisation, successor organisation to the GATT, following the successful completion of its final Uruguay Round; headquartered in Singapore.

Worldwide web or www:
Often used synonymously with 'Internet' of which it is the part that allows communication via text, graphics, audio and video.

ZeeTV:
A pioneer transnational satellite broadcaster in Hindi, first targeted at India and subsequently diversified into other South Asian dialects/languages and diasporic/expatriate markets.

BIBLIOGRAPHY

Acharya, Rabi Narayan (1987). *Television in India*. Delhi: Mass Publications.

Adorno, Theodor W. and Max Horkheimer (1972). "The Cultural Industry: Enlightenment as Mass Deception", extracted from *Dialectic of Enlightenment* [trans. John Cumming]. New York: Seabury Press.

Ahmed, M. (1993). "Television Maldives". Paper presented at the AMIC seminar on Legal and Regulatory Aspects of Satellite Broadcasting, New Delhi.

Alfian and Godwin C. Chu (eds) (1981). *Satellite Television in Indonesia*. Honolulu: East-West Center.

Al-Hail, Ali (2000). "The Age of New Media: The Role of Al-Jazeera Satellite TV in Developing Civil Society in Qatar", *Transnational Broadcasting Studies*, Spring.

Al-Makaty, Safran S. (1995), Direct Satellite Broadcasting in the Arab World: A Descriptive Study of DBS's Impact in Saudi Arabia, Doctoral dissertation, University of Kentucky.

Al-Thawadi, Khalil Ebrahim and Sarah Callard (1997). "Broadcasting in Bahrain", *Middle East Broadcasting and Satellite*, July.

Ali, Owais Aslam and Shelton A. Gunaratne (2000). "Pakistan", in Shelton A. Gunaratne (ed.), *Handbook of the Media in Asia*. New Delhi, Thousand Oaks and London: Sage Publications.

Amin, Samir (1982). "Crisis, Nationalism and Socialism", in Samir Amin, Giovanni Arrighi, Andre Gunder Frank, Immanuel Wallerstein (eds), *Dynamics of Global Crisis*. London and Basingstoke: MacMillan Press.

——— (1984). "Self-reliance and the New International Economic Order", in Herb Addo (ed.), *Transforming the World-Economy?* London: Hodder and Stoughton.

Anderson, Benedict (1983). *Imagined Communities*. London: Verso.

Ang, Ien (1985). *Watching Dallas: Soap Opera and the Melodramatic Imagination*. London and New York: Methuen.

Anwar, M. Tawhidul (1993). "The Social and Cultural Impact of Satellite Broadcasting in Bangladesh". Paper presented at the AMIC Seminar, 1–3 February, Singapore.

Appadurai, Arjun (1990). "Disjuncture and Difference in the Global Cultural Economy", in Mike Featherstone (ed.), *Global Culture: Nationalism, Globalization and Modernity*. London: Sage Publications.

Atkins, William (2002). *The Politics of Southeast Asia's New Media*. England: Curzon Press.

Babbie, Earl (1992). *The Practice of Social Research* (6th edn.). Belmont, CA: Wadsworth Publishing Co.

Badarudin, Noor Bathi (1997). "Programming Content in Malaysian Television: Implications of Recent Trends", *Media Asia*, 24 (3).

Barraclough, Steven (2001). "Pakistani Television Politics in the 1990s", *Gazette*, 63 (2–3).

Baudrillard, Jean (1988). "The Masses: The Implosion of the Social in the Media", in Mark Poster (ed.), *Selected Writings*, Stanford: Stanford University Press.

Berger, Peter (1991). *The Capitalist Revolution*. United States: Basic Books/Harper Collins.

Bergensen, Albert (1990). "Turning the World-System Theory on its Head" in Mike Featherstone (ed.), *Global Culture: Nationalism, Globalization and Modernity*. London: Sage Publications.

Bhargava, G.S. (ed.) (1991). "Introduction" in *Government Media: Autonomy and After*. New Delhi: Institute of Social Sciences and Concept Publishing Co.

Bhatt, S.C. (1994). *Satellite Invasion of India*. New Delhi: Gyan Publishing House.

Bhuiyan, Serajul I. and Shelton A. Gunaratne (2000). "Bangladesh", in Shelton A. Gunaratne (ed.), *Handbook of the Media in Asia*. New Delhi, Thousand Oaks and London: Sage Publications.

Bishop, Robert L. (1989). *Qi Lai! Mobilising One Billion Chinese: The Chinese Communication System*. Ames: Iowa State University Press.

Boyd, Douglas (1999). *Broadcasting in the Arab World* (3rd edition). Ames: Iowa State University Press.

Boyd-Barrett, Oliver (2000). "Pan-Arab Satellite Television: The Dialectics of Identity" in Howard Tumber (ed.), *Media Power, Professionals and Politics*. London and New York: Routledge.

Braman, Sandra and Annabelle Sreberny-Mohammadi (eds) (1996). *Globalization, Communication and Transnational Civil Society*. Cresskill, NJ: Hampton Press.

Brewer, John and Albert Hunter (1989). *Multimethod Research: A Synthesis of Styles*. Newbury Park: Sage Publications.

Callinicos, Alex (1994). "Against postmodernism", in *The Polity Reader in Social Theory*. Cambridge and Oxford: Polity Press.

Chan, Joseph Man (1994). "National Responses and Accessibility to StarTV in Asia", *Journal of Communication*, 44 (3), Summer.

——— (2000). "When Capitalist and Socialist Television Clash: The Impact of Hong TV on Guangzhou Residents", in Lee Chin-Chuan (ed.), *Power, Money and Media: Communication Patterns and Bureaucratic Control of Cultural China*. Evanston, IL: Northwestern University Press.

Chang, Yu-Li (2001). "From Globalization to Localization: The World's Leading Television News Broadcasters in Asia", *Asian Journal of Communication*, 11 (1).

Chase-Dunn, Christopher (1975). "The Effects of International Economic Dependence on Development and Inequality: A Cross-National Study", *American Sociological Review*, 40.

Chen Guo-Ming and William J. Starosta (2000). "Communication and Global Society: An Introduction" in Chen Guo-Ming and William J. Starosta (eds), *Communication and Global Society*. New York: Peter Lang Publishing.

Chen, Ping Hung (1999). "Market Concentration in Taiwan's Cable Industry", *Media Asia*, 26 (4).

Chirot, D. and T.D. Hall (1982). "World-System Theory", *Annual Review of Sociology*, 8.

Chu, Godwin, Wilbur Schramm and Alfian (1991). *The Social Impact of Satellite Television in Rural Indonesia*. Singapore: Asian Mass Communication Research and Information Centre.

Ciochetto, Lynne (2001). "Outdoor Advertising and Social Change in Contemporary Russia", *Media International Australia*, 101, November.

Cioffi-Revilla, Claudio and Richard Merritt (1981–82). "Communication Research and the New World Information Order", *Journal of International Affairs*, 35 (2).

Cooper, Harris M. (1984). *The Integrative Research Review: A Systematic Approach*. Beverly Hills, CA: Sage Publications.

Creswell, John W. (1994). *Research Design: Qualitative and Quantitative Approaches*. Thousand Oaks: Sage Publications.

Crook, Stephen, Jan Pakulski and Malcolm Waters (1992). *Postmodernization: Change in Advanced Society*. London: Sage Publications.

Curran, James and Myung-Jin Park (2000). "Beyond Globalization Theory" in James Curran and Myung-Jin Park (eds), *De-Westernizing Media Studies*. London and New York: Routledge.

D'Agostino, Peter (1995). "Virtual Realities: Recreational Vehicles for a Post-Television Culture", in Peter D'Agostino and David Tafler (eds), *Transmission: Towards a Post-television Culture* (2nd edition). Thousand Oaks: Sage Publications.

Dahrendorf, Ralf (1973). "Towards a Theory of Social Conflict", in Eva Etzioni-Halevy and Amitai Etzioni (eds), *Social Change: Sources, Patterns, and Consequences* (2nd edition). New York: Basic Books.

Daniel, Kate (2003). *SBS World Guide* (11th edition). Melbourne: Hardie Grant Books.

Demers, David (2002). *Global Media: Menace or Messiah?* (revised edition). Cresskill, NJ: Hampton Press.

Denzin, Norman D. (1991). *Images of Postmodern Society*. London, Newbury Park and New Delhi: Sage Publications.

Downing, John (1996). *Internationalizing Media Theory: Transition, Power, Culture*. London, Thousand Oaks and New Delhi: Sage Publications.

Drucker, Peter (1993). *The Post-Capitalist Society*. New York: Harper Business.

Eisenstadt, Shmuel Noah (1973). *Tradition, Change and Modernity*. New York: John Wiley & Sons.

Ellul, Jacques (1985). *The Humiliation of the Word* [trans. Joyce Main Hanks]. Grand Rapids, MI: Wm. B. Eerdmanns Publishing Co.

Esslin, Martin (1982). *The Age of Television*. San Francisco: W.H. Freeman and Co.

Featherstone, Mike (1990). "Global Culture: An Introduction", *Theory, Culture and Society*, 7 (2–3), June; and in Mike Featherstone (ed.), *Global Culture: Nationalism, Globalization and Modernity*. London, Newbury Park and New Delhi: Sage Publications.

——— (1995). *Undoing Culture: Globalization, Postmodernism and Identity*. London, Thousand Oaks and New Delhi: Sage Publications.

Ferguson, Marjorie (1993). "Globalisation of Cultural Industries: Myths and Realities", in Marcus Breen (ed.), *Cultural Industries: National Policies and Global Market* (Proceedings of a CIRCIT conference, 10 December 1992). Melbourne: Centre for International Research on Communications and Information Technologies.

Fontana, Andrea and James H. Frey (1994). "Interviewing: The Art of Science", in Norman D. Denzin and Yvonna S. Lincoln (eds). *Handbook of Qualitative Research*. Thousand Oaks: Sage Publications.

Forrester, Jan (1998). "Instant Noodle Propaganda: Vietnamese Television in the Late 1990s", in David Marr (ed.), *Mass Media in Vietnam*. Canberra: Australian National University.

Foucault, Michael (1978). *The History of Sexuality: An Introduction*, Volume One [trans. Robert Hurley]. London: Penguin.

Frederick, Howard H. (1993). *Global Communication and International Relations*. Belmont, CA: Wadsworth Publishing.

French, David and Michael Richards (1996). "Open Markets and the Future of Television—Fiction and Fact: GATT, GATS and the World Trade Organisation", in David French and Michael Richards (eds), *Contemporary Television: Eastern Perspectives*. New Delhi, Thousand Oaks and London: Sage Publications.

Friedman, Thomas (2000). *The Lexus and the Olive Tree*. London: HarperCollins.

Fukuyama, Francis (1992). *The End of History and the Last Man*. London: Penguin.

Fung, Anthony Y.H. and Lee Chin-Chuan (1994). "Hong Kong's Changing Media Ownership: Uncertainty and Dilemma", *Gazette*, 53.

Fung, Anthony and Eric Ma (2002). "Satellite Modernity: Four Modes of Televisual Imagination in the Disjunctive Socio-Mediascape of Guangzhou", in Stephanie Hemelryk Donald, Michel Keane and Yin Hong (eds), *Media in China: Consumption, Content and Crisis*. London: Routledge Curzon.

Gershon, R.A. (1997). *The Transnational Media Corporation: Global Messages and Free Market Competition*. Mahwah, NJ: Lawrence Erlbaum.

Gher, Leo and Hussein Amin (1999). "New and Old Media Access and Ownership in the Arab world". *Gazette*, 61 (1).

Giddens, Anthony (1990). *The Consequences of Modernity*. Cambridge: Polity Press.

Gilani, Ijaz S. and Nisar A. Zuberi (1993). "Communication Scene in Pakistan", in Anura Goonasekara and Duncan Holaday (eds), *Asian Communication Handbook*. Singapore: Asian Mass Communication Research and Information Centre.

Gilpin, Robert (1987). *The Political-Economy of International Relations*. Princeton: Princeton University Press.

Glazer, Rashi and Rajeev Batra (1989). "Cable TV Advertising: A Strategic Overview", in Rajeev Batra and Rashi Glazer (eds), *Cable TV and Advertising: In Search for the Right Formula*. Wesport, CN: Quorum Books.

Gramsci, A. (1978). *Selections from the Political Writings*. London: Lawrence and Wishart.

Gray, John (1998). *False Dawn: The Delusions of Global Capitalism*. London: Granta Books.

Greider, William (1997). *One World, Ready or Not: The Manic Logic of Global Capitalism*. New York: Simon & Schuster.

Gumpert, Gary and Robert Cathcart (1984). "Media Stereotyping: Images of the Foreigner", in L.A. Samovar and R.E. Porter (eds), *Intercultural Communication: A Reader*. Belmont, CA: Wadsworth.

Gunaratne, Shelton and Chanuka Lalinda Wattegama (2000). "North Korea", in Shelton A. Gunaratne (ed.), *Handbook of the Media in Asia*. New Delhi, Thousand Oaks and London: Sage Publications.

Gunaratne, Shelton and Shin Dong Kim (2000). "Sri Lanka", in Shelton A. Gunaratne (ed.), *Handbook of the Media in Asia*. New Delhi, Thousand Oaks and London: Sage Publications.

Handy, Charles (1997). *The Hungry Spirit: Beyond Capitalism—A Quest for Purpose in the Modern World*. London: Random House.

Harvey, David (1989). *The Conditions of Postmodernity*. Oxford: Blackwell.

Haverkamp, Hans and Neil J. Smelser (eds) (1992). *Social Change and Modernity.* Berkeley: University of California Press.

Heo, Chul, Ki-Yul Uhm and Jeong-Heon Chun (2000). "South Korea", in Shelton A. Gunaratne (ed.), *Handbook of the Media in Asia*. New Delhi, Thousand Oaks and London: Sage Publications.

Herman, Edward S. and Noam Chomsky (1988). *Manufacturing Consent: The Political Economy of the Mass Media.* New York: Pantheon Books.

Hobsbawm, Eric J. (1990). "Nationalism and Ethnicity", *Intermedia*, 20 (4–5), August–September.

Holaday, Duncan Alan (1996). "Social Impact of Satellite TV in Indonesia: A View from the Ground". *Media Asia*, 23 (2).

Hong Junhao (1998). *The Internationalization of Television in China: The Evolution of Ideology, Society and Media since the Reform.* Westport, CT: Praeger.

——— (1999). "Globalization and Change in Taiwan's Media: The Interplay of Political and Economic Forces", *Asian Journal of Communication*, 9 (2).

Hoselitz, Bert (1957). "Economic Growth and Development: Noneconomic Factors in Economic Development", *American Economic Review*, 47, May.

Howkins, John (1982). *Mass Communications in China.* New York and London: Longman.

Huang Changzhu and Zhong Wanyi (1993). "Communication Scene of People's Republic of China", in Anura Goonasekera and Duncan Holaday (eds), *Asian Communications Handbook*. Singapore: Asian Mass Media Information and Research Centre.

Hudson, Heather (1990). *Communication Satellites: Their Development and Impact.* London: The Free Press/Collier MacMillan.

Huntington, Samuel (1998). "The Coming Clash of Civilizations or, the West against the Rest" in *The Global Agenda: Issues and Perspectives.* Boston: McGraw-Hill.

Husband, Charles (2000). "Media and the Public Sphere in Multi-Ethnic Societies", in Simon Cottle (ed.), *Ethnic Minorities and the Media: Changing Cultural Boundaries.* Buckingham and Philadelphia: Open University Press.

Hutchinson, David (1999). *Media Policy: An Introduction.* Oxford: Blackwell Publishers.

Inglehart, Ronald (1990). *Culture Shift in Advanced Industrial Society.* Princeton: Princeton University Press.

Inkeles, A. and D.H. Smith (1974). *Becoming Modern: Individual Change in Six Developing Countries.* Cambridge, MA: Harvard University Press.

Jameson, F. (1984). "Post-modernism or the Cultural Logic of Late Capitalism", *New Left Review*, 146.

Jeffrey, Robin (2000). *India's Newspaper Revolution: Capitalism, Politics and the Indian-language Press, 1977–99.* New Delhi: Oxford University Press.

Joshi, S.R. and K.M. Parmar (1992). *International Television and Video Flow in India: A Case Study.* Ahmedabad: ISRO.

Jussawalla, Meheroo (1988). "Information Economies and the Development of Pacific Countries", in Meheroo Jussawalla, Donald M. Pemberton and Neil D. Karunaratne (eds), *The Cost of Thinking: Information Economies of Ten Pacific Countries.* Norwood, NJ: Ablex.

Kakabadse, Mario A. (1995). "WTO and the Commodification of Cultural Products: Implications for Asia", *Media Asia*, 22 (2).

Karan, Kavita and K. Viswanath (2000). "Maldives", in Shelton A. Gunaratne (ed.), *Handbook of the Media in Asia*. New Delhi, Thousand Oaks and London: Sage Publications.

Karthigesu, R. (1994). "Broadcasting Deregulation in Developing Asian Nations: An Examination of Nascent Tendencies using Malaysia as a Case Study", *Media, Culture and Society*, 16.

Katz, Elihu and Paul F. Lazarsfeld (1955). *Personal Influence: The Part Played by People in the Flow of Mass Communication*. Glencoe, IL: Free Press.

Keane, Michael (1996). "China's New Revolutionary Role Models: Television Drama and Urban Consumerism". Paper presented at the *Culture and Citizenship Conference*, September-October, Brisbane.

Kellehear, Allan (1993). *The Unobtrusive Researcher: A Guide to Methods*. St. Leonard's, NSW: Allen and Unwin.

King, Anthony D. (1991). "Introduction: Spaces of Culture, Spaces of Knowledge", in Anthony D. King (ed.), *Culture, Globalisation and the World-System: Contemporary Conditions for the Representation of Identity*. Binghampton: State University of New York.

——— (1995). "The Times and Spaces of Modernity (Or Who Needs Postmodernism)", in Mike Featherstone, Scott Lash and Roland Robertson (eds), *Global Modernities*. London, Thousand Oaks and New Delhi: Sage Publications.

Kinnear, Thomas C. and James R. Taylor (1996). *Marketing Research: An Applied Approach* (5th ed.). New York: McGraw-Hill.

Kitley, Philip (1994). "Fine Tuning Control: Commercial Television in Indonesia", *Continuum: Australian Journal of Media and Culture*, 8 (2).

——— (1997a). "Television Institutions in Indonesia". Paper presented at the Modernisation in Bali seminar, University of Wollongong, July.

——— (1997b). "Deregulation and the Public Debate on Television". Paper presented at the Modernisation in Bali seminar, University of Wollongong, July.

——— (2000). *Television, Nation and Culture in Indonesia*. Athens, OH: Ohio University Center for International Studies.

Knox, Paul L. (1995). "World Cities in a World-System", in Paul L. Knox and Peter J. Taylor (eds), *World Cities in a World-System*. Cambridge: Cambridge University Press.

Kumar, Keval (2000). "Cable and Satellite Television in India: The Role of Advertising", in David French and Michael Richards (eds), *Television in Contemporary Asia*. New Delhi, Thousand Oaks and London: Sage Publications.

Lash, Scott and John Urry (1987). *The End of Organized Capitalism*. Cambridge: Polity.

——— (1994). *Economies of Signs and Space*. London: Sage Publications.

Lauer, Robert H. (1991). *Perspectives on Social Change* (4th edition). Boston: Allyn and Bacon.

Lee, Paul S.N. (1998). "Foreign Television in Hong Kong: Little Watched but Favourably Received", in Anura Goonasekera and Paul S.N. Lee (eds), *TV without Borders*. Singapore: Asian Media Information and Communication Centre.

Lent, John (1995). "Introduction", in John Lent (ed.), *Asian Popular Culture*. Boulder: Westview Press.

Lerner, David (1958). *The Passing of Traditional Society: Modernizing the Middle East*. Glencoe, IL: Free Press.

Lewis, Glen (2000). "Communications Deregulation and Democratization in Thailand", *Media Asia*, 27 (3).

Lo Ven Hwei, Chen Jei-Cheng and Lee Chin-Chuan (1994). "Television News in Government News in Taiwan: Patterns of Television News Sources Selection and Presentation", *Asian Journal of Communication*, 4 (1).

Lovelock, Peter and Charles Goddard (1999). "Hongkong's Television Policy in an Era of Convergence", in Venkat Iyer (ed.), *Media Regulations for the New Times*. Singapore: Asian Media Information and Communication Centre.

Lowe, Barry and Shelton Gunaratne (2000). "Mongolia", in Shelton A. Gunaratne (ed.), *Handbook of the Media in Asia*. New Delhi, Thousand Oaks and London: Sage Publications.

Lull, James (1990). *Inside Family Viewing: Ethnographic Research on Television's Audiences*. London: Routledge.

————— (1995). *Media, Communication, Culture: A Global Approach*. Cambridge: Polity Press.

Lyon, David (1994). *Postmodernity*. Buckingham: Open University Press.

Lyotard, J-F. (1984). *The Postmodern Condition: A Report on Knowledge*. Manchester: Manchester University Press.

MacBride, Sean (ed.) (1980). *Many Voices, One World: Communication and Society, Today and Tomorrow* (Final report of the International Commission for the Study of Communication Problems, a.k.a the MacBride Commission). Paris: Unesco; London: Kogan Page; and New York: Unipub.

MacBride, Sean and Colleen Roach (1993). "The New International Information Order", in George Gerbner, Hamid Mowlana and Kaarle Nordenstreng (eds) , *The Global Media Debate: Its Rise, Fall and Renewal*. Norwood, NJ: Ablex Publishing.

Martin-Barbero, Jesús (1993). *Communication, Culture and Hegemony: From the Media to Mediations*. [Translated by Elizabeth Fox and Robert A. White]. London: Sage Publications.

McDaniel, Drew O. (1994). *Broadcasting in the Malay World: Radio, Television and Video in Brunei, Indonesia, Malaysia and Singapore*. Norwood, NJ: Ablex Publishing Company.

McGrew, Anthony (1992a). "A Global Society?", in Stuart Hall, David Held and Tony McGrew (eds), *Modernity and its Futures*. Oxford: Polity Press, Open University and Blackwell Publishers.

————— (1992b). "Global Politics in a Transitional Era", in Anthony McGrew and Paul Lewis (eds), *Global Politics*. Cambridge: Polity Press.

McLuhan, Marshall (1964). *Understanding Media: The Extensions of Man*. New York: McGraw-Hill/Signet Books.

Melkote, Srinivas R., Peter Shields and Binod Agrawal (eds) (1998). *International Satellite Broadcasting in South Asia: Political, Economic and Cultural Implications*. Lanham, New York and Oxford: University Press of America, Inc.

Melkote, Srinivas (2002). "Theories of Development Communication", in William B. Gudykunst and Bella Mody (eds), Handbook of International and Intercultural Communication, (2nd Edition). Thousand Oaks: Sage Publications.

Merriam, Sharan B. (1988). *Case Study Research in Education: A Qualitative Approach*. San Francisco and London: Jossey-Bass Publishers.

Meyrowitz, Joshua (1985). *No Sense of Place*. New York: Oxford University Press.

Miles, Mathews B. and A. Micheal Huberman (1994). *Qualitative Data Analysis: An Expanded Sourcebook* (2nd Edition). Thousand Oaks, CA: Sage Publications.

Morley, David (1980). *The "Nationwide" Audience*. London: British Film Institute.

Morley, David and Kevin Robins (1995). *Spaces of Identity: Global Media, Electronic Landscapes and Cultural Boundaries*. London: Routledge.

Mowlana, Hamid (1986). *Global Information and World Communication*. New York and London: Longman.

Mulhearn, Chris (1996). "Change and Development in the Global Economy", in Charlotte Bretherton and Geoffrey Parton (eds), *Global Politics*. Oxford: Blackwell.

Myagmar, Munkhmandakh (2000). "Mongolian Mass Media in the 90s", *Media Asia*, 27 (1).

Myagmar, Munkhmandakh and Poul Erik Nielsen (2001). "The Mongolian Media Landscape in Transition", *Nordicom Review*, 22 (2).

Nain, Zaharom (2002). "Globalized Theories and National Controls: The State, the Market and the Malaysian Media", in James Curran and Myung-Jin Park (eds), *De-Westernizing Media Studies*. London and New York: Routledge.

Naisbitt, John (1984). *Megatrends: Ten New Directions Transforming Our Lives*. London and Sydney: Futura/Macdonald and Co.

——— (1995). *Megatrends Asia: The Eight Asian Megatrends that are Changing the World*. London: Nicholas Brealey Publishing.

Negrine, Ralph and S. Papathanassopoulos (1990). *The Internationalisation of Television*. London, New York: Pinter Publishers.

Ninan, Sevanti (1996). *Through the Magic Window: Television and Change in India*. New Delhi: Penguin Books.

O'Connor, James (1970). "The Meaning of Economic Imperialism", in R.I. Rhodes (ed.), *Imperialism and Underdevelopment: A Reader*. New York: Monthly Review Press.

Ohmae, Kenichi (1990). *The Borderless World: Power and Strategy in the Interlinked Economy*. London: Fontana/Harper Collins.

Page, David and William Crawley (2001). *Satellites over South Asia: Broadcasting, Culture and the Public Interest*. New Delhi, Thousand Oaks and London: Sage Publications.

Park Myung-Jin, Kim Chang-Nam and Sohn Byung-Woo (2000). "Modernization, Globalization, and the Powerful State: the Korean Media", in James Curran and Myung-Jin Park (eds), *De-Westernizing Media Studies*. London and New York: Routledge.

Parsons, Talcott (1973). "A Functional Theory of Change", in Eva Etzioni-Halevy and Amitai Etzioni (eds), *Social Change: Sources, Patterns, and Consequences* (2nd edition). New York: Basic Books.

Patton, Micheal Q. (1990). *Qualitative Evaluation and Research Methods* (2nd Edition). Newbury Park: Sage Publications.

Peacock, Walter Gilis, Greg A. Hoover and Charles D. Killian (1988). "Divergence and Convergence in International Development: A Decomposition Analysis of Inequality in the World-System", *American Sociological Review*, 53, December.

Pek Siok Sian (1998). *The Establishment of Television in a Developing Nation: Lessons for Bhutan*. Unpublished master's thesis. Sydney: Macquarie University.

Pieterse, Jan Nederveen (1994). "Globalisation as Hybridisation", *International Sociology*, 9 (2), June.

Porter, Michael E. (1990). *The Competitive Advantage of Nations.* London: Macmillan Press.

Raghavan, Chakravarthi (1991). *Recolonization: GATT, the Uruguay Round & the Third World.* Penang: Third World Network.

Rao, Sandhya and Bharat Koirala (2000). "Nepal", in Shelton A. Gunaratne (ed.), *Handbook of the Media in Asia.* New Delhi, Thousand Oaks and London: Sage Publications.

Real, Michael (1989). *Super Media: A Cultural Approach.* London: Sage Publications.

Reeves, Geoffrey (1993). *Communications and the "Third World".* London: Routledge.

Richards, Thomas and Lyn Richards (1993). Non-numerical Unstructured Data Indexing, Searching and Theorising (*NUD.IST*). Melbourne: La Trobe University/Qualitative Solutions and Research.

Robertson, Roland (1992). *Globalization: Social Theory and Global Culture.* London, Newbury Park and New Delhi: Sage Publications.

Rogers, Everritt (1962). *The Diffusion of Innovations.* New York: Free Press.

Rosenau, J. (1990). *Turbulence in World Politics.* Brighton: Harvest Wheatsheaf.

Rostow, Walt W. (1960). *The Stages of Economic Growth: A Non-Communist Manifesto.* Cambridge: Cambridge University Press.

Safar, H.M. and Yussof Ladi (2000). "Brunei Darussalam", in Shelton A. Gunaratne (ed.), *Handbook of the Media in Asia.* New Delhi, Thousand Oaks and London: Sage Publications.

Saidkasimov, Saidmukhtar and Bobir Tukhtabayev (1998). "Role of Mass Media in the Democratisation of Society: Lessons from Malaysian Experience", in Mohd. Safar Hashim, Samsudin A. Rahim and Bobir Takhtabayev (eds), *Mass Media and National Development: Experiences of Malaysia and Uzbekistan.* Kuala Lumpur: International Centre for Media Studies.

Saito, Shinichi (2000). "Japan", in Shelton A. Gunaratne (ed.), *Handbook of the Media in Asia.* New Delhi, Thousand Oaks and London: Sage Publications.

Samarajiva, Rohan and Peter Shields (1993). "Integration, Telecommunications and Development: Power in the Paradigms", in Anura Goonasekara and Duncan Holaday (eds), *Asian Communication Handbook.* Singapore: Asian Media Information Communications Centre.

Sassen, Saskia (1996). *Losing Control: Sovereignty in an Age of Globalization.* New York: Columbia University Press.

Schlesinger, Philip (2000). "The Nation and Communicative Space", in Howard Tumber (ed.), *Media Power, Professionals and Politics.* London and New York: Routledge.

Schiller, Dan (2000). *Digital Capitalism: Networking the Global Marketing System.* Cambridge, MA: MIT Press.

Schiller, Herbert I. (2000). "Digitised Capitalism: What has Changed?", in Howard Tumber (ed.), *Media Power, Professionals and Politics.* London and New York: Routledge.

Schramm, Wilbur (1964). *Communication and National Development: The Role of Information in the Developing Countries.* Stanford: Stanford University Press.

Sen, Krishna (1994a). "Changing Horizons of Television in Indonesia", *Southeast Asian Journal of Social Science*, (22).

——— (1994b). *Indonesia Cinema: Framing the New Order.* London and New Jersey: Zed Books Ltd.

Shannon, Thomas R. (1989). *An Introduction to World-System Perspective.* London: West View Press.

Shoesmith, Brian (1994). "Asia in their Shadow: Satellites and Asia", *Southeast Asian Journal of Social Science,* 22.

—— (1998). "No sex! No violence! No news!: Satellite and Cable Television in China", *Media Asia,* 25 (1).

Sinclair, John and Linda Hemphill (1997). *The Social Determinants of Demand for Convergent Communications Services in the Asian Region: The Case of India—A Status Report.* Melbourne: Victoria University of Technology.

Sinclair, John G., Elizabeth Jacka and Stuart Cunningham (eds) (1996). *New Patterns in Global Television: Peripheral Vision.* Oxford: Oxford University Press.

Singhal, Arvind and Everett M. Rogers (1989). *India's Information Revolution.* New Delhi, Newbury Park and London: Sage Publications.

Siochrú, Seán Ó., Bruce Girard and Amy Mahan (2002). *Global Media Governance: A Beginner's Guide.* Oxford: Rowman and Littlefield Publishers.

Smith, Anthony D. (1992). "Is there a Global Culture?", *Intermedia,* 20 (4–5), August–September.

So, Clement, Joseph Man Chan and Chin-Chuan Lee (2000a). "Macau SAR (China)", in Shelton A. Gunaratne (ed.), *Handbook of the Media in Asia.* New Delhi, Thousand Oaks and London: Sage Publications.

—— (2000b). "Hong Kong SAR (China)", in Shelton A. Gunaratne (ed.), *Handbook of the Media in Asia,* New Delhi: Sage Publications.

Sonwalkar, Prasun (2001). "India: Makings of Little Cultural/Media Imperialism?", *Gazette,* 63 (6).

Speake, Jennifer (ed.) (1993). *The Hutchinson Dictionary of World History.* Oxford: Helicon Publishing.

Spybey, Tony (1996). *Globalization and World Society.* Cambridge: Polity Press.

Sreberny-Mohammadi, Annabelle, Dwayne Winseck, Jim McKenna and Oliver Boyd-Barrett (1997). *Media in Global Context: A Reader.* London: Arnold. *Foundations in Media* series, edited by Oliver Boyd-Barrett.

Stearn, Gerald E. (ed.) (1968). *McLuhan Hot and Cool.* Harmondsworth, UK: Penguin.

Stewart, Randall G. (1999). *Public Policy: Strategy and Accountability.* Melbourne: MacMillan.

Straubhaar, Joseph D. (1990). "Context, Social Class, and VCRs: A World Comparison", in Julia R. Dobrow (ed.), *Social and Cultural Aspects of VCR Use.* Hillsdale, NJ: Lawrence Erlbaum Associates, Publishers.

Sussman, Gerald and John A. Lent (eds) (1991). *Transnational Communications: Wiring the Third World.* Newbury Park, London and New Delhi: Sage Publications.

Tehranian, Majid (1999). *Global Communication and World Politics.* Boulder and London: Lynne Rienner Publishers.

Thomas, T.K. (1990). *Autonomy for the Electronic Media: A National Debate on the Prasar Bharati Bill, 1989.* New Delhi: Konark Publishers.

Thurow, Lester (1993). *Head to Head: The Coming Economic Battle among Japan, Europe and America.* London: Nicholas Brealey Publishing.

To Yiu Ming (1998). "China", in Albert Albarran and Sylvia Chan-Olmsted (eds), *Global Media Economics.* Ames: Iowa University Press.

Tomlinson, John (1991). *Cultural Imperialism.* London: Pinter Publishers.

Tracey, Michael (1988). "Popular Culture and the Economics of Global Television", *Intermedia*, 16 (2), November.

Tunstall, Jeremy (1977). *The Media are American: Anglo-American Media in the World*. London: Constable.

Turner, Mark and David Hulme (1997). *Governance, Administration and Development: Making the State Work*. London: Macmillan Press.

Vanden Heuvel, Jon and Everette E. Dennis (1994). "Trends and Developments in the Media of South Korea", in Chie-Woon Kim and Jae-Won Lee (eds). *Elite Media Amidst Mass Culture: A Critical Look at Mass Communication in Korea*. Seoul: NANAM Publishing House.

Wallerstein, Immanuel (1979). *The Capitalist World Economy*. New York: Cambridge University Press.

———— (1991). "The Lessons of the 1980s", *Geopolitics and Geoculture*. Cambridge: Cambridge University Press.

Walsh, James (1994). "Sky Static", *Time*, 19 September.

Waters, Malcolm (1995). *Globalization* (Key Ideas series, Peter Hamilton, ed.). London: Routledge.

Westerway, Peter (1990). *Electronic Highways: An Introduction to Telecommunications in the 1990s*. Sydney: Allen and Unwin.

Wilson, Rob and Wimal Dissanayake (1996). "Introduction: Tracking the Global/Local", in Rob Wilson and Wimal Dissanayake (eds), *Global/Local: Cultural Production and the Transnational Imaginary*. Durham and London: Duke University Press.

Wittkopf, Eugene R. and Charles W. Kegley, Jr (1998). "Vanishing Borders: The Globalization of Politics and Markets", in Charles W. Kegley, Jr and Eugene R. Wittkopf (eds), *The Global Agenda: Issues and Perspectives*. Boston: McGraw-Hill.

Won Ho-Chang (1989). *Mass Media in China: Its History and the Future*. Ames: Iowa State University Press.

Wong Kok Keong (2001). *Media and Culture in Singapore: A Theory of Controlled Commodification*. Creskill, NJ: Hampton Press.

About the Author

Amos Owen Thomas is an Associate Professor of International Business at the Maastricht School of Management. Much as his research critiques the globalisation of business and communications, economy and culture, he seeks to challenge graduate students from around the developing world to do likewise. For some 15 years now Dr Thomas has been an academic at five universities in Australia, Netherlands, Papua New Guinea and Singapore, plus visiting stints in about a dozen other countries. In the 14 years prior to that he worked at three transnational advertising agencies servicing the Pacific Rim region, as well as in consulting, government and non-profit organisations.